AFROCENTRICITY
in AFROFUTURISM

AFROCENTRICITY
in AFROFUTURISM

Toward Afrocentric Futurism

Edited by

AARON X. SMITH

Foreword by Molefi Kete Asante

University Press of Mississippi / Jackson

The University Press of Mississippi is the scholarly publishing agency of the Mississippi Institutions of Higher Learning: Alcorn State University, Delta State University, Jackson State University, Mississippi State University, Mississippi University for Women, Mississippi Valley State University, University of Mississippi, and University of Southern Mississippi.

www.upress.state.ms.us

The University Press of Mississippi is a member
of the Association of University Presses.

First printing 2023
∞

Library of Congress Cataloging-in-Publication Data

Names: Smith, Aaron X., editor. | Asante, Molefi Kete, 1942– author of foreword.
Title: Afrocentricity in AfroFuturism : toward Afrocentric Futurism / Aaron X. Smith, Molefi Kete Asante.
Description: Jackson : University Press of Mississippi, 2023. | Includes bibliographical references and index.
Identifiers: LCCN 2023031750 (print) | LCCN 2023031751 (ebook) | ISBN 9781496847836 (hardback) | ISBN 9781496847843 (trade paperback) | ISBN 9781496847850 (epub) | ISBN 9781496847867 (epub) | ISBN 9781496847874 (pdf) | ISBN 9781496847881 (pdf)
Subjects: LCSH: Afrocentrism. | African Americans—Race identity. | Black people—Race identity. | African Americans—Social conditions. | African diaspora. | African Americans—Music.
Classification: LCC DT15 .A376 2023 (print) | LCC DT15 (ebook) | DDC 305.896—dc23/eng/20230719
LC record available at https://lccn.loc.gov/2023031750
LC ebook record available at https://lccn.loc.gov/2023031751

British Library Cataloging-in-Publication Data available

Dedicated to Jeniece and Bakari,
my greatest present gift, my future, and my forever.
Daddy loves you!

In this great future, you can't forget your past.

—BOB MARLEY, "No Woman, No Cry"

CONTENTS

PART ONE: REPRESENTATIONS

PART TWO: TRANSFORMATIONS

FOREWORD

Molefi Kete Asante

In this provocative and intellectually stimulating anthology, *Afrocentricity in AfroFuturism: Toward Afrocentric Futurism*, Aaron Xavier Smith, known as the "Rapping Professor," has assembled a forward-looking cadre of young and seasoned academics to examine all aspects of the new future movement given an accelerant by the imaginative Wakanda art-technic-scientific creativity seen in the film *Black Panther* (2018). In fact, Smith created the original idea of "Afrocentric Futurism" as a new stage of what Mark Dery once called "AfroFuturism." Unlike what Dery and those who followed his lead did in launching the term AfroFuturism, several scholars who have examined the contours of this term have arrived at the conclusion that Afrocentricity is a necessary platform for any innovation in AfroFuturism. Therefore, Smith has called his approach Afrocentric Futurism, indicating that a conscious attitude grounded in the present and past narratives of African agency is at the core of this new movement.

Of course, all the writers are not on the same page, and that is as it should be since the writers have arrived at their positions from different angles on the same landscape, that is, the future as imagined and envisioned in the minds of Black people. There is no violent rejection of the Derian idea, only an expansion and perhaps a multiplicity of directions for such an idea. Since Afrocentric Futurism is an intellectual, social, and artistic movement, it finds literature, comics, hip-hop, and other forms of music and lifestyles, as well as iconic African symbolisms, as a part of a formal expression of presentations of techno-cultural realities.

Afrocentricity allows one to experience the meaning of a future where African agency converges with what we know about technology and art. I have always believed that the most creative individuals are those who are capable of using their historical knowledge and cultural imagination to bring into existence something that is really new. To say that something is new is not to say that it has not appeared in some form before but that the newness, the innovation, is how those images and technics are combined in a novel way.

Clearly, what Smith has seen is the impact the digital revolution has had on the mental energy unleashed toward building a future of techno-cultural achievements. Indeed, the writers in this book have brought about imagery, angles, and perspectives on all the human issues confronting us now and in the future. What I find so fascinating in this work is that it has taken into consideration the demographic and cultural changes happening in the society in the same way that Joseph Biden as president has investigated the need for diversity in government. Smith is intent on placing Africa and Africans in the future in a conscious manner. As a scholar, teacher, and media performer, Smith has seen up close the convergence of agency and technology in the age of digital realities.

A few years ago, I attended a conference on AfroFuturism at Temple University where Reynaldo Anderson and Jennifer Williams led hundreds of people in vibrant discussions and encounters about the African future. There was something special in the energy in Gladfelter Hall when I walked through the corridors where comic-book authors, toymakers, video creators, history-book authors, and illustrators were displaying their works at one end, and the speakers were delivering impassioned discourses in the auditoriums around the lobby. It was phenomenal because I had never seen such a centered, that is, Afrocentric, relationship to technology and the future as I saw at that conference. Pulsating with energy, clarity, and dedication to the African past with its icons of *sankofa*, ankhs, the eye of Heru, and so forth, the devotees of an Afrocentric Futurism gave me hope that the music, poetry, and comics that created the *Black Panther* movie would expand to become one with the future the attendees were so willing to speak about. It is this movement that Smith and his energetic cadre of scholars join in this book. Indeed, Smith notes that his aim in presenting this work is to go beyond the ordinary amazement at what the artists, singers, painters, musicians, and intellectuals are doing to make sense of their creativity in the twenty-first century.

Smith is a well-known professor among students at Temple University because of his dynamic lectures, commentaries on contemporary lifestyles, and research interests into Afrocentric Futurism. As a former media personality with a high-energy persona, Smith has been able to translate his relationships with hip-hop culture into a serious academic pursuit in the area of African culture. His scholarship and writings on Afrocentricity and popular culture are accompanied by his mentorship of younger scholars. In this book, *Afrocentricity in AfroFuturism: Toward Afrocentric Futurism*, he has combined his skill, commitment to excellence with a powerful orientation toward understanding the trajectory of African and African American culture.

African American speculative artists and astro-Blackness specialists will love this book because they will find discussions of science fiction, cosmological issues woven together with talks about digital vibrations and innovative ways to view art, music, and technological inventions. Ultimately, they will see the vision that the editor has articulated in his chapter for an Afrocentric Futurism with all the consciousness of culture, tradition, and values linked to whatever techno-future comes into being.

PREFACE

I felt intellectually enraptured as if looking into a literary looking glass while reading the unbelievably exciting news about a researcher named Mogomme Masoga. This innovative thinker recently directed the first dissertation on Indigenous Batswana astronomy, which was defended successfully by his groundbreaking student Motheo Koitsiwe, one of the first people in Africa to get a doctorate in Indigenous astronomy. Molefi Kete Asante, an Afrocentric innovator and mentor of both Masoga and myself, has envisioned the future of Afrocentric research in the stars!

In addition to contributions from scholars such as Ian Brenner (GZERO World), John S. Mbiti, George Lewis, Kamau Brathwaite, Filippo Tommaso Marinetti (future studies), Octavia Butler, and many others, this volume presents an Afrocentric Futuristic lens that is more unique with regard to methodological standpoints into the realms of Futurism. This Afrocentric Futurist approach differs from scholars who assume a decidedly more Marxist, feminist, LGBTQIA, communist, or animist Eurocentric analytical outlook. These distinctions speak to an entirely different relation to cosmogony, which undoubtedly impacts our perception of future potential and related purposes.

The future being conceived through an Afrocentric paradigm presents a dramatically different perception of the discipline of Africology often held by those who muse aloud, What will you do with a degree in African American studies? For clarity and correctness concerning the depth and potential benefits of Afrocentric study, I have included excerpts from one of the most accurate and thorough descriptions of this field of study, powerfully advanced by Africologist Christel Temple (2018), who writes: "The intersectional study of African people is transcontinental and transgenerational. The discipline of Africana studies sustains comprehensive immersion in African world content to guide efforts to study, to define, to critically interpret, to map, and to comparatively engage the multi-directional continuum of African experience."

Questions around the potential benefits of Black people learning more about African history, language, and culture speak volumes about the need for a greater appreciation of self as we plot out our future. To see beyond the Van Allen belt with the clearest most transformative visions of our collective future, it would behoove us to set our gazes far beyond pessimism, self-hate, and the ignorance of racist revisionist ideologies. The shift toward a more Afrocentric conceptualization of the future, in many regards, is not merely a matter of speculative subjectivity, but a means of survival. We have more to fear concerning a separation from self than a potential transhumanistic merging with machines or an alien takeover.

In *The Connecticon: Learning for the Connected Generation* (2004) by Frank Rennie and Robin Mason, this ancient African principle is expressed as a more recent realization in contemporary Eurocentric thought spaces. "Gone are the threats that machines will replace teachers; machines can store, link and process information, but people transform it and add value to it" (Rennie & Mason, 2004, p. 6). The text introduces the idea as "a new paradigm, that of connection" (Rennie & Mason, 2004, p. 1). The Afrocentric Futurist might ask, New to whom? The ancient African principles of *ma'at*, which include harmony, truth, justice, and reciprocity, express an understanding of the interconnectedness of all things as a foundational component to reasonable, divinely inspired African thought and culture. These African perspectives maintained balance and kept away chaos and have been expressed through numerous African ideologies throughout the ages.

In *Muntu: An Outline of the New African Culture*, by Janheinz Jahn and Marjorie Greene (1961, p. 102), an excerpt reads "space and time fall together into the category of hantu. Hantu is the force which localizes spatially and temporally every event and every motion." Afrocentric Futurists typically take a *"both-and,"* positive, inclusive approach to the idea of technological advancement in relation to human civilization. Contrarily, the notion of *"us versus them"* rings of colonial xenophobia and other related paradigms, which are at the foundation of White supremacist thought and culture.

Diversity does not require disagreements. Race is not a zero-sum game; racism is. Misconstruing these truths can produce a mentality resulting in commonly heard phrases, including "they are going to take our jobs." This form of proverbial musical chairs, "winner-takes-all" worldview was apparently implemented by early European settlers in their engagement with the Indigenous populations in the Americas, later with so-called minorities, and later extended to exhibiting computerphobia (Lafrance, 2015), cyberphobia (Vocabulary.com, n.d.), or technophobia, the fear or dislike of advanced technology or complex devices, especially computers. The common denominator throughout the continuum of resistance to reality is found in a groundless distorted perception that increases discomfort and manifests an aversion to risk taking. For example, "technophobia does not involve fears such as job displacement or concerns over the effects of screen radiation, rather a negative affective and attitudinal response to technology which the technophobe acknowledges to be irrational" (Brosnan, 2002, p. 10).

These psychological seeds of fearful separation gave rise to a technological tug-of-war manifested in the idea of advanced technology as a potential enemy of humanity. This is the continuation of the "*either-or*," imperial domination paradigm, which paradoxically posits humankind at war with all that sustains and enriches us, from the sun to circuits. The limitations of these dislocating analytical frameworks speak to the urgency for a greater infusion of Afrocentric thought when engaging in the potential of a people, a planet, and beyond:

> Collectively, the discipline aims to expand knowledge and inspire behaviors that will increase the life chances and life experiences of people of African descent, in particular, and of humanity, in general. Students emerge from Africana Studies courses as (1) master communicators on matters related to culture, race, ethnicity, diversity, and power, and (2) as practitioners with a high cultural competency in matters related to social justice, cultural ethics, policy, and globalism. (Temple, 2018)

Not simply *Black*, but as rapper Nasir Jones (2020; aka "Nas") explains, "we going ultra-Black."

Through the silence, I can hear the ancestors congratulating in collective chorus. This is a form of scholarship that connects with ceremonial facial painting and scarification, emblematic of ancient engagements with circadian rhythms. While interstellar wombs, reminiscent of the regenerative potential of the goddess Nut pulsate with African communal consciousness, we continue to research and write to connect more deeply with Afrocentric philosophical roots. Nut was the sky goddess born of Shu and Tefnut in the mythology of ancient Kemet. Alongside her brother and husband Geb, Nut was responsible for bringing into existence Ausar, Auset, Set, and Neb-het. We are the talking drums with skins of dark matter, whose lives matter, whose thoughts matter, who brought matter in their DNA from the rich glorious past, through outer space to the Eve gene.

We are living, breathing, calculating intergalactic equations. We are quantum leaping out of all forms of mental, physical, and future bondage. We are free, were free, and will be free in the mind, body, spirit, and in the unceasing expanse of the universe. We are returning to fetch our future with the aid of our ancestors for the benefit of our present reality and our progeny. We are cosmic cool like that. We be an Afrocentric people; time and space, we glide through; we rise soon. I am because we are . . . the future.

REFERENCES

Brosnan, M. J. (2002). *Technophobia: The Psychological Impact of Information Technology.* Routledge.

Jahn, J., & Greene, M. (1961). *Muntu: An Outline of the New African Culture.* Grove Press.

Lafrance, A. (2015, March 30). When People Feared Computers. *The Atlantic.* https://www.theatlantic.com/technology/archive/2015/03/when-people-feared-computers/388919/

Nasir Jones. (2020). Ultra Black [Song]. On *Kings Disease.* Mass Appeal; Atlantic.

Rennie, F., & Mason, R. (2004). *The Connecticon: Learning for the Connected Generation.* Information Age Publishing.

Temple, C. (2018, February). *A "Value Added" Module for Introduction to Africana Studies.* [PowerPoint slides]. University of Houston, Houston, TX, United States. https://www.academia.edu/43141231/_Chapter_A_Value_Added_Module_for_Introduction_to_Africana_Studies_Speaking_in_the_Disciplines_and_Africana_Market_Value

Vocabulary.com. (n.d.). Cyberphobia. In *Vocabulary.com Dictionary.* Retrieved December 11, 2020, from https://www.vocabulary.com/dictionary/cyberphobia

ACKNOWLEDGMENTS

THANK YOU to Dr. Molefi Kete Asante and everyone associated with the Department of Africology and African American Studies at Temple University for helping to make my future amazingly bright in so many ways. My sincerest appreciation to all the Futurist authors who contributed to this important work: Molefi Kete Asante, Taharka Adé, Alonge O. Clarkson, John P. Craig, Ifetayo M. Flannery, Kofi Kubatanna, Lehasa Moloi, and M. Ndiika Mutere.

SPECIAL ACKNOWLEDGMENTS to the graduate-level academic voices of today and tomorrow within our Africology Department who will grow to become authorities in their respective fields of study with diligence and rigorous study: Hope Dove, Carm Almonor, Marimer Berberena Alonso, Rasheed Atwater, Eva Bohler, William Chamberlin, Anthony Dandridge, Latif Davis, Jordan Denson, Brenda Edwards, Jennifer Gardner, Lindsay Gary, Jessica Hamilton, Carmella Harris, Abdul-Jabaar Isiaq, Mariama Khan, Tracey McPherson, Raven Moses, Olivia Patton, Maurice Robinson, Naaja Rogers, Matthew Simmons, Stephanie Smith, Michelle Taylor, Priscilla Thermidor, Christopher Viscuso, Louis Walee, Shane Weaver, and Christina M. Hudson.

SPECIAL THANK YOU to Taheerah Nisreen Sabb for all your assistance with this work.

To all those who believe in their ability to shape and direct their future through Afrocentric agency utilizing the lessons, culture, and ancestral connections of their roots.

From Montclair, NJ, to Philadelphia, PA, to the stars and beyond.
Afrocentric Futurism!

AFROCENTRICITY
in AFROFUTURISM

INTRODUCTION
Defining Our Future on Our Terms

Aaron X. Smith

I have been blessed to teach one of the largest elective classes on my campus at Temple University. One day, a student in my Tupac Shakur and the Hip-Hop Revolution course came up to me after I had given an energetic lecture and said, "Professor, what's the significance of Tupac for us today?" I paused, looked at the student, and asked, "Were you present for the previous lecture?" (as his question was a slight variation of the question discussed during that class). The student, almost shyly said, "I missed that class." My thought, however, was that this student really needed a substantive answer in order to move on, so I held off rushing to an interview to maximize this teachable moment. I said to the student, "Studying Tupac helps us know where we have come from so that we can know where we need to go. Everything about the life and legacy of Tupac Amaru Shakur is the merging of the past, present, and future." He thanked me and left for his next class, and luckily, I was still able to make my interview. This work, like that artistic-political legacy, reflect permeance and transcendence simultaneously, like AfroFuturism.

What I am interested in is the flow between AfroFuturism and its evolution to Afrocentric Futurism. I know, for example, as we shall see in this volume, that Afrocentricity played a representative role in the creation of AfroFuturism, but I also want to know how the speculative future is aided by the Afrocentric philosophy. Mark Dery is credited with being one of the first to use the term "AfroFuturism" (Anderson & Jones, 2016, p. viii). However, Reynaldo Anderson and Charles E. Jones (2016, p. vii) understand that a form of AfroFuturism is "speculative fiction that treats African American themes and addresses African American concerns in the context of 20th century techno-culture-and, more generally, African American signification that appropriates images of technology and a prosthetically enhanced future."

This definition of AfroFuturism has continued to expand and be interpreted and expressed through a myriad of writers, artists, scientists, and other visionary creatives. Perhaps the most significant reexamination of Dery's use of the term was conducted in 2016, with the publication of *AfroFuturism 2.0: The Rise of Astro-Blackness*, edited by Anderson and Jones. In this work, Anderson and Jones detail the evolution of the phenomenon of AfroFuturism. "What is presently called AfroFuturism was originally a techno-cultural perspective accompanying engagement in a form of cultural production, originating in practices in Black urban dwellers in North America after World War II" (Anderson & Jones, 2016, p. viii).

Anderson and Jones critique Dery's definition as not being rooted in certain elements of the 150-year history that contributed to the phenomenon of AfroFuturism. I critique existing scholarship on AfroFuturism for too often relegating Afrocentricity to the role of an equal influence among many rather than a foundational component in the roots and expansive future of this field of study. Just as Afrocentricity centers the African within her/his own historical and cultural reality, AfroFuturism will gain/grow exponentially through centering Afrocentricity in the agency-rich reshaping of the world around us, through the lens of the children of the diaspora as subject rather than the object.

Later in his introductory remarks, Anderson and Jones define AfroFuturism 2.0 as he delineates the concepts: "**AfroFuturism 2.0** is the early twenty-first century technogenesis of Black identity reflecting counter histories, hacking and or appropriating the influence of network software, database logic, cultural analytics, deep remixability, neurosciences, enhancement and augmentation, gender fluidity, posthuman possibility, the speculative sphere, with transdisciplinary applications and has grown into an important Diasporic techno-cultural 'Pan African' movement (Samatar 2015)" (Anderson & Jones, 2016, p. x, emphasis added). The question I attempt to answer with this volume is, How can an Afrocentric methodological approach to AfroFuturism effectively remedy the disproportionate influence of Eurocentrism in many

Black speculative spaces while revealing a more historically accurate and exponentially greater transformative liberatory epistemology?

In order for AfroFuturism to launch into the next generation with powerful, culturally grounded, Pan-African intentionality, the Afrocentric method must be properly implemented in the understanding and development of the phenomenon. Despite mentions of the work of Molefi Kete Asante and other Afrocentric scholars, Anderson and Jones describe a fourth dimension of AfroFuturism (the social sciences dimension), which I firmly assert requires a deeper academic dive into this *dimension*, particularly as it relates to the potential for a richer understanding of AfroFuturism through the implementation of the Afrocentric method. "**Afrocentricity** is a quality of thought or action that allows the African person to view himself or herself as an agent or actor in human history, not simply as someone who is acted upon. It provides a perspective from the subject place, not from the margins of being victims or being an object in someone else's world" (Asante, 2007, p. 7, emphasis added). One of the primary distinctions that many of the contributors to this text exhibit (in contrast to much of the previous writings on Black futurity) reflects the implementation of the Afrocentric paradigm in the process of rooting, analyzing, and predicting the future of AfroFuturism. The transformative potential of grounding existing elements of AfroFuturistic dialogue and creativity within the Afrocentric paragon will provide further avenues of historical connectivity and intellectual and cultural substantiation, as well as potential for the creation and re-creation of various modes of existing and expressing as African people throughout the diaspora.

My recognition of the numerous ways AfroFuturism emphasizes African agency and a reimagining of the world and the universe from an African/ diasporic perspective lead me to interrogate the connections between AfroFuturism and Afrocentricity. This investigation has culminated in the production of a body of Afrocentric scholarship, which takes a more in-depth look at the tensions created by the historical and cultural dislocation of African peoples and consciousness as it relates to the AfroFuturistic project and projections.

Dislocation can prove exponentially problematic when attempting to envision a future through a borrowed or superimposed methodological lens, which is unknowingly light years behind other means of expressing and engaging, despite the more sophisticated methods having been labeled primitive, reprobate, or obsolete by conquerors, colonists, and revisionist historians. In name and linguistic structure, there are similarities between Afrocentricity and AfroFuturism. The foundational dominant narrative that both seek to break free from links both terms comparatively. "AfroFuturism can be seen as a reaction to the dominance of White, European expression, and a reaction to the use of science and technology to justify racism and White or Western dominance and normativity" (Lewis, 2018, para. 2).

The utilization of technological advancement for the maintenance of European domination over the people of the African diaspora adds further layers of depth and nuance to the existing conversations around technology, futurity, and the importance of African agency coupled with Afrocentric consciousness. As a result of the foundational contributions of Afrocentricity on countless aspects of modern Black art, film, writings, and other manifestations, I found it prudent to describe this particular iteration of study and expression of Futuristic thought and creativity, as *Afrocentric Futurism*. It is the study and implementation of the early ancient Kemetic technogenesis of pioneering, cutting edge African cosmologies, creativity, and culture from an African/diasporic-centered perspective.

This foundational historiography and worldview center past, present, and future African expression, identity, evolution of thought, and civilization. Afrocentric Futurism analyzes phenomena through the foundational lens of Kemetic science, philosophy, spirituality, and related methodologies. The process of transformative forward thinking, which utilizes foundational lessons of the past, is an age-old tradition that is essential to the inception and evolution of what is commonly referred to as Africana studies. This work is designed to help readers better understand AfroFuturism within the larger context of Africana studies and how each relates to Afrocentricity. "Africana Studies is an academic extension of what Cedric Robinson has called the "Black radical tradition." This tradition is notable for emerging out of a pre-existing constellation of African intellectual work, shaped by millennia of migration, adaptation, and improvisation. Through the central acts of translation and recovery, Africana Studies seeks to theorize on the basis of long-view genealogies of African intellectual work" (Carr, 2011, p. 178).

AfroFuturism, like other more recent fields that fall under the umbrella of Africana studies, must defer chronologically and, to some extent, methodologically to the seminal components of the field, such as Afrocentricity. The Afrocentric paradigm has helped to make many of the subsequent, innovative, intellectual outgrowths possible within this imaginative, transformative space. This book "seeks to remind scholars in African studies [and beyond] that the Afrocentric idea has been the guiding paradigm of the discipline and it not only needs to be defended, but Afrocentric scholarship needs to be vigorously pursued" (Alkebulan, 2007, p. 410). Afrocentricity will not become an invisible, unrecognized, and underappreciated steppingstone in the process of Black self-determination and redefinition, which it must be thoroughly credited with encouraging and informing. Afrocentricity has helped to make much of this empowering, speculative AfroFuturistic thought possible through introducing new perceptual paradigms and literally creating numerous spaces within and outside the academy where new intellectual creative frontiers are forged.

Many of these new frontiers have deep roots in previous eras of innovation. The rich connections to the African past and the most innovative modern technology cannot be overstated. For example, this Afrocentric chronology reveals the origins of the binary code, which governs computer technologies (Platts, 2018; McIntyre, n.d.), and neurology: "In the realm of neurosurgery, ancient Egyptians were the first to elucidate **cerebral and cranial anatomy**, the first to describe evidence for **the role of the spinal cord** in the transmission of information from the brain to the extremities, and the first to invent **surgical techniques** such as trepanning and stitching" (Fanous & Couldwell, 2012, abstract, emphasis added). Alongside alchemy (Roberts, 2019), posthuman potentialities (Cockburn et al., 1998), and other realities, Afrocentric Futurism is a self-defining liberation movement, which manifests an independently driven future through the utilization of lessons and connections to the traditions and deep structures of the ancient African past. Afrocentric Futurism is an effort to further anchor, connect, and reconnect contemporary consciousness and our Futuristic innovations with the immovable power of our African culture and past and future potential as a methodological hedge of protection against cultural appropriation, which often leads to whitewashing of African history. "A more accurate term for its name would be erasure" (Anderson & Fluker, 2019, p. xi). The synthesis between Afrocentricity and AfroFuturism serves to bolster the defensive capabilities of each on the battlefield of ideas and the struggle for the independence of Black redefinition and self-determination. The weapons of this war are numerous and none more important than the other from a wholistic, interconnected, communal, Afrocentric perspective.

Our creations—our visual, digital, performative art, our stories, poems, plays, our musical compositions and sonic contextualizations, our fashion and architectural design, our medical, scientific breakthroughs, our philosophical, cultural innovations and paradigms shifts, our artistic activism—all of it serves as an undeniable witness to our survival, to Black genius, Black art, Black innovation in a world that would deny its existence, then turn around and claim it as its own. (Anderson & Fluker, 2019, p. xi)

As we move forward into the world created in large measure by Futuristic thought, the preservation of African traditions is critical. The shoulders we stand on must continuously be acknowledged in order to be most powerfully guided by ancestral forces and to utilize the lessons of the past. A leading voice in the field, Ytasha Womack, expressed homage to those who cracked the limiting literary lenses of patriarchy and racism in her crucial work *AfroFuturism: The World of Black Sci-Fi and Fantasy Culture* (2013). "AfroFuturists are not the first women to do this. Fine artist Elizabeth Catlett, author Zora Neal Hurston, and anthropologist/choreographer Katherine Dunham, among others, used imagination, art and technology to redefine Black and female expressions" (Womack, 2013, p. 101). Similarly, AfroFuturists are not the first speculative thinkers to engage in similar forms of redefinition through innovative and imaginative creativity. Scholars like John Henrik Clarke, Frances Cress Welsing, Cheikh Anta Diop, Molefi Kete Asante, Maulana Karenga, and Ama Mazama have used imagination, theory, and methodology to redefine diasporic existence. It is of vital importance that we know our past as we move forward and the benefits of the transformative potential of truly knowing ourselves.

Knowledge of the Afrocentric Self as a Conquering Compass for Futuristic Thought

The critical importance of knowledge of self was a message engraved prominently on the walls of ancient African temples over five thousand years ago (later attributed erroneously to Socrates). African self-awareness represented the spiritually conscious roadmap to finding the kingdom of heaven (note that inscribed on the Temple of Amun-Mut-Montu is "the kingdom of heaven is within you; and whosoever shall know thyself shall find it"), connecting with your God force within, as well as the stars above. These admonishments express the imperative of knowing one's past in order to know one's path.

A large portion of AfroFuturistic expressions and thought center technology in a traditionally Eurocentric sense; examples include metallics, computers, space travel, and the merging of humans and machines (technological singularity, neuromorphic computing, and neurotransmitters). Many of these expressions leave some AfroFuturist thinkers more aligned with Elon Musk than the African polymath Imhotep. This current conundrum regarding the recognition of the liberatory potential of technology when analyzing progress from the perspective of the oppressors of African people brings to mind a line from a scene in the movie *Black Panther* in which the character Killmonger accuses, "Your technological advancements have been overseen by a child who scoffs at [African] tradition" (Coogler, 2018).

Viewing the notion of Futuristic technology from a European compartmentalized standpoint could drastically limit the analytical scope of the investigation. When a culturally dislocated Futuristic lens is utilized to cast an AfroFuturistic vision, problems with practical relevance, historical accuracy, and potential benefits toward African liberation can arise. This illustrates the imperative for an Afrocentric Futurist voice to be included and centered in the larger AfroFuturism conversation. The value of the Afrocentric methodology has been championed by scholars (Asante, Karenga, James Conyers, and others for decades). According to Asante:

> "[The] Afrocentrist is concerned with discovering in every place in all circumstances the subject position of the African person. . . . Asante further argues that Africans who are operating from a Eurocentric perspective are dislocated. They are removed from their own cultural center, which has been replaced with a Eurocentric understanding of how they are in the world. . . . If a person is dislocated, then they are operating from a marginal place or within the confinements that their oppressor has outlined. (Conyers, 2018, p. 290)

Cultural and historical dislocation can contribute to degrees of self-hatred, which may result in the perversion of purpose for technological advancements and the adverse utilization of African innovations against the Afrocentric growth and development of the masses of African people. For these reasons, the distinction between AfroFuturism and Afrocentric Futurism may at first appear less significant. The nuance, when accurately delineated, has some connections to the more polarized, foundational, ana-lytical, cultural, and methodological debates concerning Eurocentric versus Afrocentric education.

Afrocentric Futuristic Theory Leaps Away from Eurocentric Domination

"Rather than grounding the imagination of counter-futures in Eurocentric philosophical and political arguments, Afrocentrism is grounded in a vari-ety of inspirations: technology (including Black cyberculture), myth forms, indigenous ethical and social ideas, and historical reconstruction of the African past" (Lewis, 2018, para. 4). This differentiation between Eurocentric and Afrocentric thought can be expressed as looking inward versus looking outward for the most advanced technologies and answers concerning the universe and our future. Afrocentric views of nature as the highest techno-logical superstructure and the human body as its crowned cosmic jewel of symbiotic, synergistic sophistication deserves greater attention. Even when ancient Africans were looking to the heavens and charting the stars, there remained a clear connection between the earthly and celestial beings. This interplay is evidenced through the merging of stars and human imagery, cre-ation stories about beings from the heavens coming to Earth, and the archi-tectural reflection of solar configurations manifested through an in-depth study of the great pyramids. Rather than a Christopher Columbus-styled, conquering exploration view of space as the great unknown, the ancient African interpretation of intergalactic connections appears to deal more with notions of a great reflection of self and a great return.

This contrast of concepts may explain the contentment toward nature and related reverence for the natural order in its untampered state, differing greatly from the engagement with nature expressed historically from the European standpoint, which constantly seeks to subdue, subvert, or improve upon nature rather than emulate the evidence of boundless genius present in even the most cursory observations of natural laws and related reali-ties. Absent the Afrocentric values of the self and the body, we increasingly encounter tales of human-computer interaction (HCI), which underestimate the sophistication of the human body, while focusing more consistently on the ways outside technologies can enhance the body and life rather than the importance of the technology of the body and nature and how it relates to the cosmos. Something as seemingly basic as drinking water can be viewed as a technological wonder when viewed through the complex lens of detoxification. "During the detoxification, waste that has been stored and disposed tissues are dumped into the blood stream and lymph [*sic*] and then sent to the liver and kidneys for processing and elimination" (Idizol, 2007, p. 393).

Viewing humans as the highest technological manifestations in history and engaging the future with that reality ever present in our mind's eye could produce drastically different visions for our collective future. Afrocentricity, communal thinking with esteem for nature and a connection and reverence to the ancestors, should be at the foundation of building the world anew toward the goal of full liberation for African people. Mentioning, referencing, and even drawing connections between AfroFuturism and African history, culture, and traditions differs greatly from centering our creative visions, Black speculative thought, scholarship, and other advancements within the Afrocentric paragon. Our future can be most powerfully and beneficially manifested through a knowledge of self and the implementation of Afrocentric culture rooted in ancestral connections.

Looking Back to See Forward: The Sankofa Foundation of Afrocentric Futurism

If early African civilizations were ahead of our current conceptualization concerning architectural feats of complex, enduring grandeur (alchemy, astrology, Waset, Abydos, the Great Zimbabwe, etc.), then it stands to reason that our future may include numerous realizations that were previously understood yet lost along the evolutionary journey of civilized humankind. In this alternate understanding, our future could very well be a return in many respects. Perhaps best expressed as an updated, improved edition of a previous foundational African program that will be understood, accessed, and manifested through a culturally and chronologically connected understanding and proper appreciation of Afrocentric Futurism.

Before we take any more quantum analytical leaps into the *dark unknown* as it relates to Futuristic visions and potential of the direct descendants of the African diaspora, it is imperative that we further assert our agency from a historically and culturally sound, self-defining, Afrocentric context.

Thus, in the spirit and speech of the ancestors, I want to engage in the practice of *sankofa*, a patient and persistent research and reasoning that enables
a critical recovery and reconstruction of the past in order to enhance our
insight into the motion and meaning of African history as the ground of the
present and the unfolding of our future (Tedla, 1995; Keto, 1994, 1995). (Asante
& Karenga, 2006, p. 166)

This work is dedicated to the importance of African chronologies, self-
awareness, and agency and the value of historical context in the shaping of
our collective future. Although, this study in a methodological sense emanates from a more targeted historically contextualized vantage point. Many
of the more general observations about the role of perspective and alternative
understandings in the shaping of AfroFuturism have been acknowledged.
The direct connections to Afrocentricity and the Afrocentric method, however, are typically mentioned in passing, as peripheral, alluded to briefly,
or completely omitted despite the undeniable connections and analytical
overlap between the two modes of thought and expression. It is crucial to
recognize the internationally interconnected ramifications of colonization
and globalism impacting AfroFuturism. "AfroFuturism implicitly recognizes
that the status quo globally—not just in the United States or the West—is one
of political, economic, social, and even technical inequality. As with much
other speculative fiction, by creating a separation of time and space from
current reality, a different kind of 'objectivity' or ability to look at possibility
arises" (Lewis, 2018, para. 3).

Alternate Chronologies and the Manifestation of Alternate Realities

Afrocentricity emphasizes a new outlook and the value of taking an objective
alternative view of traditionally Western/European influences on African
thought and creativity. Historically, the predominant predictions of the future
of humanity have come from the continent of Africa where two-thirds of
human history had taken place before any migration to other continents ever
occurred. The origins of humankind are often discussed in the context of
African history, yet seldom is similar attention devoted to the complex technological realities that are involved in the story of Africa, existing as a Futuristic
civilization for generations in comparison to other parts of the world:

Authorities in anthropology and archaeology concede that Africans were the first to discover iron, the element most useful to man. They learned how to extract iron from the ore that abounds in the interior of Africa and to refine it in furnaces, and blacksmiths throughout Africa worked the metal into useful tools. Other peoples learned to use iron only much later. In Africa, the Black was a discoverer and inventor in spite of his lack of contact with the so-called progressive parts of Asia and Europe. Scientists now give Africans credit for first discovering iron, developing stringed instruments, domesticating the sheep, goat, and cow, and learning about the planetary system. (Haber, 1970, p. viii)

Too often, complex science and modern technological advancements are juxtaposed, and any notion of ancient African existence and expression is typically deconstructed in historian circles of analysis. However, Western technological spaces are similarly plagued with these misconceptions. These perceptual impediments persist despite Africa being the home of the first civilizations and the first technologies. "In fact, everything indicates that the Egyptians had arrived at some remarkable results in certain areas of astronomy" (Sauneron, 1960, p. 152). The myth of Africa as a dark continent devoid of evolved concepts and creations contributes to the failure of some to access the Futuristic potentialities of previous African civilizations. The lie of this dangerous, dark continent states:

Africans, on this view, had never evolved civilizations of their own; if they possessed a history, it could scarcely be worth the telling. And this belief that Africans had lived in universal chaos or stagnation until the coming of Europeans seemed not only to find its justification in a thousand tales of savage misery and benighted ignorance; it was also, of course, exceedingly convenient in high imperial times. (Davidson, 1959, p. ix)

A prime example of this need for visionary realignment is elucidated through an exploration of the advanced deep sciences of the Dogon people of Mali in West Africa. The Dogon people have a rich and sophisticated astrological and astronomical infusion into the foundational aspects of their concepts of creation and their culture. The Dogon have evidenced recognition of extrasolar entities, including Sirius and two other accompanying stars, which researchers claim would not be possible to view without the aid of complex telescopic technologies. African civilizations existed on the planet thousands of years before Socrates and Plato came to Africa to study and years before the Moors ruled, educated, and uplifted Spain. "A Dogon Sage Ogotemmeli, took up thirty-three days in explaining Dogon cosmological ideas to the French ethnologist Griaule" (Davidson, 1966, p. 170). These historical realities challenge the notion of the universal benefits of a European technological worldview for Africans throughout the diaspora.

The reinterpretation of technology/technological advancement as an Afrocentric Futuristic conceptualization of Hollywood (which has often displayed the future as highly computerized, sterile, with bland or nonexistent color schemes) focuses more on humankind in harmony with nature rather than the human versus the machine. Nature is the highest form of true technology in existence. The human brain, the balance between plant life and humans in relation to oxygen and carbon dioxide, photosynthesis, the connection between bees and human life, and the magnetic pull of the moon are natural technologies yet to be replicated by computers.

Africa has predated Europe in many technological realities and continues to be the epicenter for many of the raw materials (e.g., cobalt, mica, coltan) needed to help power everything from cellular phones to automobiles. The dependency upon African natural resources in the international journey forward places Africa in a precarious geopolitical position, which can serve to contrast the future of Africa with the continued domination of the world by European powers. Is the future of AfroFuturism simply an imaginative, Eurocentric manifestation of expressions and technological advancements with an overemphasis on aesthetics masked in blackface? The distinguishing factors necessary to effectively delineate between the possibilities presented by the previous question rest heavily upon issues of culture, agency, liberation, and the identification, deconstruction, and opposition to what I label "negative aesthetics."

Negative Aestheticism

Numerous African expressions have been appropriated, commodified, and defanged by racism, capitalism, and cultural/historical dislocation. One of the primary tactics implemented in this detrimental process involves an overemphasis on the aesthetic components of African phenomena, which results in a misrepresentation of the deeper meanings, messages, and movements that undergird many African contributions to the world. This unfortunate truth can be viewed in recent memory through the drastic reduction of the Afrocentric cultural messages in hip-hop coupled with rap artists displaying an exponentially increased focus on money and fashion. Negative aestheticism may be interpreted through house speaker Nancy Pelosi kneeling for a quasiwoke photo op, draped in kente cloth, or when a Kardashian dons Bantu knots or cornrows (not boxer braids). Negative aesthetics could be bleached skin, the problematic reinterpretation of the ancient Sambo, or the demonization of African features and spiritual systems.

One way to prevent distortions and problematic appropriation is to beneficially couple culture with accurate African historical chronologies. The key to Afrocentric Futurist thought is Afrocentric agency for the liberation of African people to be self-defining: "The Afrocentrist seeks to build the foundation for full self-recognition of his or her people and their culture, a necessary condition for this empowerment. Afrocentricity defines as its priorities the deconstruction of dominant notions of African history and culture, distorted by Eurocentrism, and the reconstruction of the content obscured by them" (Nascimento, 2007, pp. 35–36).

Recognition of the powerful potential of chronologies in the process of worldview construction has resulted in a battle of storytelling, retelling, revising, whitewashing, and even erasing historical truths, which have impacted the development of AfroFuturism as a field of study. Libraries have been destroyed as a consequence of conquest since ancient times. The relationship between what master teacher Clarke referred to as the "colonization of information" and the need for greater Afrocentric grounding of AfroFuturist thought could be recognized in comments from Reynaldo Anderson given in 2017 concerning potentially problematic European perspectives of African people and others attempting to relate to and recognize the Afrocentric potential of AfroFuturism. Anderson (2017) shares one of the weaknesses expressed by "a Eurocentric perspective related to early formulations of AfroFuturism that have wondered if the history had been erased. And too many previous commentaries are little more than European studies of AfroFuturism."

Seeing America's Future through the Lens of Afrocentric History

There has been an American emphasis on the importance of rhetoricians, authors, and military leaders in traditional historiographies about the foundation and evolution of the United States. Conversely, there is a severe void in analysis and appreciation for the Africans/African Americans who brought the words to life and served, created, and sacrificed to make the country a more perfect union. African minds have thought of the freedom, integration, and progressive realities that have defined the highest collective character and determined the future of America's moral trajectory at various iterations in history. One example can be illustrated by looking into the cultural and political positions and predictions of contemporaries such as Frederick Douglass in opposition to Robert E. Lee. One could empirically deduce which of these men fit best for the role of Futurist, given the freedoms envisioned by Douglass in contrast to the continued delay of the South rising again.

Analyzing Afrocentric Futurism within the context of racially codified oppression, it is worthwhile to interrogate which people would have been the most motivated to imagine and innovate at the highest transformative levels, more than those who were in bondage. While having their labor exploited, while rendered less than human with the ever-present possibility of all manner of evil being afflicted upon them with no recompense or semblance of justice, imagination, and alternative realities can serve as valuable survival mechanisms. The rhetorical founding of the nation, with its celebrated parchment, was only a loosely stitched wish list for a proverbial "to-do list," which was primarily completed by Africans and others, boldly manifested through spontaneity, inventive genius, speculative thought, artistic innovation, and struggle. The American dream in its purest form was first envisioned and manifested by the enslaved African who believed, worked for, invented, read, wrote, prayed, lived, and died for freedom, liberty, and justice for all.

Popular Cultural Connections

The public sphere has consistently infused elements of ancient and contemporary African culture. At times, direct connections are made while other examples are linked through subtle nuance, and other examples are devoid of any manifested link to their African origin. In television, an example from my childhood comes to mind from the long-running CBS network television program *Touched by an Angel* (September 21, 1994–April 27, 2003). The series chronicles a trinity of angelic beings who roam the Earth in search of people to assist as they deal with various challenges in their lives. The most memorable character in the series is perhaps Tess (played by actress Della Reese), who is the senior angel in the trio and dispatches the other angels (Monica and Andrew) as she deems necessary.

The notion of an angelic feminine being who restores balance to people's lives and justice throughout the world was a foundational component of the spiritual cosmology of ancient Kemet (an ancient name for Egypt meaning the "Black Land"). The ancient African connection to deification may be best expressed through Ma'at. "Ma'at embodies the concept of an ideal human being. The ancients viewed the ideal human being as a silent, moderate, and sensible person who lives up to society's moral norms and values" (Okafor, 2002, p. 206). This image of perfection was powerfully feminine.

Long before any television series, the original arms of an angel were Auset piecing Ausar back together. In film, most recently, the dominant pop-culture discussion around African aesthetics, values, traditions, and technologies on screen can all be summed up in two words: "Wakanda forever." The film *Black Panther* shows actress Letitia Wright portraying Shuri, sister of King T'Challa, who utilizes the latest technologies to empower and repair (Auset style) her male familial counterpart (brother) portrayed by the late actor Chadwick Boseman. An Afrocentric Futuristic approach would pay more attention to a woman restoring the order of the universe through a reascending to the emblematic throne of divine femininity rather than simply flying through space or merging with machines.

"Black Panther is an ok hero, but where is Nat Turner, Zumbi Thutmoses III, Ramses II, Opoku, Ware I, Sundiata, Nehanda, Mansa Musa, Abubakari II, Yenenga, Hatshepsut, Fredrick Douglass, Marcus Garvey, Antenor Firmin, or Steve Biko" (Madhubuti & Boyd, 2019, p. xvi). The time has come to merge the AfroFuturist movement more thoroughly with the established Afrocentric foundation, upon which many aspects of AfroFuturist contributions emerge.

This is Octavia Butler meets Oshun. These are the cosmic philosophies of Sun Ra, connecting with the pro-Black raps and Afrocentric attire of King Sun, analyzed through the lens of the Sun rays of Ra. These are the potentialities of speculative fiction, manifested through the *Ka* (i.e., "vital life force, spirit"; Nehusi, 2016, p. 75) of the innovative imagination of Womack, cutting through the stagnation of African forward progress with the determination of Yaa Asantewaa in defense of the golden stool of Ashanti and the sacred nature of her nation.

This is where the Parliament-Funkadelic Mothership meets the biblical wheel, within a wheel of Ezekiel/Elijah, soaring through the solar system with Outkast-inspired ATLiens, on a path to reunite the African diaspora with the divinity of the Annunaki. From the wisdom teachings of Anansi, the spider, to the depths of the dark web and Sheree Thomas's work *Dark Matter* (2000), this is a process of using Afrocentricity as our guide and *sankofa* as our cultural catapults into an Afrocentric future through the practical and imaginative utilization of ancient wisdom and traditional African technologies, cosmologies, and Futuristic thought.

REFERENCES

Alkebulan, A. A. (2007). Defending the Paradigm. *Journal of Black Studies*, 37(3), 410–27. https://doi.org/10.1177/0021934706290082

Anderson, R. (2017, November 7–12). *Enter AfroFuturism at the OCC | Renaldo Anderson: Interstellar Black Power and AfroFuturism* [Video]. YouTube. https://www.youtube.com/watch?v=QqgOUzy2xII&t=3379s

Anderson, R., & Fluker, C. (2019). *The Black Speculative Arts Movement: Black Futurity, Art+Design*. Lexington Books.

Anderson, R., & Jones, C. E. (2016). Introduction: The Rise of Astro-Blackness. In R. Anderson & C. E. Jones (Eds.), *AfroFuturism 2.0: The Rise of Astro-Blackness* (pp. vii–xviii). Lexington Books.

Asante, M. (2007). The Resurgence of the African World in the 21st Century. In A. Mazama (Eds.), *Africa in the 21st Century: Toward a New Future* (pp. 3–16). Routledge.

Asante, M., & Karenga, M. (2006). *The Handbook of Black Studies*. Sage Publications.

Carr, G. (2011). What Black Studies Is Not: Moving from Crisis to Liberation in Africana Intellectual Work. *Socialism and Democracy*, 25(1), 178–91.

Cockburn, A., Cockburn, E., & Reyman, T. (1998). *Mummies Disease & Ancient Culture* (2nd ed.). Cambridge University Press.

Conyers, L., Jr. (2018). *African Methodology: A Social Study of Research, Triangulation and Meta-Theory*. Cambridge Scholar.

Coogler, R. (Director). (2018). *Black Panther* [Film]. Marvel Studios; Walt Disney Studios Motion Pictures.

Davidson, B. (1959). *The Lost Cities of Africa*. Little, Brown and Company.

Davidson, B. (1966). *A History of West Africa to the Nineteenth Century*. Anchor Books.

Fanous, A., & Couldwell, W. (2012). Transnasal Excerebration Surgery in Ancient Egypt. *Journal of Neurosurgery*, 6(4), 743–48. https://doi.org/10.3171/2011.12.JNS11417

Haber, L. (1970). *Black Pioneers of Science and Invention*. Harcourt.

Idizol, A. (2007). *Directory of Priests and Priestesses 2008–2009* (8th ed.). National African Religion Congress.

Lewis, J. (2018, February 19). *AfroFuturism: Imagining an Afrocentric Future, Rejecting Eurocentric Dominance and Normalization*. ThoughtCo. https://www.thoughtco.com /AfroFuturism-definition-4137845

Madhubuti, H., & Boyd, H. (2019). *Black Panther, Paradigm Shift or Not?* Third World Press Foundation.

McIntyre, L. (n.d.). *Ancient Egyptian Mathematics and Computers*. University of Georgia Mathematics Education Program, J. Wilson, EMAT 6690. http://jwilson.coe.uga.edu/ EMAT6680Fa11/McIntyre/6690%20Egyptian%20Math%20and%20Computers/Essay %201%20EgyptianMathComputers.htm

Nascimento, E. (2007). *The Sorcery of Color, Identity, Race, and Gender in Brazil*. Temple University.

Nehusi, K. (2016). *Libation: An Afrikan Ritual of Heritage in the Circle of Life*. University Press of America.

Okafor, V. (2002). *Towards an Understanding of Africology* (4th ed.). Kendall Hunt.

Platts, J. (2018, April 16). *Ancient Egyptians: The Original Computer Scientists?* Medium. https://medium.com/@jillplatts/ ancient-egyptians-the-original-computer-scientists-ab97322d48dd

Roberts, A. (2019). *Hathor's Alchemy: The Ancient Egyptian Roots of the Hermetic Art*. Northgate.

Sauneron, S. (1960). *The Priests of Ancient Egypt*. Grove Press.

Womack, Y. L. (2013). *Afrofuturism: The World of Black Sci-Fi and Fantasy Culture*. Chicago Review Press.

Part One

REPRESENTATIONS

1

HANTU FROM THE ORAL-AESTHETIC PERSPECTIVE
AfroFuturism Transcending the Matrix Space-Time Warp

M. Ndiika Mutere

AfroFuturism has been defined by Alondra Nelson as "a critical perspective that opens up inquiry into the many overlaps between technoculture and Black diasporic histories" (qtd. in Gunkel & Lynch, 2019, p. 28). The term itself was coined in 1994 by Mark Dery to define philosophical inquiries into aesthetic trends that evolved in conjunction with America's space race, a Euro-patriarchally constructed technocultural era that was triggered around the 1957 launch of Russia's Sputnik satellite.[1] A pioneering example was musician Sun Ra's space-themed links to Kemet/ancient Egypt in the 1950s. Music artists such as George Clinton, Lee Scratch Perry, Earth, Wind & Fire, OutKast, and Janelle Monáe followed, charting new frontiers through the interview "Black to the Future" and its creative visions (Dery, 1994, p. 736), AfroFuturistic explorations, and vehicles built on oral-aesthetic traditions (Mutere, 1995). Black culture was thus asserting its own unique and sovereign agency in navigating this pivotal era in human history.

Academically, the same 1957 launch of Russia's Sputnik coincided with the establishment of African studies in American universities. In order to be competitive within the larger Cold War circumstances of the times, the

US government funded the development of American expertise on Africa so as to gain and maintain access to key natural resources from the geopolitically designated region of "sub-Saharan" (Eurocentric terminology) Africa. The Kemet/Egypt of Sun Ra's AfroFuturistic explorations were assigned to a Middle Eastern– or Near Eastern–studies annex—alongside Arabic, Armenian, Jewish, and Islamic studies—within campuses such as the University of California at Los Angeles where African studies programs were initially installed. Thus, the political impact upon academic constructions of African time-space at various US campuses can be seen, including historically Black Howard University. Black studies would not be formalized in the American academy until over a decade later and then only through African American struggles for civil rights and as a separate entity from US studies of Africa.[2]

Africa's space-time continuum referred to in this writing and within Bantu philosophical thought as *hantu* has been warped on multiple levels by competing Western ideologies and political agendas. These will be examined and evaluated in terms of what sets each apart from the other as sovereign entities, thus forces within the *universe*-as-theater of human affairs. The role played by the *university* in constructing humanity's controlling narratives makes the institution a pivotal link within the pipeline of Western industrial processes and alienating ideas of "progress" which have been largely dependent upon African resource control, including claims to ancient Egypt. In contrast, an Africa-centered perspective values a balanced chronological worldview in the spirit of *sankofa*, where looking back is essential to most effectively and productively moving forward.

The curation, preservation, and advancement of *hantu*—the Bantu philosophical category of space-time implied in "AfroFuturism" as a term—thus becomes the raison d'*être* or process of self-reparations *sankofa* directs. This writing will discuss how, from diasporic theaters, African oral traditions have uniquely and significantly contributed toward human well-being through their culturally mandated *art-for-life's-sake* role—a communication problem that has yielded time-tested empirical data when regarded on its own sovereign terms of existence. Black pop music is a significant paradigm of proof in this regard (Mutere, 2012). In his study on the technologizing of the word, Walter Ong (1982, p. 8.) accedes that "oral expression can exist and mostly has existed without any writing at all, writing never without orality." Yet writing became the latter-day cultural aggressor in human communication and affairs (McLuhan, 1964) evolving as a weapon of "creative destruction" (Schumpeter, 1975, p. 83) to create a matrix of containment, order, and control (Carey, 1989) in contrast to African oral-aesthetic praxis (Mutere, 2012) and Bantu philosophical principles (Kagame, 1976).

The American Theater of *Hantu*: "Manifest Destiny" versus *Ubuntu*

Ubuntu—meaning "I am, because we are" (Mbiti, 1969, p. 141)—is a term that encapsulates the philosophical core and cultural worldview of Bantu, meaning "persons" and/or "of *ntu*"—the great "I am." Bantu concepts of the universe thus manifest as unity-consciousness from the collective of theaters where "we are" in the global village as cocreators. From America, in particular, the Bantu presence has been one of the world's great civilizing forces. Robert F. Thompson provides several examples in a documentary entitled *New York: The Secret African City* (Kidel, 1989) and in his chapter titled "Kongo Influences on African American Artistic Culture" (Thompson 2005, 283–325). Joseph E. Holloway—a scholar of Africanisms in the New World after such pioneers as Lorenzo Dow Turner, Carter G. Woodson, Melville J. Herskovits—explains from his research data that 40 percent of all enslaved Africans in America were Bantu from Central Africa. Originating largely from Congo and Angola, Holloway (2005, p. 19) asserts that Bantu were "the largest homogeneous culture among the imported Africans and [had] the strongest impact on the development of African American culture."

> Once the Bantu reached America, they were able to retain much of their cultural identity. Enforced isolation of these Africans by plantation owners allowed them to retain their religion, philosophy, culture, folklore, folkways, folk beliefs, folk tales, storytelling, naming practices, home economics, arts, kinship, and music. These Africanisms were shared and adopted by the various African ethnic groups of the field slave community, and they gradually developed into African American cooking (soul food), music (jazz, blues, spirituals, gospels), language, religion, philosophy, customs, and arts. (Holloway 2005, pp. 36–37)

According to renowned musician and trumpeter Wynton Marsalis, "The bloodlines of all important modern American music can be traced to Congo

Square" (qtd. in Evans, 2011, front matter). Situated in what is now the Louis Armstrong Park in Tremé—the oldest African American neighborhood in New Orleans's port city of Louisiana, this historic birthplace of jazz and rhythm and blues was the area in which enslaved Africans were permitted to gather on Sundays for music, dance, and merrymaking. Beginning in the early 1700s under French, Spanish, and then American rule, the trans-Atlantic trafficking of enslaved Africans from Congo and Angola, in particular, thus turned New Orleans into a formidable Bantu cultural theater. Conversations between ancient oral traditions and new world elements manifested around the *ubuntu* consciousness they practiced, which has been described thus:

> Africans believe in something that is difficult to render in English. We call it *ubuntu*, *botho*. It means the essence of being human. You know when it is there and when it is absent. It speaks about humaneness, gentleness, hospitality, putting yourself out on behalf of others, being vulnerable. It embraces compassion and toughness. It recognizes that my humanity is bound up in yours, for we can only be human together. (Tutu, 1989, p. 71)

Angola—an eight-thousand-acre Louisiana plantation about 150 miles northwest of Congo Square named after the African homeland—was originally owned by Isaac Franklin, a wealthy slave trader. In 1880, it was turned into the Angola State Prison where inmates housed in old slave quarters would do plantation work. Despite the 1807 act prohibiting the further importation of slaves, New Orleans fast became the nation's largest slave market in the antebellum South through forced migration, illegal shipments of slaves from the Caribbean, the domestic resale of enslaved Africans through the Mississippi valley, and by becoming the largest exporter of slave-picked cotton. Eli Whitney's 1793 invention of the cotton gin played a decisive role in evolving a technoculture that was increasingly dependent on slave labor to fulfill industry demand and increase capital gain for those in control. Meanwhile, Angola (which grew to eighteen thousand acres by 2008)— America's largest maximum-security prison—became known as the "Alcatraz of the South" due to its harsh conditions.

Between the War of 1812 and the American Civil War in 1860, an ideological fervor known as "Manifest Destiny" had also taken hold. Overtly Eurocentric, the central belief of Manifest Destiny held that White settlers were destined to expand across North America and, by extension, the world—promoting and defending their worldview. Later labeled "American exceptionalism," its three basic programs were: (1) White people and their institutions have special virtues; (2) the US has a mission to redeem and remake the world in its own image, which was plantation based at the time; and (3) accomplishing this goal is America's duty to god—hence it's Manifest Destiny. Author of *The Sovereign Psyche*, Ezra Aharone (2016, p. 17), notes in his discussion on the three dimensions of sovereignty: "Simply put, in order for sovereignty to function with the highest efficiency, these 3 Dimensions must always operate in singular and synchronized fashion. . . . In the final analysis the effectiveness of a sovereign psyche hinges heavily on intellect and willpower."

Consider their motives and psychology behind the likes of the Magna Carta of 1215; the Westphalian Sovereignty Accord of 1648; Chattel Slavery; American Exceptionalism; the Treaty of Paris 1783; Manifest Destiny; the Berlin Colonial Congress of 1884; the White Man's Burden; and Globalism of today. Each instance puts their *Sovereign Psyche* on display whereby ideals of freedom, government, and development are interworked for their societies to flourish. Congo Square thus became one of several ideological crossroads for Bantu who had arrived to this American theater through a time-space warp (the "Middle Passage") in the most profoundly traumatizing and culturally disenfranchising of ways. With *ubuntu* as the overriding cultural mandate preserved in their oral traditions, against the greatest odds, Congo Square became a cultural and spiritual intersection where empirical contrasts in the interface of two separate "sovereignties" became apparent. Here, ancient oral-aesthetic techniques manifested a certain civility within American discourse; oftentimes by the way musicians improvised on instruments and in tongues that suited the mixed comfort levels of those in attendance, e.g., merging French songs that came in from Haiti or reconstructing songs from British colonies through African rhythms. Similarly, they'd bring instruments from a range of cultures into conversation with each other, like bamboula drums, gourds, violins, banjos, *banzas*, quill pipes, marimbas, bells, flutes, triangles, tambourines, and Jew's harps. (These rhythms and arrangements are heard today in jazz funerals, second lines, and Mardi Gras parades.) By manifesting inclusive, conversational, and democratic arrangements—jazz, among other art-for-life's-sake expressions, African oral-aesthetic communication systems were a civilizing force that transformed the American theater and the universe beyond.

Creative Destruction: The Matrix and Transportation Communication Modes

Cornel West (1993, pp. 14–20) has contended that Black American existence is under the threat of nihilism, which he describes as a lived experience of "horrifying meaninglessness, hopelessness, and . . . loveless-ness." In *Prophetic Fragments* (1988), he critiques religion for not warding off this nihilistic threat by being the key support structure it once was for Black life in America. He argues that it instead accommodates the political and cultural status quo and becomes one more addictive stimulant in America's consumerist, narcissistic, and hedonistic culture. Accusing religion of complicity in fueling consumption and breeding existential emptiness, West (1988, pp. ix–xi) writes of the urgent need to generate cultural agency that confronts and converts Black self-destruction through a love-centered ethic of self-valuation with modes of political resistance and transcendence.

Though Africology, under the leadership of Molefi Asante (2015), provides such an intellectual platform, West and other notable Black scholars have tended to argue from a perspective that views the African American identity as being forged in America rather than Africa—as if slavery's historical outcome irrevocably severed cultural continuity. The term "natal alienation," coined by Orlando Patterson in his book *Slavery and Social Death* (1982), is taken by West (1988, p. 4) to mean "a form of social death in which people have no legal ties of birth in both ascending and descending generations, [and] no right to predecessors or progeny." Edward F. Frazier (1928) similarly argues that the devastation of slavery was so complete as to render African cultural antecedents obsolete in America. Such arguments from notable Black scholars raise concerns about their submission to the controlling narratives of those whose modus operandi to maintain rule over African descendants is to deny their identity and agency as cultural sovereigns and instead diminish and cast them as racialized Black "others."

The 2013 International Association for Media and Communication Research conference missed an opportunity to speak to such concerns. Its theme (and event title)—Crises, "Creative Destruction" and the Global Power and Communication Orders—provoked thought on the possibility of a plurality of *communication orders* from the separate accounts of global sovereigns (Mutere, 2013) and their contrasting narratives for humanity. "Creative destruction" is an economic term coined by Austrian American economist Joseph Schumpeter (1975, pp. 82–85) to describe how the development of

Western capitalism requires the destruction and reconfiguration of previous economic orders and the ceaseless devaluation of existing wealth through dereliction, war, or periodic economic crises. The ceaseless devaluation and expropriation of Africa's "existing wealth"—*human, natural, spiritual*, and *cultural* resources—as modalities to engineer "social death" under the auspices of slavery, colonialism, and industrialism should have been on the agenda, which would frame the dilemma of a single, industrially biased, Eurocentric controlling narrative.

Martin Bernal (1987, pp. 27–28) addresses this dilemma by exposing the matrix of Western knowledge as an *industry* founded upon racist myth making, effecting creative destruction through a core "paradigm-of-progress" thesis. According to Bernal, modern disciplinary scholarship was pioneered in 1734 at the University of Göttingen (Germany), where scholarly accounts of civilization featured imperialistic, religious, romantic, and racist elements that reflected a Christian reaction *against* Greek religious identification with its Egyptian antecedent. Instead, a "Romantic Hellenism" evolved to promote the myth of Greece as the epitome of European civilization and its "pure" genesis, casting ancient Egypt as a static civilization by comparison. Eurocentric notions of "later is better" and "the conqueror is superior to the conquered" were endorsed by and constructed upon this academically engineered bedrock of propaganda Bernal refers to as the "paradigm of progress." These notions fueled the rise of racism, which Bernal (1987, pp. 27–28) contends was needed as justification for African enslavement and colonialism as well as the American policy to exterminate Indigenous peoples.

Thus, the academic portal in African space-time was initially breached in Kemet where knowledge, a sacred custodianship, was taught by priests in the *per-Ankh*—"Houses of Life"—attached to temples. One such temple is Ipet Resyt—the "Southern Sanctuary" built for God/dess consorts Amun-Mut, known today as the Luxor Temple. It is partly renowned for its architecture resembling a human figure in repose on African soil (Schwaller de Lubicz, 1981). Several proverbs inscribed throughout the temple of Ipet Resyt mention religious iconography and the relationship between the spiritual self and divine purpose and power. Many of the spiritual teachings and admonishments present in the inscriptions found in ancient Kemet have made their way into works that are foundational to the Abrahamic faith (Carlos Bustamante Restrepo, 2015).

Djehuti, a chief priest and creator of hieroglyphs ("holy writing"), among other significant accomplishments, referred to Kemet itself thus: "Art thou not aware that Egypt is the image of heaven, or rather, that it is the projection below of the order of things above? If the truth must be told, this land is indeed the temple of the world" (qtd. in Trismegistus, 1885, p. 71). He then prophetically lamented times ahead when this land would become a place where "strangers will fill the earth" (qtd. in Trismegistus, 1885, p. 71).

The commandeering of Kemet's sacred knowledge in service to Greco-Roman empire building transitioned human affairs over the BCE–CE threshold to a linear Julian-Gregorian timeline, a highly abstract alphabetic communication technology and its controlling narratives, including that of a savior derivative from the Annunciation record at Ipet Resyt. Of the Greek role in this process, George G. M. James (2013, p. 1) writes:

> The Egyptian Mystery System was a Secret Order. . . . After nearly five thousand years of prohibition against the Greeks, they were permitted to enter Egypt for the purpose of their education. . . . From the sixth century BC to the death of Aristotle (322 BC) the Greeks made the best of their chance to learn all they could about Egyptian culture; most students received instructions directly from the Egyptian Priests, but after the invasion by Alexander . . . the Royal temples and libraries were plundered and pillaged, and Aristotle's school converted the library at Alexandria into a research center.

Thus, creative destruction of the mysteries was set in motion through Greco-Roman modalities of writing, interpretation, and record keeping. Marshall McLuhan (1964) defines Western communication orders that subsequently arose as *transportation* models concerned with moving data from point *A* to point *Z* efficiently and with minimal distortion—an industrial-mechanical process that is intimately tied to the West's abstract and linear phonetic alphabet. McLuhan cautions that, as technology, the alphabet exhibits aggressive tendencies in human affairs unlike hieroglyphs, which, as pictographs, connect one's consciousness with the organic world. Over the course of history, abstract and linear European orientations led to conquest and hegemonic control of outer space (the matrix) justified by a thesis of "rationalism" and "progress." "Rational" for the West has long meant "uniform, continuous and sequential," McLuhan (1964, p. 15) elaborates, concluding that the West has thus confused "reason"/"rationalism" with its particular form of literacy and "progress" with a single aggressive technology of abstraction.

Thus, ideologies of Western exceptionalism originally founded at the University of Göttingen (Bernal, 1987) were made "official" through an aggressive linear communication modality and the technoculture it reinforces (McLuhan, 1964). Africology (Asante, 2015) argues against Eurocentrism's universalist claims and on behalf of an antecedent sovereignty whose communication *tkhn* culture (Mutere, 2012)—informed by ideologies of *ma'at* and *ubuntu*—acts on behalf of Africa's descendants and nurtures humanity, unlike the other which is referred to in popular parlance as the "matrix." Controlled by a hegemonic elite, this false "matrix" masquerades as "universal" but is generally experienced by its socially engineered/controlled masses as alienating and oppressive.

James Carey concurs with McLuhan by confirming the American knowledge industry's normative mindset being driven by an allegiance to *transportation communication models*. The movement of goods, people, and information is regarded within this industrially oriented technoculture as identical communication transactions. Carey (1989, pp. 13) says that although these processes were initially formulated through an agenda for the "extension of God's kingdom on earth" (as in Manifest Destiny and American exceptionalism), Western transportation models nonetheless developed as a matrix of containment, order, and control. Among its negative consequences was the demise of creativity within academia, an outcome lamented by education reformist Ken Robinson (ARC 2016) who attributes this manifestation to the environment of standardization fostered by and policed within Western industrial systems.

Not surprisingly, Göttingen's *knowledge-industry model* (Bernal, 1987) was forged when slavery was well underway—during the mid-1700's Industrial Revolution, during which the emphasis was placed on extraction, higher yield, objectification, compartmentalization, standardization, accumulation, etc. German feminist scholar, Heide Göttner-Abendroth (1985, 83) critiques the detachment from human life that is systemically fostered by such a Euro-patriarchal model of industrialism, presenting as evidence the extended communication chains (e.g., artist-creative product-dealer-agent-critic-marketplace audience) that typically exist between art-for-art's-sake productions on one end and a programmed/standardized consumer base on the other. Like Robinson who recommends that the ideal educational process would be one that develops creative/artistic powers linking organically to the ecosystem where humans naturally belong, Göttner-Abendroth argues for a matriarchal alternative.

The Oral-Aesthetic Perspective: A Transformation Communication Flow

In Cheikh Anta Diop's (1990) "two-cradle" theory of humankind, he distinguishes between the northern Euro-patriarchal cradle and the ideologically dissimilar ancient African matriarchal cradle of the southern hemisphere. Diop contends that northerners espouse ideals of violence, war, and conquest and promote pessimistic religious systems based on guilt, original sin, and alienation from nature[3] and the feminine-principle[4]; whereas southerners engender a humane ethos based on the cocreational partnership between genders and their organic *mind-body-spirit* pact with nature. This pact is integral to Sema Tawy, the formal unification of Upper (south) Egypt and Lower (north) Egypt in 3100 BCE that took place under Pharaoh Menes, also known as Narmer, as ancient Egypt entered its dynastic period. Sema Tawy's symbol depicts the human trachea arising from the lungs and entwined with local plants, which represent the south (lily) and the north (papyrus). This bond continued to be upheld in the sacred rituals enacted between Ipet Resyt and Ipet Isut, Amun-Mut's southern (Luxor) and northern (Karnak) sanctuaries.

The beneficial interplay between north and south continues to play a significant role throughout the African continent. The Congo Square, for example, is a crucible of the "south" from which Africa's oral traditions manifested as a traceable civilizing force over the four-hundred-year period in the northern hemisphere that began in slavery. Below are summaries of motifs from these transformative traditions—tools by which to understand and evaluate how well these south-north bonds met their own art-for-life's-sake cultural mandates, as measured through Black pop music (Mutere, 2012).

Ubuntu is the first and overarching oral-aesthetic motif that encompasses its meaning; "I am because we are" is the guiding cultural mandate that informs Africa-centered communication orders, mechanisms and missions, and guides human imagination toward creating a more organic and perfect union. *Ubuntu* expresses dynamically, interactively, and transformatively as art for life's sake within an aesthetic field that is understood in Bantu thought to be the *universe of forces*—a quantum field that is conceived of in four categories:

- **Muntu** (singular)/**Bantu** (plural) refers to human beings who, because of their endowment of intelligence, also have exclusive control of *nommo* (the generative power of the word).
- *Kintu* refers to forces that cannot act for themselves, e.g., inanimate objects such as tools.
- *Kuntu* is the modal force with an art-for-life's-sake mission and goal of aesthetic beauty. Failure in that high-stakes mission "anaesthetizes" and therefore, as art for art's sake, lacks *kuntu* or aesthetic quality/beauty.
- *Hantu* is the category of space-time that, like the term "AfroFuturism," responds to questions of *where* and *when* but from within a nonlinear Africa-centered consciousness of the quantum field. In contrast to Eurocentrism's three-dimensional matrix of the material world where the fourth and fifth dimensions of "time" and "spirituality" are constructed linearly and regulated from within compartmentalized hierarchic arrangements, the Bantu universe is realized as a dynamic space-time continuum of several interactive dimensions and forces at once. It's a consciousness in which, for instance, environmental events accompanying one's birth would inform a child's traditional naming, thus encoding and protecting their organic/sovereign place, purpose, and journey in Africa's space-time continuum. Otherwise, *hantu* itself has been colonized by Greco-Roman weekdays/months invoking latter-day gods from Gregorian calendars manufactured with a seven-year Euro-Futuristic differential ahead of the ancestral timelines still used in Africa's horn.

"**Ntu**" is the creator principle residing in and unifying the above-mentioned categories in the Bantu universe of forces and dimensions, which go well beyond those of the material and largely Euro-patriarchal 3D construct. However, *ntu* is not suited to be the object of worship. It neither proselytizes nor disenfranchises in the name of an abstract religion or for self-glorification. *Ntu* operates on principles of harmony and coherence between these forces as they interact, necessitate, and complement each other in the quantum theater through the agency of Bantu cocreators. Hence the philosophical and moral understanding of *ubuntu*: I am because we are.

Following *ubuntu* as the overarching oral-aesthetic motif, the six others (summarized briefly below) are as follows:

- *Mojo* is an Ebonics term from the Bantu word *kimoyo*, meaning "[language] of the spirit." Mojo—the flow of this spirit or creator principle (*ntu*)—is operationalized outwardly into the arena of human affairs through oral articulation or *nommo*. Mojo often mediates between the detached, alienating field of oppositional dualities (e.g., good/evil, spirit/flesh, sacred/secular) representing mind-body-spirit divisions of Euro-patriarchal thought imposed on the Bantu universe of forces. Mojo is working when *ntu* organically engenders life from the aesthetic language, form(s), and flow between cocreational forces that explain, necessitate, and interact with each other, collectively informing the structure and harmonious workings of the universe or *ubuntu*.

- *Call response*, fundamental to African oral communication flows, is the mechanism that assumes interactivity between individuals and within groups to establish and maintain *centralized* and/or *decentralized* forms of social and political order. *Nommo*—the generative power of the word that is aesthetically enhanced as music—is the masculine principle (seed) at cocreative play in transformations of feminine space-time (womb/Earth). Before its media-related use, the term "broadcast" referred to the literal scattering/sowing of seeds over land. Measured as *ubuntu*, the collective human experience is the final empirical authority on the success of *nommo*'s broadcast into this mission field and the *hantu* (time-space) continuum.

- *Jazz* conversations in themselves tend to reflect a *decentralized* democratic consensus, as opposed to the *centralized* leader-chorus call-response oral-aesthetic arrangements that typically emerged from Black churches. As such, jazz is a performer's art rather than a composer's art. Jazz is reflective of group success being driven by everyone's input—similar to the oral-aesthetic dynamics of hunting-and-gathering societies—rather than a leader's charisma, which may or may not serve the group's best interests. This connects to the cultural belief that "it is the *people* who make a leader great." Etymologically linked to the masculine creative principle of *nommo* as seed, jazz discourse throughout time-space since its Congo Square genesis (discussed above) has manifested working models of democracy and inclusion while respecting and reflecting difference and aesthetic sensibilities.

- *Kinetic orality* occurs when Bantu who hear music understand and transcribe it in dance. "Walking the talk" or the inseparability of dance and its music is a principle of balance and harmony in the oral-aesthetic life-world—a spirit-mind-body dialogue/call response that kinetically extends *nommo* outwards and manifests socially. It's an integrated art-for-life's-sake process with creational flows (Mojo) governing narratives (art for life's sake), communal imperatives (*ubuntu*), transcendental passageways, etc. Detaching dance from its music impacts the navigational settings of the Bantu oral-aesthetic continuum. As Robert Farris Thompson (1974, p. xii) says, "Sculpture is not the central art, but neither is the dance, for both depend on words and music and even dreams and divination."

- *Masquerade* is the motif representing survival strategies/techniques in which outward forms (masks) would be created to appease hostile authorities while protecting the deeper integrity and mission of Bantu cultural source codes. An African mask might hold two designations: the first being the visual codes the artisan provides; the second being provided by the dancer who wears it in performance. Without the masquerade certain masks would be considered incomplete because they lack efficacy as *nommo*. A master drummer would know how best to activate and navigate these oral-aesthetic masks and/or "code-switch" on behalf of the community.

  The masquerade motif also reflects upon entertainment-industry history, which began in the 1830s with minstrel performances, consisting of White actors in Blackface, warping the cultural expression and lives of enslaved Africans. "Ethiopian delineators," as the minstrels called themselves, created caricatures such as "Jim Crow" and "Zip Coon," codifying the public imagination with negative Black stereotypes and Whiteness as the antithesis (creative destruction). The minstrelsy era came to a close around the 1920s with the cultural assertiveness of the jazz age, as it had evolved from Congo Square and through northern migrations.

- *Talking drum* is an African musical instrument. Drums, in particular, represent the communal heartbeat and spoken language, extending the body and oral communication patterns (*nommo*) of the human prototype in their roles as secondary 3D models and cocreators, amplifying rhythmic portals of access to the quantum Bantu universe. Efforts by slave masters to sabotage African communication networks by destroying traditional instruments were thwarted by culturally conscious adaptations of the human prototype.

The talking-drum motif pays attention to the specialized role and revered status of master drummers from societies with strong drumming traditions, including those with sacred drums, like the Nyabingi (discussed below). Each of the six motifs is a highly significant link in our understanding of the oral-aesthetic substance that connects Bantu and governs *hantu* throughout the diaspora. Related myths/mysteries provide codes that aid in that process of curating Bantu space-time and resurrecting gods put to "sleep" by Euro-patriarchal antagonists and false narratives.

For instance, part of the mystery of the *tkhn*—an obelisk and architectural symbol of resurrection from ancient Kemet—is its identical spelling to the hieroglyph that refers to drums, drumming patterns, and related musical gifts (Budge, 1920). Ausar, Kemet's popular king who was said to have had a great passion for song and dance, had his reign cut short by a jealous antagonist named Set—a reputed god of foreign invasion and chaos who murdered and dismembered Ausar. Set then scattered the fourteen pieces of Ausar into the wilderness—an allegory for the African diaspora traumatized and reconfigured from slavery, colonialism, and apartheid—through which Auset's widow must travel on a search-and-recovery mission. Auset's crown, a symbolic heaven-on-Earth throne, represents her consciousness and mission as Ausar's divine counterpart. She mummifies the thirteen pieces she's able to locate of her deceased husband's body and then receives divine intervention to posthumously conceive Heru, their son who is destined to battle Set for the restoration of Kemet's throne. From an oral-aesthetic perspective, Ausar's fourteenth piece (represented by the *tkhn* symbol) is an AfroFuturistic testimonial of this fertility god as an ascended master drummer within the quantum Bantu theater.

The Global Drum Circle and *Ma'atrix*: From Nyabingi to Hip-Hop

When one "returns to the source to reclaim that which may have been lost, forgotten, or stolen," AfroFuturism becomes a lens that potentially resets us to a qualitatively different account from the linear story of human "progress" found(ed) within parasitic Greco-Roman myths and the predatory/controlling University of Göttingen narratives and timelines (Bernal, 1987), which exposes flaws in the matrix system's core. *Sankofa* is a reparations mandate for Bantu to circle back around in response to the cultural drum—a collective rendering of ancestral heartbeats that creates the organic time-space frequencies (*hantu*) of a global African odyssey (Mutere, 1997) and its unity-conscious mission, *ubuntu*. In Kemet—"the temple of the world" (Trismegistus, 1885, p. 71), this ideal state of truth, balance, and justice that remains tied to "source" in the geographic heart of Africa is referred to as *ma'at*.

According to the papyrus of Hunefer (1300 BCE), "We came from the beginning of the Nile where God Hapi dwells, at the foothills of the Mountains of the Moon" (Van Auken, 2011, p. 50). Rwenzori, as these mountains are also named, are located on the colonial border separating present-day Congo and Uganda in Toro—one of several traditional Bantu kingdoms surrounding a major source of the Nile River in Africa's Great Lakes region, which plays a role as cultural caretaker of humanity's sacred womb. Other Bantu kingdoms include Ankole, Buganda, Bunyoro, Busoga, and Abaluyia. The latter, a Buganda offshoot in present-day western Kenya, "have it in their oral tradition that they came from Misri [Egypt]" (Osogo, 1966, p. 140).

Other consciousness of the sacredness of humanity's organic *Ma'at*rix is evident in the Swahili term for the Great Lakes and waters of the Nile as "*Maziwa Mkuu*" (meaning "great milk"), a recognition of the Milky Way mirrored on Earth and flowing from humanity's cradle to blossom in ancient times as Kemet—present-day Egypt, which is still referred to as "the gift of the Nile." The south-north geographic journey of the Nile is ingrained within the quantum Bantu universe as a navigational setting that is organically aligned with the heavens. In America, for instance, this same consciousness guided Benjamin Banneker's 1791 role in the mapping of what is referred to in Afrocentric circles as "Egypt on the Potomac" (Browder, 2004) in Washington, DC, where the National Museum of African American History and Culture (opened in 2016) now stands next to America's *tkhn* replica—the Washington Monument (built 1848–1884). Later, during the Underground Railroad era (through the 1860s), Africans escaping slavery in the South knew through "map songs" that in order to "steal away to Jesus," they had to "wade in the water" (to confuse hunting dogs) and "follow the drinking gourd" (the Big Dipper constellation) to freedom via the North Star.

The seminal heartbeat of this consciousness within Mama Africa's womb is represented by Goddess Nyabingi's sacred drum. According to mythology, Nyabingi's rule was disrupted by the theft of her sacred drum in the late 1800s along with the arrival of explorers searching on behalf of Britain's Queen Victoria for the Nile River source. Nyabingi's powers had already earned her a reputation in the colonial mind as a great sorceress. Nyabingi, along with her followers, waged war against the intrusion into Africa's Great Lakes region by colonials whose missionaries were pushing Christianity, resulting in the deaths of colonial-puppet chiefs. The British response was to pass the Witchcraft Act (Goodare, 2005), which threatened burnings at the stake. Although the Nyabingi resistance was eventually subdued and the region colonized, by the 1930s, it had caught fire in the Caribbean.

Nyabingi, oldest of the Rastafari subgroups that emerged in Jamaica, is a name meaning "death to all oppressors." In Rastafari observances, *bingi* is chanted in prayer, music, dance, and biblical reasonings through which adherents call on the destruction of "Babylon" by natural forces. Nyabingi's heartbeat is played on a trinity of drums: thunder (a bass drum referred to as the "pope smasher" or "Vatican basher"); *funde* (the middle drum, which maintains the dominant heartbeat); and *akete* or repeater (the smallest, highest pitched drum, which plays the most improvisational role as carrier of spirit). In concert with Jamaican *kumina* practices inherited from the BaKongo, this heartbeat pulses in the reggae, ska, and rock-steady musical stylings of artists such as Peter Tosh, Black Uhuru, Count Ossie, Burning Spear, and Bob Marley, the latter of whom preached *ubuntu* in his song "One Love." Musical recordings were initially broadcast via mobile disc jockey (DJ) units in Jamaica, an island tradition that became key to the development of hip-hop's seminal heartbeat in early 1970s America. Dawn Norfleet (2006, p. 357) notes:

> DJs were the focal points in the early stages of hip-hop, providing the musical backdrop for the other forms of hip-hop expression. They served as the foundation and unifying element of hip-hop culture. In rap music, DJs were crucial in defining musical features that distinguished rapping from poetry recitation and other types of oral performance. Even though they provided music from prerecorded discs, DJs used various strategies to make this musical practice equivalent to a live event. Using complex technical maneuvers, hip-hop DJs (known as "turntablists" in the 1990s) transformed their phonographs, turntables, and mixing units into musical instruments. . . . Three

Bronx DJs—Kool Herc, Afrika Bambaataa, and Grandmaster Flash—are most frequently credited with the development of hip-hop.

Jamaican-born DJ Kool-Herc arrived in the Bronx as an adolescent already versed in the island tradition of toasting, mobile DJ performances and battles held for status between partygoers. He went further to develop a technique of isolating the musical breaks on vinyl records, repeating them through a hands-on technique of scratching, which evolved into him using two turntables simultaneously. Afrika Bambaataa, a west Indian descendant who informally studied Kool Herc's style, emerged as his competitor in the mid-1970s, promoting hip-hop through the Universal Zulu Nation he'd founded. Grandmaster Flash, a Barbados-born resident of the Bronx, distinguished his role in hip-hop's development by introducing the beat box. These DJs thus innovated the traditional African role of master drummers within the *tkhn* culture of hip-hop, evolving the signature heartbeat around which the other elements of being a master of ceremony (MC), break dancing, and graffiti took form.

Other DJs followed, but it would be GrandMixer DXT who, with his 1984 Grammy performance of "Rockit" with Herbie Hancock, brought turntablism or scratching to the world's attention. During a separate ceremony, DXT conferred the title of "Grand Mixer" onto Filipino-American DJ Qbert for his mastery of turntablism, essentially inducting him into the master-drummer ranks. Traditionally, this honored status is conferred by other master drummers upon initiates who've successfully proven their worth to this life calling. Grand Mixer Qbert describes turntablism as "the zone . . . or Nirvana. It's like you're not playing the instrument. It's like you're the instrument and the universe is playing you." He adds: "I believe everyone is one . . . connected . . . everyone affects everyone . . . everyone is part of you" (Pray, 2001).

This 5D level of perception is the sacred *ubuntu* consciousness, which custodians of Africa's oral-aesthetic traditions evolve into as would-be initiates into the master ranks of Africa's sovereign *tkhn* culture. Technical agility alone is not sufficient in performing a role that organically curates and navigates the communal pulse. The art-for-life's-sake stakes remain a Bantu cultural mandate, even to post-"Rockit" turntablists, such as QBert, who transcended the industry's art-for-art's-sake modalities of cultural appropriation and/or creative destruction. A proverb from Ipet Resyt describes the importance of critical analysis in the process of engaging and understanding widely held beliefs. When examined from the *transformation*-communication perspective of oral-aesthetic *tkhn* culture, the evolution of Black popular music in the diaspora provides evidence of its African identity and of what should be the limited *transportation* role of industry—a model that has typically overextended its interests in Bantu existential reality and sovereign space. This scenario played out ironically in the 1972 relocation of Berry Gordy's Motown from Detroit, America's "motor town"—birthplace of the Black-owned record label whose phenomenal success was in part built on the assembly-line business model of its hometown car-manufacturing industry.

With chart-topping hits from legendary acts, including Stevie Wonder, The Supremes, The Miracles, The Marvellettes, Marvin Gaye, and The Jackson 5, Gordy's global marketing of Motown as a soundtrack for the youth of America captured the zeitgeist of optimism spreading with the independence and civil rights gains of the early 1960s African diaspora. In part, Gordy's original intent was to rebrand and overcome the stigma of "race music"— the mainstream industry label that had been attached to African American musical expression. Gordy's assembly-line team of songwriters, producers, quality-control inspectors, and musicians each had a role in perfecting Motown's sound and "sweetening" it to cross over into the mainstream. Black artists who were the voice and face of Motown were then trained in etiquette, dress, and stage presence at the campus finishing school (artist development) so their presentation would more closely resemble and therefore appeal to the target White audience.

Though financially successful from a legacy forever forged in hearts and minds the world over, Gordy's art-for-art's-sake formula eventually rendered the Motown sound as out of touch and even irrelevant as a drum of the Black community, which was suffering psychically from the Vietnam war, John F. Kennedy's and Martin L. King Jr.'s assassinations (1963 and 1968), and failing civil rights promises—concerns outside Motown's mainstream brand. Billboard editor Nelson George (2003) argues that Motown ultimately lost touch with its community voice, thus ushering in the death of a cultural language, namely rhythm and blues. The community's "existing wealth" had been compromised by pandering to mainstream consumer sensibilities and appetites. Motown's literal transportation communication modalities had hence become part of the capitalist arc of creative destruction which spurred the company's 1972 relocation to the industry capital of American fantasy—Los Angeles.

Meanwhile (as discussed above) in 1972, a new oral-aesthetic generation had begun to *transform* the landscape from the Bronx boroughs of America's news-industry capital, New York. Hip-hop—"Black America's CNN," as Public Enemy's Chuck-D characterized it—became the community's new drum or *tkhn* culture (qtd. in Eichler, 2010).

This process of purging and recycling sovereign *transformation* communication orders and narratives in the forward progress of Bantu diaspora space-time has, through such processes, gifted the world several music genres. The community has had to be self-policing, vigilant consumers of entertainment trends and the low frequency/dysfunctional, for-profit narratives (e.g., drugs, violence, misogyny, cultural erasure, hypersexuality, etc.) that are pushed via compliant agents.

"If you don't own your masters, your masters own you" (Lussenhop, 2016), Prince advised, referencing his struggle against the Warner Brothers record label where he'd been contracted since 1977 at the age of 19. "WB took my name, trademarked it, and used it as the main marketing tool to promote all of the music I wrote. . . . The company owns the name Prince and all related music marketed under Prince. I became merely a pawn used to produce more money for WB" (Lussenhop, 2016). In 1993, he fought back by sporting the word "slave" on his cheek and changing his name to an ankh-like "love symbol."[5] "It is an unpronounceable symbol whose meaning has not been identified" (Lussenhop, 2016), the artist explained as he disabled contract enforcers, copy editors, and others in the *transportation* communication chain from speaking, let alone writing, his new name. Prince had effectively taken his name out of the "massa's" mouth, and for a season became "the artist formerly known as Prince."

"It's all about thinking in new ways, tuning in 2 a new free-quency" (Lee, 1999), Prince elaborated, his cultural symbolism and oral-aesthetic *transformation* modalities hinting at a higher sovereign order. "Know thy self" is the cardinal concept underlying the timeless proverbial guidance from Ipet Resyt, which conveys the enduring wisdom of God/dess consorts Amun and Mut. Thus, Prince's Africa-centered activism reverse engineered the warping of diaspora space-time and collapsed low-frequency industry timelines and claims in his particular case (Mutere, 2018).

Hantu, the spiritually ordered space-time "free-quency" of a quantum Bantu universe may seem like a new way to seekers trapped in the 3D matrix of industrially enforced containment and linear constructions of time in which Futurism has been claimed as a spoil of patriarchal conquest. *Sankofa* directs AfroFuturism away from such alienating frequencies— "transportation" technocultures built upon the disordering and realigning of *hantu* along hegemonic routes with justifications such as Manifest Destiny. At this point during the four-hundred-year journey in Africa's American diaspora, *ubuntu* has proven itself as the time-tested governing narrative of Bantu sovereignty through the cultural agency and humanizing/civilizing impacts of its "transformation" communication modes (Mutere, 2012) and *ennobling* philosophical grounding.

Recognizing human experience as the final empirical authority, Africology's work of dismantling Eurocentric hegemony (Asante, 2003) is made more urgent by a knowledge-industry built upon the University of Göttingen model (Bernal, 1987). AfroFuturism implies by its very terminology that there are cultural differences in the reckoning of Africa-centered versus Eurocentric (Gregorian) timelines, the latter of which hegemonically orders the global matrix and its industrial technocultures around itself. *Hantu* organically quarantines the latter within its larger context and the alienating justifications of artificial intelligence in order to facilitate the clarifying pursuit of AfroFuturism as directed by *sankofa*.

The record of industrial overreach (predatory/parasitic "plantation paradigms") with compliance/control modes that stripped and replaced authentic identities and imposed uniform dehumanizing codes (social death), dates back to the construction of Set's northern, homo-social Greco-Roman cradle and the slave-master relationships that live on in the modern-day music industry, as Prince pointed out. As cosmologist Carl Sagan (Manuscript Films, 2022) observes, within this cradle of Western civilization and religion "the permanence of the stars was questioned. The justice of slavery was not." Biblical mandates issued to subdue/control nature (creative destruction) became a focal concern in Diop's distinguishing of the predecessor southern matriarchal cradle as its own organically aligned, culturally identified, and spiritually mandated (*ubuntu/ma'at*) sovereignty (1990).

"Know thy self" is irrevocably encoded within the proverbial instructions found on the walls of Ipet Resyt in humanity's motherland—the "temple of the world" (Trismegistus, 1885) where ancient mystery systems were originally sourced and *ma'at* established prior to Greco-Roman ventures. The best and shortest road toward knowledge of truth is Nature. All organs work together in the functioning of the whole, suggesting that such knowing of one's inner truth is organically and inextricably linked to mysteries of the quantum universe. This relationship to the great "I am . . ."—*ubuntu*—continues to be supported through the art-for-life's-sake cultural mandate and oral-aesthetic transformation praxis evident in Black pop music.

Sankofa provides the door of return through which Africa's south-north global kingdoms reaffirm their enduring unity and organic *tkhn* cultural bonds, a journey which pioneering AfroFuturist Sun Ra undertook through music in the 1950s as America entered the space race and began instituting formal studies of Africa as a strategy of its Cold War footing. *Hantu*—encoded psycho-geographically in the south-to-north flow of *Maziwa Mkuu*, the sacred "Milky Way" on Earth—has brought humanity back to the source following a prophetic four-hundred-year testing/initiation period. Named after three source elements, Earth, Wind & Fire reorients us through the group's AfroFuturistic artistry of enduring alignments between humanity and the life-renewing rhythms and mysteries of the quantum universe encoded within the ancient temple that is the ultimate gift of the Nile to the world and its organic memory.

As an inquiry into the crosscurrents between technoculture and Black diasporic histories, AfroFuturism has such organic space-time source codes, directives, and diasporic custodianships from which to anchor its "back-to-the-future" discourses and evaluate the antagonistic paradigms and karmic cycles of the derivative, hegemonic matrix. Reclaiming *hantu* on its own cultural terms as a sovereign force to be reckoned with would empower humanity's mothership in her conscious ascension and reentry to the *ubuntu/ma'at* timeline and "free-quency" that ennobles all.

NOTES

1. Sparked by the 1957 launch of the Sputnik satellite, American fears of Russia's military control of space led to competition for achievements in space explorations and locked America into the Cold War era.

2. The first Black studies program in America was achieved at San Francisco State University in 1968.

3. God blessed the humans by saying to them, "Be fruitful, multiply, fill the earth, and subdue it! Be masters over the fish in the ocean, the birds that fly, and every living thing that

---

crawls on the earth!" (Gen. 1:28). According to Christopher Brown (2009), "*kabash*" is the Hebrew word for "subdue," meaning "enslave," "molest," and/or "rape."

4. In his *Symposium*, Plato reasons: "the love of man and woman, when it is mentioned at all, is spoken of as altogether inferior, a purely physical impulse whose sole object is the procreation of children" (qtd. in Atkinson, n.d.). In Greco-Roman homo-social relations, the "penetrator" is culturally regarded as master and the "penetrated," as slave, a perspective implemented as "buck-breaking" on slave plantations.

5. The ankh—"key of life"—from Kemet is a gendered representation (female oval in relation to a male crucifix) of Ubuntu. Prince referred to his stylized version of the ankh as the "love symbol" (Lussenhop, 2016).

REFERENCES

Aharone, E. (2016). *The Sovereign Psyche: Systems of Chattel Freedom vs. Self-Authentic Freedom*. AuthorHouse.

ARC. (2016, September 15). *Sir Ken Robinson: The Need for a New Model in Education* [Video]. YouTube. https://www.youtube.com/watch?v=fAb9PMs8bEg

Asante, M. K. (2003). *Afrocentricity: The Theory of Social Change* (Rev. 2nd ed.). African American Images.

Asante, M. K. (2015). *African Pyramids of Knowledge: Kemet, Afrocentricity and Afrocentricity and Africology*. Universal Write Publications.

Atkinson, P. (n.d.). *Introduction (2 of 3): The Symposium by Plato*. ourcivilization.com. https://www.ourcivilisation.com/smartboard/shop/plato/intro2.htm

Bernal, M. (1987). *Black Athena: The Afroasiatic Roots of Classical Civilization. Vol. 1: The Fabrication of Ancient Greece 1785–1985*. Rutgers University Press.

Browder, A. T. (2004). *Egypt on the Potomac: A Guide to Decoding Egyptian Architecture and Symbolism in Washington, D.C.* Institute of Karmic Guidance.

Brown, Christopher. (2009, January 3). *Genesis 1:28, to "Subdue" and "Have Dominion Over" Creation*. Poiesis Theou. https://christopherbrown.wordpress.com/2009/01/03/genesis-128-to-subdue-and-have-dominion-over-creation/

Budge, E. A. W. (1978). *An Egyptian Hieroglyphic Dictionary*. Dover. (Original work published 1920).

Carey, J. W. (1989). *Communication as Culture: Essays on Media and Society*. Unwin Hyman.

Carlos Bustamante Restrepo. (2015, December 1). *John Anthony West in the Temple of Luxor - 2015* [Video]. YouTube. https://www.youtube.com/watch?v=LA49SReP_OI

Dery, M. (1994). Black to the Future: Interviews with Samuel R. Delany, Greg Tate, and Tricia Rose. In M. Dery (Ed.), *Flame Wars: The Discourse of Cyberculture* (pp. 179–222). Duke University Press.

Diop, C. A. (1990). *The Cultural Unity of Black Africa: The Domains of Patriarchy and of Matriarchy in Classical Antiquity*. Third World Press.

Eichler, A. (2010, October 12). Rap Isn't "Black America's CNN." *The Atlantic*. https://www.theatlantic.com/culture/archive/2010/10/rap-isn-t-black-america-s-cnn/339862/

Evans, F. W. (2011). *Congo Square: African Roots in New Orleans*. University of Louisiana at Lafayette Press.

George, N. (2003). *The Death of Rhythm and Blues*. Penguin.

Goodare, J. (2005). The Scottish Witchcraft Act. *Church History, 74*(1), 39–67.

Gordy, B. (1995). *To Be Loved: The Music, the Magic, the Memories of Motown*. Warner Books.

Göttner-Abendroth, H. (1985). Nine Principles of a Matriarchal Aesthetic. In G. Ecker (Ed.), *Feminist Aesthetics* (pp. 81–94). Beacon Press.

Gunkel, H., & Lynch, K. (2019). Lift Off . . . an Introduction. In H. Gunkel & K. Lynch (Eds.), *We Travel the Space Ways: Black Imagination, Fragments, and Diffractions* (pp. 21–44). Transcript Verlag.

Frazier, E. F. (1928). The Negro Family. *Annals of the American Academy of Political Science, 140*(1), 44–51.

Holloway, J. E. (2005). The Origins of African American Culture. In J. E. Holloway (Ed.), *Africanisms in American Culture* (pp. 18–38). Indiana University Press.

James, G. G. (2013). *Stolen Legacy*. Simon and Schuster.

Kagame, A. (1976*). La Philosophie Bantu Compare*. Presence Africaine.

Kidel, M. (Director). (1989). *New York: The Secret African City* [Film]. BBC Arena.

Lee, W. (1999, June 4). The Artist, Formerly Known as Prince. *Entertainment Weekly*. https://ew.com/article/1999/06/04/artist-formerly-known-prince-2/

Lussenhop, J. (2016, April 22). *Why Did Prince Change His Name to a Symbol?* BBC News. https://www.bbc.com/news/magazine-36107590

Manuscript Films (2022, October 8). *Carl Sagan - Cosmos - The Library of Alexandria and Hypatia* [Video]. YouTube. https://www.youtube.com/watch?v=eI5PSCBtJ6s&t=90s

Mbiti, J. S. (1969). *African Religions and Philosophy*. Heinemann.

McLuhan, M. (1964). *Understanding Media: The Extensions of Man*. McGraw Hill.

Mutere, M. N. (1995). *The Oral-Aesthetic: An Africa-Centered Perspective of Music*. Temple University.

Mutere, M. (1997). *An Introductory Guide to African History and Cultural Life*. John F. Kennedy Center for the Performing Arts.

Mutere, M. (2012). Towards an Africa-Centered and Pan-African Theory of Communication: Ubuntu and the Oral-Aesthetic Perspective. *Communication: South African Journal for Communication Theory and Research, 38*(2), 147–63.

Mutere, M. (2013, June 28). *Mature Oral-Aesthetic Discourse and the Schooling of "New" Media in Ubuntu: The Case of Hip-Hop* [Working group presentation]. International Association for Media and Communications Research 2013 Conference, Dublin, Ireland.

Mutere, M. (2018, September 5) *Towards a Transformation Communication Theory: Ubuntu, Prince, and the Oral-Aesthetic Perspective*. The Journalist. http://www.thejournalist.org.za/academic-papers/towards-a-transformation-communication-theory-ubuntu-prince-and-the-oral-aesthetic-perspective

Norfleet, D. M. (2006). Hip-Hop and Rap. In M. V. Burnim & P. K. Maultsby (Eds.), *African American Music: An Introduction* (pp. 353–89). Taylor and Francis.

Ong, W. J. (1982). *Orality & Literacy: The Technologizing of the Word*. Routledge.

Osogo, J. (1966). *A History of the Baluyia*. Oxford University Press.

Pray, D. (Director). (2001). *Scratch* [Film]. Palm Pictures.

Schumpeter, J. A. (1975). *Capitalism, Socialism and Democracy*. Harper Colophon. (Original work published 1942).

Schwaller de Lubicz, R. A. (1981). *The Temple in Man: Sacred Architecture and the Perfect Man* (R. Lawlor & D. Lawlor, Trans.). Inner Traditions.

Thompson, R. F. (1974). *African Art in Motion*. University of California Press.

Thompson, R. F. (2005). Kongo Influences on African American Artistic Culture. In J. E. Holloway (Ed.), *Africanisms in American Culture* (pp. 283–325). Indiana University Press.

Trismegistus, H. M. (1885). *The Virgin of the World* (A. B. Kingsford & E. Maitland, Trans.). George Redway.

Tutu, D. (1989). *The Words of Desmond Tutu*. Newmarket Press.

Van Auken, J. (2011). Edgar Cayce's Tales of Ancient Egypt. ARE Press.

West, C. (1988). *Prophetic Fragments*. Africa World Press.

West, C. (1993). *Race Matters*. Beacon Press.

2

AGENCY-PRODUCING INTELLECTUAL SYSTEMS IN THE DIGITAL AGE
Resisting Domination

Aaron X. Smith

There is a growing and profound recognition of the impact of the Afrocentric perspective on the interpretation of African phenomena. In fact, Ana Monteiro-Ferreira (2009, p. 327) declares: "One of the leading intellectual paradigms in the study of African phenomena during the past two decades has been the idea of Afrocentricity. Conceived and developed in the writings of Linda James Myers, Maulana Karenga, Ruth Reviere, and others, Afrocentricity has become the dominant theoretical method in the critique and examination of African and African American phenomena." I shall extend this method of interrogation and critique more deeply into AfroFuturism and related digital spaces through the implementation of what I have called an Afrocentric Futuristic, philosophical, research-driven journey across the digital divide from avatars to Afrocentric agency. In addition to extending Afrocentricity into Futurism, I am also recognizing how agency reduction formation (Michael Tillotson) relates to the possibilities of the future.

Agency reduction formation (ARF) is defined as "any system of thought that distracts, neutralizes, or reduces the need and desire for assertive collective agency by African Americans" (Tillotson, 2011, p. 60). The World Wide Web in many ways is a mecca for ARF with consistently distracting pop-up ads, clickbait, and otherwise deceptive and misinforming links. With an ever-changing assortment of notions related to agency, the need and desire for a cooperative African American thrust are often lost in virtual translation. However, there are many bright spots worth highlighting within an often trivializing, redundant, and culturally misleading online matrix.

In this increasingly technological age, it is imperative to recognize the origins and evolution of the algorithms and equations, which contribute foundationally to the operating systems of some of the world's most powerful and popular technologies. While AfroFuturism as articulated by Mark Dery is limited to the idea of Africans and African ideals in the future, the term "Afrocentric Futurism" adds consciousness to the creation and execution of the past, present, and future political and speculative imagination of artists and intellectuals. In effect, they are creators of something that is based fundamentally on a historical awareness of African and African American assertion of consciousness and agency.

Therefore, I am using an Afrocentric Futuristic chronological connection to modern technology in two primary ways. (1) Realize the natural, historical relationship between Africa and advanced technologies, which could significantly serve to increase agency and confidence of Afrocentric Futurists engaging with digital innovation. (2) Increase abilities to utilize technology as a form of resistance to neocolonial domination through attaining a more in-depth understanding of the racialized realities of technological history and contemporary advancements.

Cell Phone

"One of such unrelenting Black personalities is the inventor of the digital cellphone Jesse Eugene Russell. He is an electrical engineer, and a business executive" (Aidoo, 2019, para. 2).

GPS Technology

"Gladys West never knew that her work at a US Navy base in Virginia back in the 1950s and '60s would play a pivotal role in creating a popular form of technology that is now incorporated into cell phones, cars, and social media" (Hill, 2018, para. 1).

Early Internet Innovations

"There were many mathematicians and scientists who contributed to its development; computers were sending signals to each other as early as the 1950s. But the Web owes much of its existence to Philip Emeagwali, a math whiz who came up with the formula for allowing a large number of computers to communicate at once" (Gray, 2007, para 1).

It is the purpose of this chapter to demonstrate how Afrocentric Futurism expounds a comprehensive resistance to the emergence or construction of ARFs (those acts and behaviors that are used to prevent African people from exercising and reaching their full potential in any capacity) in the digital age. In fact, it is clear that millions of people are currently engaged with their digital phones instead of libraries, creating and being created by the ever-advancing encroachment of nuanced digital forms of influence and domination. This work is a cultural reconnection through the aesthetic aligning of disciplinary dots, which seeks to accurately and powerfully ground Black speculative Futuristic thought within the Afrocentric methodological paradigm. It is fitting to explore one of the most popular and influential literary voices early in this interrogation, Octavia Butler. One of the primary literary voices that has come to undergird and inform the AfroFuturism movement is the late Butler, who explored various dimensions of the Black imagination as a response or a resistance to any form of domination.

Butler was born in 1947 in Pasadena, California, and began to seriously develop her passion for writing in the 1970s. Her ability to shift the literary paradigm in an otherwise male-dominated field adds layers of literary nuance to her creative genius. In the text titled *Changing Bodies in the Fiction of Octavia Butler* (2010), Gregory Jerome Hampton expresses the wide-ranging cultural and academic influence of Butler in the world of AfroFuturistic science fiction. Hampton (2010, p. xii) explains: "There are approximately sixty-six PhD dissertations and thirteen master theses written since 1993 that engage some aspect of Butler's fiction directly or at least mentions of her writing in a significant manner in relationship to other writers inside and outside of the science fiction genre."

Some notable distinctions recognized in Butler's writings provide a different creative perspective, which appears to deviate from the majority of White-male-dominated science fiction. "To be clear, Butler's fiction is dystopian, not utopian. Instead of the goals of perfection and homogeneity, Butler's fiction negotiates violence and difference" (Hampton, 2010, p. 120). This negotiation and reconfiguring of the world of fiction and the imaginative world around African genius and potential mirror the inspirational, psychological realignment that often occurs for readers first introduced to the writings of authors such as W. E. B. Du Bois, Reynaldo Anderson, Molefi Kete Asante, and Nah Dove concerning the perspective-shifting African contributions to past, present, and future agency. African liberation has been significantly promoted through the proper understanding and implementation of Afrocentric agency in theories, actions, and Futuristic projections.

Both Afrocentricity and AfroFuturism serve to take the mind and understanding of African potentialities out of this world, whether through fiction, as with Du Bois's "Comet" (1920), or fundamental pursuits of freedom through action and art. In Marleen Barr's (2008, p. 4) book *Afro-Future Females: Black Writers Chart Science Fiction's Newest New-Wave Trajectory*, she writes:

> Among Black women writers in the genre of science fiction, Octavia E. Butler has created entire alternative worlds that uncannily reflect reality and deflect and undermine it at the same time by generating subjects who improve on the available human models; in that regard, science fiction puts into play something that we know, that is rather familiar, while it so rearranges the signposts that the outcome is strange and defamiliarized.

This rearrangement of the marginalizing traditional depictions and perspectives of African people occurred within academia when Afrocentricity was introduced as an analytical challenge to the existing intellectual order. Butler, like Asante, challenged and Blackened the status quo, leaving literary legacies of African assertion and agency of personal and collective power in spite of political, literary, and social obstacles.

There exists a consistent artistic history, detailing the attempts to reimagine and redefine Blackness from the perspective of African people throughout the world. One of the most popular creative periods of African American literary liberation can be found in the famed Harlem Renaissance. *The Encyclopedia of the Harlem Renaissance* (S. L. West & Aberjhani, 2003) contains a foreword by Clement Alexander Price that places the movement in an undeniably esteemed context. Price explains: "Our interest in the flourishing of Black artistic talent, racial chauvinism, and group expressiveness known as the Harlem Renaissance is both durable and understandable. No other period in 20th century African-American history with the possible exception of the modern Civil Rights movement, has drawn as much of our attention or encouraged as many exemplary works of scholarship" (Price, 2003, p. xi).

One of the more notable creatives who helped to define this artistic period and offered a new perspective and lens through which African Americans could view themselves and the world was Alain Locke. In 1927, writer/poet/composer Locke described the cyclical nature of artistic expression and the power of creative mediums being rooted in the strength of culture, history, and tradition. I find it worthy of note here the dialectic (cynical versus creative) is similar to the dystopian-utopian comparison related to the writings of Butler.

Black Arts and Afrocentric Futurism

In the essay titled, "The Negro and the American Theatre," Locke asserts:

> A race of actors can revolutionize the drama quite as definitely and perhaps more vitally than a coterie of dramatists. The roots of drama are after all action and emotion and our modern drama for all of its frantic experimentation, is an essentially anemic drama, a something of gestures and symbols and ideas and not overflowing with the vital stuff of which drama was originally made and to which it must return for its rejuvenation, cycle after cycle. (qtd. in Gayle, 1971, p. 249)

This need for a return in order to most effectively rejuvenate is at the base of Afrocentric thought. The mental, spiritual, scientific, moral, and artistic return to classical African concepts and context is what undergirds much of Asante's (2007) location theory. This artistic cycle of return, rejuvenation, and reemergence can be recognized readily in a cursory chronology of Black music in America: spirituals, gospel, blues, jazz, rock 'n' roll, and rap. The

Black Arts Movement, in particular, resonates powerfully with the tradition of culturally, and artistically divorcing from the artistic whims of the West.

There exist cultural community connections in relation to the departure from traditional Western artistic expressions.

> The Black Arts Movement is radically opposed to any concept of the artist that alienates him from his community. Black Art is the aesthetic and spiritual sister of the Black Power concept. As such, it envisions an art that speaks directly to the needs and aspirations of Black America. In order to perform this task, the Black Arts Movement proposes a radical reordering of the Western cultural aesthetic. It proposes a separate symbolism, mythology, critique and iconology. (Neal., 1989, p. 55)

The AfroFuturism movement has been baptized in the deep Black theoretical, artistic, methodological, and aesthetic womb of Afrocentric, victorious consciousness and agency. Numerous iterations of African American art contain utilization of the past in an effort to envision and construct a better future for African people. It is here that we see the effective resistance to domination so imagined in the theoretical work of Tillotson toward formations that attack African assertion. It seems that the history of Blackness is always the history of resilience in the face of the most terrible examples of denial, persecution, and agency reduction.

The creative methods prominent within Afrocentric Futurism embody the African understanding of the instructive symbolism of the *sankofa* bird, often presented looking backward while progressing onward. The *sankofa* bird is looking over its hind feathers in perfect preparation to powerfully propel forward. The idea of going back and fetching what is necessary and beneficial for the future of African people is propelled exponentially into the envisioned future or Futuristic worlds of the AfroFuturistic creative. AfroFuturism is returning and fetching the methodological, historical, and intellectual landmarks of Afrocentricity and flying with them to creative worlds unseen and yet to be developed from the minds of said innovators.

These artists have continued to define and redefine AfroFuturism in an autonomous Afrocentric way, viewing themselves and their artistic creations as liberating entities in a universe created by self-determined African agency, which refuses any forms of reduction. AfroFuturists have been particularly adept in manipulating the digital worlds in the areas of creation, promotion, and innovative cooperation. The power and potential of digital spaces as a means to maintain a liberated Afrocentric Futuristic consciousness is an ever-evolving and adapting convergence of creative realities.

AfroFuturism manifests the digital, abstract, fictional, space-aged, or alternative technological expressions of autonomy, agency, envisioned reality, and African centering. Afrocentric Futurism represents an African-centered resurrection, inspiring communion with ancestors through the exhalation of classical African iconography and related traditions. An analysis of AfroFuturism reveals a significant methodological connection to the foundations of Asante's (1998) Afrocentric idea.

AfroFuturism has originally developed within a context that has admittedly been detached from the defining academic, sociological, and cultural underpinnings, which have indirectly contributed to much of the aesthetic and creative inspiration represented therein. "During the discipline's formative stage (1968–1972), minimal attention was devoted to the relationship between scientific and technological issues and Africana Studies" (Anderson & Jones, 2017, p. xii). This lack of Afrocentric methodological grounding may have contributed to the vulnerabilities of AfroFuturistic dialogue, leaving it, in some cases, disproportionately influenced by a more Marxist- or Feminist-leaning philosophy rather than a more African-centered starting point. The potentially disjointed dislocation could result in leaving elements susceptible to analytical encroachments stemming from the marginalization or removal of Afrocentric agency. Attacks on agency have been a consistent obstacle, obstructing the self-definition and imaginative, creative liberation of African people for generations. In order to properly historically contextualize current dilemmas of racial inclusion and marginalization in digital spaces, I will first explore an academic methodological approach articulating the attempted omission of Blackness for various spaces.

Properly infusing Afrocentric agency and racial reality into our collective consciousness and imaginative discussions can serve to empower the potential for greater liberatory Afrocentric Futuristic creativity. Being definitively rooted in an African-inspired speculative criterion encourages resistance to antiegalitarianisms that are social, political, and psychological formations meant to undermine the functional and productive capacity of African people. The questions of cultural production should not be separated from the producer. Afrocentric methodologies describe cultural and historical dislocation as a motivating factor for adherence by many creatives to manifest

Eurocentric ideas and other cultural expressions despite being children of
the African diaspora. The increased foundational presence of Afrocentricity
within the Futurist conversations can enable greater connections with Pan-
African progress rather than culturally arbitrary (solely aesthetic) examples
of transhumanistic merging with machines.

Applied Afrocentric Futuristic Theories in the Digital World

For many African Americans throughout recent history, technological innovations like the gun led to great degrees of subjugation, while inventions
such as Eli Whitney's cotton gin helped to stimulate productivity and inspire
greater potential to manifest Black genius. The African American vision of
freedom and Futuristic manifestations (as alluded to in my introduction)
have contributed greatly to the growth and identity of the nation. While
European oppressors envisioned a future of ignorance with penalties for
learning to read and antilynching laws, African Americans were becoming
literate, drawing up their own freed person papers and later writing computer
codes, which have changed the course of the future internationally. Other
failed racialized predictions include chattel slavery existing in perpetuity for
Africans and segregation lasting forever, as suggested by racist segregation-
ists, like George Wallace. These historical realities properly posit African
Americans as the proverbial canaries in the mine when it comes to what the
future will hold. The African American Futuristic vision of America is more
likely what the future will resemble based on past levels of accuracy regarding Futuristic predictions. The influence and accuracy of these Afrocentric
and related scholars speak to the need for greater focus on their works and
perspectives, as we shift from the age of literature through the age of the
download into the age of the digital unknown.

There have been significant scholars (Akbar, 1984; Ani, 1994; Asante, 2003;
Baldwin, 1993; Du Bois, 1994; Dyson, 2003; Goldberg, 1993; Gordon, 1997;
Kardiner & Ovesey, 1951; Marable, 1995; Mills, 1997; Omi & Winant, 1986;
Reed, 2003; Sutherland, 1997; Welsing, 1991; C. West, 1993; Wilson, 2005;
Wright, 1984) who have examined racism and African Americans. Yet, despite
these works, people of African descent remain at the bottom of every posi-
tive sociological indicator in American society (Powell, 2007; Winant, 2001).
In effect, the study of African people does not necessarily mean the uplift

of African people when all the social indices are considered. Furthermore, all the discourses on race, as Patricia Reid-Merritt (2017) has shown, do not necessarily eliminate racism.

In order to effectively employ the Afrocentric Futuristic theories and methodologies within a technologically contemporary digital context, we can start with the dominance of social media. The online juggernaut Facebook has been a driving force in areas of politics, culture, entertainment, and even identity shaping for years. College-age students are notoriously engaged on the site. Authors Laura A. Wankel and Charles Wankel discuss the power of social media sites among members of the collegiate demographic in their informative work titled *Misbehavior Online in Higher Education: Cutting-Edge Technologies in Higher Education* (2012). They explore various aspects of the intersection between academia and modern technology. It is generally accepted that over 80 percent of students enrolled in higher education use Facebook. It is not an unusual platform for discussions and conversations about social issues among students and young adults. Using Facebook to assert historical facts, social ideas, and rational discourse around race is now a common practice. While some use the medium to expand agency, others have employed these technologies as weapons of digital destruction against the self-defining, liberating, innovative thoughts and creativity of African/African American people.

However, Afrocentric Futurism can inspire unique strategies to minimize, neutralize, or overcome new age efforts to silence Black expression and reduce the formation of African identity. Afrocentric Futurism exists as a perceptually strategic hack to surpass metaphorical firewalls of Eurocentric definitions, concepts, and actions that serve to block African agency online. The internet is filled with numerous misinformation campaigns. One popular example of negative online efforts has been the Russian interference in the 2016 presidential elections, which attempted to mislead African American voters throughout the United States. Disinformation, traveling at light speed reportedly posed a serious threat to the sound political engagement of African Americans and the democratic future of the United States. The technological problematics present in contemporary politics represent the tip of an online iceberg composed of a varied collection of challenges. When online bullying, all manner of aesthetic depravity, and deception are combined with the exhalation of the Eurocentric perspective as a universal online standard, the need for effective educational alternatives increases exponentially. It is no wonder that Afrocentric thinkers like Ama Mazama and Garvey Musumunu (2015) have contended that Eurocentric curricula in certain social and educational circles have driven African American parents to homeschooling. This form of Afrocentric education is often geared toward overcoming and fostering greater degrees of self-awareness concerning history, culture, and Afrocentric Futuristic thought. The manifold manifestations of Afrocentric influence on Futuristic expression can be observed through science-fiction movies, novels, memes, and computer code. These forms of digital resistance and redefinition embody and involve the communal concern, spontaneity, colorful motifs, ancestral veneration, and the central role of nature and universal balance present throughout African cultures.

The key is to link cultural identity, imagination, and technological innovation. "Imagination is a magic carpet / Upon which we may soar / To distant lands and climes / And even go beyond the moon to any planet in the sky" (Youngquist, 2016, p. 6). The connection between the existing theoretical methods and emerging technologies can be described by the term "Connecticon." "The complex merging of a networked technological infrastructure with the flexibility of the human resource of knowledge users and their opportunities for hyper-interactivity can be regarded as an example of a complex adaptive system that we have termed the Connecticon" (Rennie & Mason, 2004, p. 78). This term perfectly embodies the convergence between the intellectual infrastructure of Afrocentricity and the flexibility of the human imagination reflected in AfroFuturism, hence "Afrocentric Futurism."

Agency Reduction Formation and Technological Colorism

The racially reprobate hashtags on social media read like an announcement for a new age Willie Lynch divide-and-conquer Olympics pitting #teamlightskin versus #teamdarkskin. This is not the enslavement period during which quadroons, octoroons, and mulattoes were systematically divided and forced to do battle with one another for the pleasure of White masters, who organized fights between children, with the competitions referred to as "Royal Rumbles." Today the domination through separation runs on applications like Instagram and Twitter in which young people perpetuate age-old programs of problematic separations from the love of themselves. According to Mark Pegrum of *From Blogs to Bombs: The Future of Digital Technologies in Education* (2009), search engine strategies are a great place to begin to realign technological trajectories.

> Most online experiences start at Google (the world's dominant search engine), YouTube (in second place as of late 2008) and other common search engines or portals like Yahoo!, Microsoft's Bing, Baidu (in China) or Naver (in South Korea). Searching, according to Google CEO Eric Schmidt, "is empowering for humans like nothing else. It is the antithesis of being told or taught. It is about self-empowerment." (Pegrum, 2009, p. 36)

Unfortunately, we often find potential empowerment replaced with an uncivil, online war rooted in self-hatred and self-deception. There has recently been an antebellum return to the emphasis on racial categorization that is completely detached from the generations of the 1960s and '70s, when Black people would routinely refer to one another as "brothers" and "sisters" with far less emphasis (if any) on the shade of one's skin. In this context, young people seem to be utilizing their access to technology and social media to reduce their agency voluntarily at 5G speed.

This quantum lurch back to extreme colorism needs to be countered by an Afrocentric Futuristic leap forward, including more effective, self-determined utilization of the internet. Innovation has progressed from the age of techno-color programming to an unfortunate age of technological colorism in which, in a tragic case of twisted irony, the chromatic binary boundaries are simply light or dark. These harmful hashtags have left our Afrocentric agency out of focus for the future. This destructive distortion is, unfortunately, more present on certain social-media timelines than other racial elements of prior ages, which could better inform and undergird the growth of Afrocentric awareness. This deterioration of self-determination could be compared to a virus in the digital world. "Viruses are programs that can potentially harm or even destroy your data" (Lewis, 2009, p. 21). There are many anti-Afrocentric viruses that need to be exposed in order to give people the power to know what seeks to reduce their agency. Many members of this generation have engaged in a detrimental process of historical rotten cherry picking, extracting the worst racial elements of our history and carrying them into a generational, current collective consciousness while abandoning the more beneficial components, traditions, and realities associated with the African experience in America.

Racial Domination and the Digital Age

It is an aim of Afrocentric Futuristic thought to examine the impact of ideological domination on African American life while projecting a more powerful, agency-filled future. The contemporary manifestations of age-old trajectories of inequalities create cautionary tale-laden launching pads for revolutionary Afrocentric Futuristic visions, which utilize relevant lessons and inspiring African achievements as fuel for creativity. Conversely, historically contextualizing modern manifestations of European hegemonic domination highlights themes of racial privilege, which may continue to reverberate in numerous forms of dislocation and agency reduction of African people. The societal struggles and the conversations concerning them are represented in the digital space, as virtual reality often mirrors reality. Technological advances, complete with international reach, options for anonymity, and mass reproduction of content, typically magnify existing voices and offer opportunities to create new ones. "So, in an environment where communication is highly valued in many formats (oral, written, film, etc.), technology is providing additional opportunities to share and discuss ideas" (King, 2003, p. 52).

What previous generations have attempted to do with paradigm-shifting legislation, a new generation of hackers and content creators are attempting to accomplish through the manipulation of the internet and computer programs. This brave new negative world is first created in the mind, manifested through binary codes and fiber optics, to later manifest as a major component of the lived experiences of billions of people. This ability to harness such significant influence has some concerning elements as well. As previously mentioned, the act of influencing political outcomes through the manipulation of computer technology is becoming increasingly concerning in this era of apps and political mishaps. There is virtually no way the Black community can escape this powerful yet potentially perilous environment. Ben Wofford (2016, para. 1) wrote in *Politico Magazine*: "When Princeton Professor Andrew Appel decided to hack into a voting machine; he didn't try to mimic the Russian attackers who hacked into the Democratic National Committees database last month. He didn't write malicious code, or linger near a polling place where the machines can go unguarded for days. Instead, he bought one online." The idea of deception, anti-Afrocentric Futurism, and agency reduction formation becoming big tech business is concerning to those who approach the technological future from an Afrocentric perspective. Perhaps, not since the enslavement of Africans during the European enterprise of trafficking human beings (chattel slavery), has the potential for profit been so intimately linked to attempted dehumanization, domination, and negative redefining of African/African American people. What was known as the *slave-breaking process*, which was part of the larger slave-making process, is being mirrored in multifaceted sophistication online every day where people are being lied to about race and racism. Their humanity is being attacked while others are being pressured to and sometimes beyond their breaking point. As a result of this challenging set of circumstances, many endure degrees of stress that they consistently seek relief from. This is where the Afrocentric connections to the universal principle of *ma'at* (truth, balance, righteousness, reciprocity) could be utilized to improve mental health within the Black community.

Afrocentric Futurism must reinvigorate the ancient African notion of maintaining balance and order while staving off chaos within our world, our communities, our homes, and our minds. Suicide is the tenth leading cause of death in the United States. Each year 44,965 Americans die by suicide. Every year, suicide attempts cost the United States $69 billion. These statistics are relevant because, with each passing year (primarily young) Black men and women are increasingly being added to these growing yet tragic statistics. For generations, suicide was looked at as a White problem, and although the numbers for Blacks (6.03 percent) were recently reported as drastically lower than Whites (15.17 percent), there exists concern about the potentially growing numbers concerning this expression of self-destructive behavior (American Foundation for Suicide Prevention, 2020).

The Politics of Stereotypes versus Afrocentric Futuristic Affirmations

Today, we see far less centralization regarding the control and dissemination of images that can result in the increased potential for media manipulation, predictive programming, and technological persuasion. In this largely unrestricted technological age, tweets and memes have significantly encroached upon space once almost completely dominated by billboards and newspapers. We have an increasing segment of the population who are assuming greater degrees of agency by becoming content creators and being the articulate and aesthetic authors of their own future. Perhaps more than any other time in recorded history, the idea of iconographic gatekeepers is being significantly challenged by those who have comparable access to the technologies that allow them to create images, record and edit film, and implement CGI (computer-generated imagery) to formulate their own alternate reality that others can interact with at the touch of a button. The future is truly in their hands.

There is unbelievable power in having the ability to literally take a vision and make it the reality for millions of people. The age-old adage that emphasizes "if you conceive it and believe, then you can achieve it" takes on exponentially greater importance for those willing and capable of affirming agency through the physical/visual transformation of the world around us. AfroFuturistic agency-affirming strategies are used to resist the structural promotion of ARF and Eurocentric speculative domination of Black spaces and Black minds. The misuse of potential has often been promoted by politicians who have proudly positioned themselves as open enemies of African self-determination. Two such polarizing political figures include former President Ronald Reagan and former West Virginia Senator Robert Byrd. "The stereotyping of Black women by welfare reformers does not exist in a contained space. The description of Black female welfare recipients as 'breeders' by [then] West Virginia Senator Robert Byrd in the 1960s laid the groundwork that set the climate for racial insensitivity that lingers and is inherent in conservative and Neoliberal reforms" (Tillotson, 2011, p. 43). Figuring out a way to infuse the relevance of historical context in a tech-savvy era of headlines and sound bites for future prosperity is of critical importance in the effort to reassert lost agency and inform analysis in a way that centers the often-harsh realities of race rather than neutralize the impacts of race through reductive rhetoric.

An impairment to the self-affirming Afrocentric future is the mental domination enacted through influencing internalizing stereotypes and the imposition of inferiority complexes. Today there are numerous discussions around the negative impacts of cyberbullying and the negative implementation of technological capabilities in efforts to cause emotional stress and other psychological impediments. This hurtful interaction is magnified exponentially when the bully is within. The act of internalizing the hateful, harmful program, insidiously downloaded by elements of a racist, oppressive society, can present increasingly complex challenges in the pursuit of balance, agency, and the liberation of the African mind from the shackles of mental domination. We must envision from within to change that which exists outside of us, whether physically or futuristically.

A Forewarning of Potential Challenges

There is a relationship between online music and social media that overlaps and connects in significant ways. This is a symbiotic relationship in which they (music and social media) are often intimately intertwined. With new technologies, there are increasing methods of utilizing these and other related mediums in our efforts to exercise creative agency and cyber self-determination. The opportunities presented in an ever-growing virtual climate of expanded opportunity, regarding redefinition and independent expression, to positively impact the twin ideas of African agency and identity are exhaustive where the proper Afrocentric perspective and optimistic, victorious consciousness are employed. In this age of avatars, personal profiles, and Bitmojis, the concept of self-determined Afrocentric Futuristic agency and the redefinition of a culturally located identity could be seamlessly and beneficially merged with the advancement of innovative technologies. The intentionality involved in the selection of an avatar or constructing your own virtual representation using the Bitmoji application possesses numerous avenues for exploring identity and casting Futuristic visions of the self (e.g., being in better shape) and our engagement with the worlds we exist in.

One of the primary ways in which technology could exponentially increase positive identity transformations through increased levels of virtual agency can be found in the comfort of online anonymity. This technologically constructed buffer between desired forms of aesthetic expression and the actual life of the avatar's creator can offer a level of confidence with future change and experimentation, which may not exist in the actual life of the online user. People may become more courageous regarding cultural fashion expressions through an animated representation in ways that may later translate directly into their actual lived experience. The virtual world can become a safe space where new clothing, new hairstyles, and new culturally rooted names can be experimented with. This freedom can create the necessary bridge required to increase comfort levels with otherwise more challenging avenues of agency and identity transformation. A reclamation of one's African self could start small in an abstract setting and later be transferred to the tangible aspects of the lived experience.

Technology and Timelines: Listening to Our Past; Speaking Our Futures

The power of the spoken word is highly regarded in African American discourse. Scholars endeavor to understand the power of our words (through speaking, texting, or typing) throughout history to better position ourselves to speak life into our current situations in a way that can be exponentially transformative to our respective and collective futures. In order to use our words and our history to our benefit, it would behoove us to become well acquainted with our own stories and begin with our own history. Asante (2007) stresses the importance of starting with a proper chronology in order to establish a more relevant, accurate, and beneficial means of self-definition and cultural analysis. Tillotson describes the absence of accurate chronologies as a critical component in European oppression of the African self. "The abandonment of the African-self is possible only if one were to undo the historical legacy of anti-egalitarian European American domination, inflicted upon African American people" (Tillotson, 2011, p. 56). The restoration of proper chronologies from a liberating, more accurate Afrocentric perspective can work wonders in the areas of reasserting African agency, which fuels Afrocentric Futurism.

The use of interactive timelines and the proper historical organization of ideas and events related to African identity formation can be sufficiently bolstered by attractive and flexible computer programs related to accurate African history and the connection to empowering expressions of agency and identity. Central to the understanding and overcoming of dislocation, displacement, and the domination and demonization of African identity is the effective resistance to ARF. Afrocentric perceptual pushback prevents the normalizing and imposition of an Anglo-Saxon universalizing idea in the head of African people as a way of undermining Afrocentric Futuristic identity, culture, visions, and values.

Social-justice movements stand to play a crucial role in the collective African resistance to oppression and domination, which may be supported by group chats, tagging, timelines, and hashtags throughout various social media platforms. Previous generations did not have the ability to reach millions with the touch of a button from a street corner or organize simultaneously on multiple continents without ever leaving the comfort of their bedroom. The potential good far outweighs the often more heavily promoted negative aspects of social media in terms of utilizing technology as a weapon in the resistance to ARF. Although "clearly the uncritical acceptance of postmodern anti-foundationalism by African Americans leads to a distorted sense of reality" (Tillotson, 2011, p. 61), ironically, many such distortions of reality may be brought into focus through the effective implementation of virtual reality.

Without the aid of sophisticated technology, it would be an arduous task indeed to truly investigate the depths and various ramifications of American racism as it denies agency and sometimes life to African people. A positive reality exists in the fact that we currently live in an age of information in which millions have advanced computers in the form of smartphones as accessible as their pants pocket, and children are learning the intricacies of computer coding at the same time that they begin to learn the parts of speech. The computer and related applications can take a great deal of the difficulty out of the previous process of figuring out ways to engage in consistent study, while steadily conveying in real-time and down-to-earth terms to the masses of people how to best access and implement the information provided. In the near future, with the proper fusion of Afrocentric Futurism and advanced technology, we will see an app developed that could define and help people historically contextualize and contemporarily implement the research and analysis set forth by numerous Afrocentric scholars.

Social Media and the Modern World through the Lens of Afrocentric Futurism

Social media is an international network, which has the capabilities of linking people from countless countries on every continent. One potential benefit from this degree of direct communication is the bypassing of the typically propagandized filter of traditional mass media. In the contemporary world, we do not have to rely on the post office or some corporately owned media outlet to access information about African people throughout the diaspora. Receiving accurate, first-hand data from around the world can be as simple and affordable as a friend request or direct message. An increase in the quality and truthfulness of the information received can contribute to Afrocentric improvements in the future.

The interconnected nature of modern technology must be mirrored by the online practices and shared connection of those who seek to achieve a stronger sense of identity more firmly rooted within the international African community. There is great potential strength in the ability for African people to utilize technology for greater degrees of cooperation and the expansion of a network of Afrocentric agency and identity. There are, however, certain concerns about a backlash to technological identity formation and utilization based upon historical precedence, including the formation of the KKK after emancipation and the election of Donald Trump after the presidency of Barack Obama.

As others work to trivialize and minimize the impacts of racial oppression through their reductionist, broad-reaching racial philosophies and Futuristic visions, others must use various means (including technological) in efforts to resist this return to prior levels of widespread historical denial. The abundance of history that can be located through technology (access to archives, census information, databases regarding racial classifications, and newspaper stories explaining how they relate to Black people) can dramatically offset emerging notions serving to promote the insignificance of race or African people in the vision for the future.

The hard, factual histories being available online can serve to properly locate recent sociological trends within the larger historical context of the Black experience. Implementing these Afrocentric Futuristic strategies can be coupled with other powerful agency-producing intellectual/creative systems, which include conscious musical expressions and even Hollywood depictions of African brilliance and genius.

Is Tech Your King? *Black Panther* and African Reimagination

One major example of agency-producing systems has been witnessed with the release of the movie *Black Panther* (2018). The film asserts agency on a number of levels that exalt African customs, aesthetics, and Afrocentric Futuristic potentialities. For example, female characters in the film (all displaying natural hair styles) have positions of nobility, technological prowess, and militaristic sophistication, representing a harmonious complimentary balance displayed across genders. This film has created a watershed, a historic international moment and movement regarding agency and Afrocentric Futuristic conversations. More mature, seasoned viewers rejoiced in the unprecedented African aesthetics and other aspects of the cinematographically triumphant production, in large part because of the connections to the period of Black Power in the 1960s and 1970s (e.g., moving the setting from New York to Oakland, California, the director's birthplace and location of the founding of the Black Panther Party for Self Defense). These layered homages plant seeds of possibility in the minds of young Africans throughout the diaspora, which can grow from imaginative fertile soil into the dawning of a newly inspired Afrocentric future.

Through the film, many viewers are introduced to the consideration of an Africa free of colonial infiltration and the motivation to reimagine the possibilities of a self-sufficient, self-determined, and self-defining African nation through the majesty and might of the fictional nation of Wakanda. Similar to the King T'Challa character in the film, Africans/African Americans are faced with decisions determining whether or not advanced technology will be a liberating force or a prison of comfort and complacency, leaving them detached from the realities of the struggles of their brothers and sisters.

AfroFuturism and Future Generations

This stands to be the first generation that spends equal or more time communicating through devices than directly to other actual people. Online activity and opinions shared in posts, comments, and direct messages increasingly determine discourses about agency, race, and identity formation. The conversations around digital engagement and cultural redefinition are shifting in more ways than one (e.g., style and medium). Consequently, it is incumbent upon those who seek to investigate and influence these aspects of phenomena to recognize and become acclimated to these potentially transformative societal advancements. However, there have been many obstacles along the road of technological evolution. One such digital impediment to the development of positive Afrocentric agency formation is cyberbullying. The act of using the internet to deny others their agency and confidence is an increasingly problematic online phenomenon.

> In an effort to better prevent and respond to bullying and cyberbullying, schools are recognizing a need to focus on positive youth development. One often-neglected developmental construct in this rubric is resilience, which can help students successfully respond to the variety of challenges they face. Enhancing this internal competency can complement the ever-present efforts of schools as they work to create a safe and supportive learning environment by shaping the external environment around the child. (Hinduja & Patchin, 2017, abstract)

The international journal *Child Abuse & Neglect* published an article titled "Cultivating Youth Resilience to Prevent Bullying and Cyberbullying Victimization" by Sameer Hinduja and Justin W. Patchin. The mention of "youth resilience" in contrast to the concept of Afrocentric Futurism brings to mind a need for increased racial resilience, which would assist in the projection and protection of positive Afrocentric, future identity formation.

An infusion of Afrocentric Futuristic cultural and historical location could assist in rejecting outward attacks, which often disguise far more insidious resistance to identity formation. One such negative tactic is the phenomena of racialized victim blaming (bootstrap, respectability politics, etc.), which manifests itself online in a variety of negative ways. These abusive accusations are typically detached from historical realities and motivated by a desire to stifle and deflect from true conversations about future possibilities concerning race and identity.

> An emerging new form of old sentiments reformulated as anti-Black responses was given birth just before, during and after the Contract with America phase of American politics. These forms of discourse seek to silence challenges to historical imbalances, suppress dissent, neutralize political opposition, and summarily deny African Americans the right to redress the quality-of-life disparities that exist in America. Housed inside of the rhetoric of the victim blame position (Ryan, 1971) is the denial of African American voices that challenge the *status quo* of the United States. (Tillotson, 2011, p. 109)

The invasive cultural and intellectual positioning of the European worldview with its concomitant African displacement is a counterproductive, agency-reducing barrier to the transformative potential of Afrocentric Futuristic thought. People cannot see themselves in a clearly Afrocentric way in the future if they continue to struggle in the present to see themselves other than through the eyes of their open enemies. Asante discusses cultural and academic dislocation and displacement in a text titled *Contemporary Critical Thought in Africology and Africana Studies* (Asante & Ledbetter, 2016). In the chapter titled "Decolonizing the Universities in Africa: An Approach to Transformation," Asante (2016) interrogates the motives and usefulness of the overemphasis of the Eurocentric perspective as it relates to African people, which could continue to negatively impact African people worldwide if not adequately addressed. "Why would Europe or Europeans see the need to 'assert' their reality into an African situation? What constitutes aggression in a conceptual sense and why was a European so set on this type of assertion" (Asante, 2016, p. 2). What began as a forced separation from self has tragically devolved into an outright rejection of cultural connections, African identity, and communal agency.

In order to utilize technology as a tool to regain this lost sense of self, it will be important to meet the new generation where they are, which is typically surfing the web, gaming, and texting on their devices. One productive idea is the potential creation of support groups around positive Afrocentric agency formation while resisting threats to the internal (mental, physical, and spiritual) security of African Americans. Utilizing texting and social media applications to inspire a more Afrocentric future can have far-reaching positive implications. For example, "the communications potential of both Facebook and Twitter can extend even beyond those students, parents, employees, or fans who use those sites" (Magette, 2015, p. 78). The metamorphic potential of these technologies is seemingly endless. There are some key points for educators regarding technology that can assist in maximizing the Afrocentric Futuristic potential of advanced technology. In order to most effectively implement these advancements for the enhancement of the educational experience, it is imperative scholars continue to interrogate relevant questions. Two such inquiries are: (1) "What do teachers need to know, believe, and be able to do in order to teach for meaningful learning using technology?" and (2) "What do district leaders need to know, believe, and be able to do in order to teach for meaningful learning using technology?" (Ashburn, 2006, p. 1).

Afrocentric Futurism is one of the latest creative, academic iterations in the continuously evolving influence of Afrocentric theory and methodologies. Afrocentric Futurism is an assertive artistic movement with the objective of projecting Africans into the future while remaining rooted in their historiographies, customs, worldviews, and traditions, with themes ranging from the speculative to the scientific to science fiction. These expressive avenues are woven together through a thematic constant that is then centered upon elements of Afrocentric history and culture. This distinction is of critical importance as many AfroFuturist theorists vacillate significantly between Afrocentric methodologies and others, including Marxism, second-wave feminism, and LGBTQIA theoretical frameworks, worldviews, and historical contexts. Afrocentric Futurism may make mention of other

theoretical approaches where appropriate but by no means is this phenomenon (Afrocentric Futurism) representative of an interdisciplinary, analytically
divided methodology. Afrocentric Futurism is a for-Africans-by-Africans
(throughout the diaspora) movement within the predominant traditions,
worldview, and cultural connections of Africa in style, methodology, and
purpose (the inspiration, elevation/liberation of African people worldwide).
The view of African people as subjects rather than objects (Afrocentricity)
extends to Futuristic visions of worlds unknown.

Afrocentric Futurism builds upon Asante's work (complemented, expanded,
and futuristically advanced by countless others), extending beyond the cultural and historical locating articulated by Asante and leaping (sometimes
light years into the future) into a predictive, fantastic concept where African
people are not only the center of their story but the center of the universe.
This is precisely where the works of Asante and Anderson (see Anderson &
Jones 2017) converge to urge the rethinking of resistance to agency reduction
in the form of astro-Blackness from an Afrocentric foundation.

REFERENCES

Aidoo, T. (2019, November 14). *Did You Know This Black Man Is Behind the Invention of the
First Digital Cell Phone?* Face2Face Africa. https://face2faceafrica.com/article/did
-You-know-this-Black-man-is-behind-the-invention-of-the-first-digital-cell-phone
Akbar, N. (1984). *Chains and Images of Psychological Slavery.* New Mind Productions.
American Foundation for Suicide Prevention. (2020, March 1). *Suicide Statistics.* https://
afsp.org/suicide-statistics/
Anderson, R., & Jones, C. E. (Eds.). (2017). *AfroFuturism 2.0: The Rise of Astro-Blackness.*
Lexington Books.
Ani, M. (1994). *Yurugu: An African Centered Critique of European Cultural Thought and
Behavior.* African World Press.
Asante, M. K. (1998). *The Afrocentric Idea.* Temple University Press.
Asante, M. K. (2003). *Erasing Racism: The Survival of the American Nation.* Humanity
Books.
Asante, M. K. (2007). *An Afrocentric Manifesto.* Polity Books.
Asante, M. K. (2016). Decolonizing the Universities in Africa: An Approach to
Transformation. In M. K. Asante & C. E. Ledbetter Jr. (Eds.), *Contemporary Critical
Thought in Africology and Africana Studies* (pp. 1–14). Lexington Books.
Asante, M. K., & Ledbetter, C. E., Jr. (Eds.). (2016). *Contemporary Critical Thought in
Africology and Africana Studies.* Lexington Books.
Ashburn, E. A. (2006). Introduction. It's Time: Technology Integrated into Meaningful
Learning Experiences. In E. A. Ashburn & R. E. Floden (Eds.), *Meaningful Learning
Using Technology: What Educators Need to Know and Do* (pp. 1–7). Teachers College
Press.

Baldwin, J. (1993). *The Fire Next Time*. Vintage Books.

Barr, M. (2008). *Afro-Future Females: Black Writers Chart Science Fiction's Newest New-Wave Trajectory*. Ohio State University Press.

Du Bois, W. E. B. (1994). *The Souls of Black Folk*. Dover.

Dyson, M. E. (2003). *Open Mike: Reflections on Philosophy, Race, Sex, Culture and Religion*. Basic Books.

Gayle, A., Jr. (1971). *The Black Aesthetic*. Doubleday.

Goldberg, D. (1993). *Racist Culture: Philosophy and the Politics of Meaning*. Blackwell.

Gordon, L. R. (1997). *Her Majesty's Other Children: Sketches of Racism from a Neocolonial Age*. Rowman & Littlefield.

Gray, M. (2007, January 12). Philip Emeagwali: A Calculating Move. *Time*. http://content
.time.com/time/specials/packages/article/0,28804,1963424_1963480_1963457,00.html

Hampton, G. J. (2010). *Changing Bodies in the Fiction of Octavia Butler*. Lexington Books.

Hill, S. (2018, February 12). *Little-Known Black History Facts: This Black Woman Helped Develop GPS Technology*. Black Enterprise. https://www.Blackenterprise.com/little
-known-Black-history-facts-87-year-old-Black-woman-helped-develop-gps-technology/

Hinduja, S., & Patchin, J. W. (2017). Cultivating Youth Resilience to Prevent Bullying and Cyberbullying Victimization. *Child Abuse & Neglect*, *73*, 51–62. https://doi.org/10.1016/j
.chiabu.2017.09.010

Kardiner A., & Ovesey, L. (1951). *The Mark of Oppression: Explorations in the Personality of the American Negro*. Meridian Books.

King, K. (2003). *Keeping Pace with Technology: Vocational Technology that Transforms*. Fordham University at Hampton Press.

Lewis, G. (2009). *Bringing Technology into the Classroom*. Oxford University Press.

Magette, K. (2015). *Embracing Social Media. A Practical Guide to Manage Risk and Leverage Opportunity*. Rowman & Littlefield.

Marable, M. (1995). *Beyond Black and White: Transforming African American Politics*. Verso Books.

Mazama A., & Musumunu, G. (2015). *African Americans and Homeschooling: Motivations, Opportunities, and Challenges*. Routledge.

Mills, C. (1997). *The Racial Contract*. Cornell University Press.

Monteiro-Ferreira, A. (2009). Afrocentricity and the western paradigm. *Journal of Black Studies*, *40*(2), 327–36

Monteiro-Ferreira, A. (2014). *The Demise of the Inhuman: Afrocentricity, Modernism, and Postmodernism*. SUNY Press.

Neal, L. (1989). The Black Arts Movement. In *Visions of a Liberated Future: Black Arts Movement Writing* (pp. 62–78). Thunder's Mouth Press.

Omi, M., & Winant, H. (1986). *Racial Formation in the United States: From the 1960s to the 1980s*. Routledge.

Pegrum, M. (2009). *From Blogs to Bombs: The Future of Digital Technologies in Education*. University of Western Australia.

Powell, J. (2007). Structural Racism and Spatial Jim Crow. In R. D. Bullard (Ed.), *The Black Metropolis in the 21st Century: Race, Power and the Politics of Race* (pp. 41–65). Rowman & Littlefield.

Price, C. A. (2003). Foreword: Race, Blackness, and Modernism During the Harlem Renaissance. In S. L. West & Aberjhani (Eds.), *The Encyclopedia of the Harlem Renaissance* (pp. xi–xiv). Facts on File.

Reed, I. (2003). *Another Day at the Front*. Basic Books.

Reid-Merritt, P. (2017). *Race in America*. Praeger.

Rennie, F., & Mason, R. (2004). *The Connecticon: Learning for the Connected Generation*. Information Age.

Sutherland, M. (1997). *Black Authenticity: A Psychology for Liberating People of African Descent*. Third World Press.

Tillotson, M. (2011). *Invisible Jim Crow, Contemporary Ideological Threats to the Internal Security of African Americans*. African World Press.

Wankel, L. A., & Wankel, C. (2012). *Misbehavior Online in Higher Education: Cutting-Edge Technologies in Higher Education*. Emerald Group.

Welsing, F. C. (1991). *The Isis Papers: The Keys to the Colors*. CW.

West, C. (1993). *Race Matters*. Beacon Press.

West, S. L., & Aberjhani (Eds.). (2003). *The Encyclopedia of the Harlem Renaissance*. Facts on File.

Wilson, A. N. (2005). *Blueprint for Black Power: A Moral, Political and Economic Imperative for the 21st Century*. Afrikan World InfoSystems.

Winant, H. (2001). *The World Is a Ghetto: Race and Democracy Since World War II*. Basic Books.

Wofford, B. (2016, August 5). How to Hack an Election in 7 Minutes. *Politico Magazine*. https://www.politico.com/magazine/story/2016/08/2016-elections-russia-hack-how-to-hack-an-election-in-seven-minutes-214144

Wright, B. (1984). *The Psychopathic Racial Personality and Other Essays*. Third World Press.

Youngquist, P. (2016). *A Pure Solar World Sun Ra and the Birth of AfroFuturism*. University of Texas Press.

3

AFROCENTRICITY'S AFROFUTURISM AND THE SIGNIFICANCE OF ASSERTING AFRICAN AGENCY IN THE PURSUIT OF AFRICAN FUTURE

Lehasa Moloi

The current chapter explores Afrocentric AfroFuturism as a transformative and combative paradigm, which seeks to restore African people to their own center in the narrative of life. This approach discredits the tendency to rewrite the narratives of African people from Eurocentric particularism, which distorts the consciousness of African people to speak and imagine their realities from dislocated philosophical grounds. Thus, the primary objective of an Afrocentric AfroFuturism is to dispose of the colonial terms of reference and replace them with African perspectives, which are germane to African cultural ethos as a way to restore the dignity of African people against five hundred years of Eurocentric humiliation. This emphasis on agency versus Eurocentric ideological domination is reminiscent of the perception of the Space Traders in Sheree R. Thomas's (2014, p. 328) AfroFuturist classic *Dark Matter*: "many American Blacks—whether watching from the shore or on their television screens—had seen the visitors as distinctly unpleasant, even menacing in appearance. While their perceptions of the visitors differed, Black people all agreed that the Space Traders looked like bad news."

There exist varying methods of promoting African self-definition and self-determination, yet a more consistent consensus that changes in this area would be extremely beneficial.

This chapter primarily argues that an emphasis on African agency is a distinction of Afrocentric Futurism, which serves as a critical pillar of the methodology. Until such time as African people are restored to their own terms, there will be no peace nor attainment of common destiny for them. To this effect, Afrocentric Futurism advances the concept, which promotes a mutual regard for various perspectives. While Europeans, for example, have a right to narrate their own lived experiences, this should not come at the expense of African people's narratives or safety. As Kodwo Eshun (2003, p. 288) argues, "the vigilance that is necessary to indict imperial modernity must be extended into the field of the future." The Afrocentric worldview (i.e., Afrocentricity) is a philosophical model predicated upon traditional African philosophical assumptions (Abarry, 1990; Akbar, 1984; Asante, 1988, 1990; Baldwin & Hopkins, 1990; Bell et al., 1990; Boykin, 1983; Boykin & Toms, 1985; Carruthers, 1999; Nobles, 2014; Schiele, 1991) that reflect the "original" cultural values (i.e., interdependency, collectivity, and spirituality) of Africans before the advent of European and Arab influences (Ben-Jochannan, 1971; Diop, 1991).

The main objective of an Afrocentric Futuristic approach is to enable Africans to look toward the future with victorious consciousness that is grounded within their history and culture. Molefi Kete Asante (2018) argues that "there are some things that are not AfroFuturism and also not Afrocentricity; there are avenues that challenge us as Africans to deconceptualize, to degenerate, to destroy, to abandon decisions, and therefore promote a future that is anti-African." These misrepresentations and other phenomena that exist outside of the Afrocentric or Afrofuturist paradigms are often the result of a lack of self-knowledge and self-love.

"When people do not know who they are, they are reduced and relegated to being imps and imitators of their oppressors" (Akua, 2020, p. 116). There is an African proverb stating, "If something is lost, we look for it first at home." Therefore, the only hope for Africans in the world hegemonized by colonial lineage (both Arabic and European) is for Africans to find their own roots and be relocated to their own center. From that center they will be able to correctly understand their own identity and fulfill their destiny. The establishment of identity determines activity. Said another way, an understanding of who one *is* determines what one *does*. According to Asante (2014, p. ix) the historical conquest of the African continent and its people began with one thousand years of Arab incursion and perpetuated through five hundred years of European invasion of African consciousness and lands. The European colonization expedition, which reached its apex during the 1884–85 Berlin Conference, enabled competing European nations to scramble the African land and divide the people of Africa to serve European interests.

This conference was part of the "European game" that emerged figuratively in 1492. According to Sabelo J. Ndlovu-Gatsheni (2013, p. 338), while the institutionalization of the slave trade became the first manifestation of this dark side of modernity, the Berlin Conference justified colonialism and laid the basis for global coloniality. Ali A. Mazrui (2010, p. xi) argues that "the scramble for and partition of Africa among European powers amounted to an open disregard and disdain for the African people's dignity, rights and sovereignty." The Conference dramatized and confirmed the fact that Europeans did not consider the people they found in Africa to be human beings who deserve to be treated with dignity. Adekeye Adebajo (2010, p.16) correctly describes the essence of the Berlin Conference in the following manner:

> Berlin and its aftermath were akin to armed robbers forcibly breaking into a house and sharing out its possessions while the owners of the house—who had been tied with thick ropes—were wide awake, but were powerless to prevent the burglary. It would be hard to find examples in the world history in which a single meeting had such devastating political, socioeconomic, and cultural consequences for an entire continent.

Much of this investigation involves the establishment of a reevaluation of existing historiographies. Similar to Sofia Samatar's (2017, p. 176) view in her writing on moving "Toward a Planetary History of AfroFuturism," a different outlook on the AfroFuturistic space includes "one that explores a Pan-African psychogeography, resists the framing of Africa as a latecomer to science fiction, and attests to the continued relevance of AfroFuturism for both Africa and the diaspora." In order to realign more Eurocentric narratives (outside and within the AfroFuturistic spaces), tensions can methodically be deconstructed around many existing mythological, primitive notions of African inferiority while extending the Futuristic innovative engagements of African peoples far beyond the more recent classifications of such ingenious speculative thought.

Prior to colonization, African people, like all other human beings, constantly and consistently improved their lives and life chances. They were inventive and innovative in many ways. Asante and Abu S. Abarry in their book *African Intellectual Heritage. A Book of Sources* (1996) captures the African works of imagination, invention, cultural dynamism, political engineering, religious and economic sophistication, and originality. In this book, Africans are presented as active and independent domesticators of plants and animals. They improved their technologies from stone to iron tools. They migrated from place to place in search of better environments that enhanced life chances. They established socio-political systems, lineages, clans, chiefdoms, kingdoms, states, and nations of varying sizes and complexities. Like all other human beings, Africans developed complex ideas as they constantly and consistently made sense of their lives and their environment.

The European invasion of Africa interfered with the progress that African people were making and fractured their ways of life and converted them into slaves that became dependent on their self-imposed masters. Ngugi wa Thiong'o (1986, p. 3) describes what was unleashed by Euro- and North American–centric modernity in its colonial and imperial phase as a "cultural bomb" and elaborates on the long-term consequences in this eloquent manner:

> The effect of a cultural bomb is to annihilate a people's belief in their names, in their language, in their environment, in their heritage of struggle, in their unity, in their capacities and ultimately in themselves. It makes them see their past as one wasteland of non-achievement and it makes them want to identify with that which is furthest removed from themselves; for instance, with other people's languages rather than their own. It makes them identify with that which is decadent and reactionary, all those forces that will stop their own springs of life. It even plants serious doubts about the moral rightness of the struggle. Possibilities of triumph or victory are seen as remote, ridiculous dreams. The intended results are despair, despondency and a collective death-wish. Amidst this wasteland which it has created, imperialism presents itself as the cure and demands that the dependent sing hymns of praise with the constant refrain: "Theft is holy."

African scholars such as Peter Ekeh (1983) use the common term "colonialism" to signify the structural straitjacket within which Africa is entrapped and the paradigm of difference it inaugurated. Ekeh (1983) argues that the process of African colonization cannot be simplistically understood as an event of conquest and rule over Africa. Rather, it must be viewed as a systemic social movement of epochal dimensions whose enduring consequences outlive the end of direct colonialism. Asante (2007, p. 10) affirms that although colonization of Africans as a direct control of the continent has ended, Africans are still mentally subjugated. The reason for this sad mental state is that we have been fighting against the evil of colonization as an economic and political problem rather than a total conceptual distortion leading to confusion (Asante, 2007, p. 10). "Whether they call it AfroFuturism or something else, scholars and artists have long been interested in the meaning and value of Black speculation" (Lavender & Yaszek, 2020, p. 7). The distinction expressed in this chapter is a question of methodology more than semantics.

Asante (2014, p. x) maintains that "we are not yet free when in the imagination of some of our young people we are still hoping to discover that Africa is not in our past." This means that the extent of our problem is severe; our children do not like themselves because if they knew, only knew, they would celebrate their Blackness, their Africanity, for the gifts Africans have given to the world (Asante, 2014). There was a time when African people led the world in literary production, scientific innovation, and wealth creation (Karenga, 2001). An understanding of that history creates an empowering identity. Sadly, this narrative is not well known among Africans and others. The restoration of African identity and retelling of African history from an African perspective are together a necessary solid foundation upon which African agency and self-determination must be created and sustained. Without relocating to our own terms of reference, we remain lost forever and will fail to become innovative and will continue to not fulfill our destiny. Asante (2014, p. x) argues: "The moral aesthetics of Afrocentricity is that it situates Africans within the center of the African narratives of place, time, and space hence demonstrating that the dislocation of Africans from the center of their own history is a form of intellectual and cultural terrorism that is a constant attack on the African's concept of self and the idea of time." When some first hear of Afrocentric Futurism, they may mistakenly assume the term is redundant considering preexisting concepts such as "AfroFuturism." They may believe: "That's what AfroFuturism is. Africa and futurism. Together" (Holbert et al., 2020, p. 342). It is imperative to recognize the profound difference between aesthetic inclusion of African symbolism, the sprinkling of African concepts throughout a creative, speculative expression, and the foundational, nation-building, Pan-African methodological superstructure of Afrocentric Futurism. This concept involves a unique vision of reclaiming our space and time in an Afrocentric way.

Eshun (2003, p. 287) posits that "in our time, the USAF (United States of Africa) archaeologists' surmise, imperial racism has denied Black subjects the right to belong to the enlightenment project, thus creating an urgent need to demonstrate a substantive historical presence." As a way to establish the historical character of Black culture, to bring Africa and its subjects into history denied by Europeans, it has become necessary to assemble countermemories that contest the colonial archive, thereby situating the collective trauma of slavery as the founding moment of modernity (Eshun, 2003, p. 288). In the words of Erique Dussel (1993, p. 65), modernity as a European constructed phenomenon appears when Europe affirms itself as the "center" of a world history that it inaugurates; the "periphery" that surrounds this center is consequently part of its self-definition. The myth of modernity as introduced by European scholars disguises the fact that it is a system of violence that represents the annihilation of others in the pursuit of European domination. Aimé Césaire in his *Discourse on Colonialism* (1955, p. 31) correctly describes European modernity as a civilization of death, "a civilization that proves incapable of solving the problems it creates . . . a civilization that chooses to close its eyes to its most crucial problems . . . a civilization that uses its principles for trickery and deceit." Thus, "Europe is unable to justify itself either before the bar of 'reason' or before the bar of 'conscience'; . . . it takes refuge in a hypocrisy which is all the more odious because it is less and less likely to deceive" (p. 31). Thus, AfroFuturism grounded in the ideals of Afrocentricity offers a new hope that seeks to restore African people cross continentally to their own base, which is, to their own history and culture, the locus of enunciation. AfroFuturism, therefore, offers a relevant avenue for a reconstruction of Africans' view of their future in a world where they have been excluded. "History, in terms of many AfroFuturist stories, involves more than the supposed 'facts' we are taught in our history lessons; it is also connected to the folktales and oral traditions that grew alongside those histories. A brief look into African American folklore studies demonstrates the interest in preserving, studying, and even reveling in this cultural past" (Lavender & Yaszek, 2020, p. 95).

Afrocentric Futurism as a Redemptive Paradigm for African Reemergence

Since the term "AfroFuturism" first appeared, scholars have seized upon the idea as a way to critique the reified distance between racialized fictions of *Black magic* and *White science*—often in satirical and even playful ways. The concept of "AfroFuturism" is normally attributed to Mark Dery (an author, critic, and essayist), coined in an interview with Samuel Delany, Greg Tate, and Tricia Rose that appeared in *South Atlantic Quarterly* in 1993. Dery (1993, pp. 735–36) explains:

> Speculative fiction that treats African-American themes and addresses African-American concerns in the context of 20th-century techno-culture—and, more generally, African-American signification that appropriates images of technology and a prosthetically enhanced future—might, for want of a better term, be called AfroFuturism. The notion AfroFuturism gives rise to a troubling antinomy: Can a community whose past has been deliberately rubbed out, and whose energies have subsequently been consumed by the search for legible traces of its history, imagine possible futures? Furthermore, don't the technocrats, science fiction (SF) writers, futurologists, set designers, and streamliners—White to a man—who have engineered our collective fantasies already have a lock on that unreal estate?

In the light of Dery's reflections, the real question is whether Africans can escape deliberate historical distortions created through five hundred years of colonial enslavement. For Asante (2007), the answer lies in the reclamation of the terms of reference, which is to situate Africans within the context of their own historical and cultural realities. AfroFuturism seeks to provide healing for people of African descent to reclaim their victorious consciousness as the panacea against European decadence. AfroFuturism is a compound of two terms: "Afro," which refers to African and "Futurism," concerning events and trends of the future and concepts, technologies, and items produced from them. AfroFuturism, therefore, is an artistic style concerned with Futuristic creations where the major elements are of African origin. "African" refers to both Africans living on the continent and those in the diaspora. The merging of AfroFuturism and Afrocentricity as a paradigm in the pursuit to recenter Africans within their own narratives of place, time, and space is the only path for Africans to pursue their liberation. Without being recentered, we will never be able to heal from the imposed colonial wounds and will continue to be defined by the very discourses that have caused Black people great pain. "This world is one in which millions of people suffer in their struggles to survive the aftermath of conquest. Their voices are ignored, silenced by a belief in a western concept of progress, an ideology that advances the notion that some members of humanity deserve to live without access to, or control over their resources" (Dove, 1998, p. xiii).

AfroFuturism is, therefore, a genre and a way of thinking that liberates and reclaims African agency through blends of Afro-culture, science fiction, magical realism, technology, and traditional African mysticism. It takes many forms and tells many different stories, but one common feature is that AfroFuturists fight for equality and Black people's rights to a place in the future—a place and a future that must not be defined by Whites. Infused with a rebellious and self-determining spirit, AfroFuturism studies the appeals that Black artists, musicians, critics, and writers have made to the future, in moments where any future was made difficult for them to imagine (Eshun, 2003). Eshun (2003, p. 293) states that "AfroFuturism is concerned with the possibilities for intervention within the dimension of the predictive, the projected, the proleptic, the envisioned, the visual, the anticipatory, and the future conditional." AfroFuturism can be seen as a reaction to the dominance of White, European expression and a reaction to the use of science and technology to justify racism and White or Western dominance and normativity. In AfroFuturism, artistic expression is used to imagine counterfutures free of Western hegemony but also as a tool to implicitly analyze the status quo (Lewis, 2018). The US-based scholar Reynoldo Anderson, the coeditor of a collection of academic essays called *AfroFuturism 2.0: The Rise of Astro-Blackness* (Anderson & Jones, 2016, p. x), defines AfroFuturism as an emerging Pan-African transnational, trans-contextual, technocultural social philosophy characterized by other "dimensions that include African or African diasporic metaphysics, aesthetics, social sciences (such as Afrocentricity, Black/African feminist and womanist thought, or Black queer practice), theoretical and applied science, and programmatic spaces" (qtd. in Kemp, 2018).

According to Asante (2018), "Anderson has been able to trace the origins of AfroFuturism and mesh it with his understanding of Afrocentricity as a theory that supports the re-centering of Africans from the marginalities inherent in many European constructions of reality and the future." Asante (2018) further states that there is no "Black secret technology, as there is no

White or Asian secret technology." Technological innovations are not demarcated or compartmentalized according to racial classification. Everyone has opportunities to add their technological contributions for the benefit of humanity. This availability of progressive innovation also includes opportunities to express agency. The ability of Africans to tell their own narratives silences the predominant culture of European intellectual dictatorship and advances African greatness. Africans cannot be future oriented if Africans cannot conceive of themselves as subjects and agents responsible for freedom. As such, Anderson has become one of the leading voices announcing the agency of African people in the assertion of the future. Asante (2018) emphatically states, "there is no future for Africans if Africans no longer exist." By employing science fiction to tell their stories, Africans have created a platform to revisit the historical past, demystify the present, and frame their futures. According to Eshun (2003), Afrocentric Futurism's first priority is to recognize that Africa increasingly exists as the subject of Futurist projections. African social reality is overdetermined by intimidating global scenarios, doomsday economic and weather projections, medical reports on AIDS, and life-expectancy forecasts, all of which predict a hopeless future for Africans as reported through Western media powerhouses. Eshun (2003) argues that these powerful descriptions of the future demoralize Africans; they command us to bury our heads in our hands and groan with sadness. This style of reporting by Eurocentric poets, artists, academics, and musicians has continued to portray a negative view of Africa, continuing to cement Georg Wilhelm Friedrich Hegel's false notion of Africans as people without history and culture. What is significant to understand about African history is that it does not begin with European enslavement of Africans. To this effect, Asante (2018) emphasizes that our history is not simply four or five hundred years of resistance to the imperial domination of White racism. In this regard, Afrocentric Futuristic approaches to education are in line with revolutionary pedagogy as defined by Asante (2018): "Revolutionary pedagogy obliterates cultural ignorance at every turn by employing the techniques of transmitting knowledge based on facts with an eye toward community values of truth, order, balance, harmony, justice and reciprocity. A revolutionary pedagogy therefore is a projection of the will to be human among other humans and to protect the legacies of humanity."

We were and have been free human beings resisting and refusing domination from the very beginning of our encounters with Arabs and Europeans.

Therefore, ours is not just the history of subjugation but also the fact that the colonization of Africa by Arabs and Europeans interfered with Africans' journey to Africa's future.

Asante (2018) posits: "AfroFuturism must mean that the people of African descent can project the best ideals and values of a multiplicity of mythological-historical narratives into speculative space to create a techno-aesthetic ethic based on the best qualities of African people. The only way for African future to be guaranteed is if Africans themselves claim their own agency." A future defined by others on our own behalf renders us as victims of domination and as people incapable of creating and managing our own lives and destiny. Whoever controls myths controls destiny. Afrocentric AfroFuturism, therefore, acts as a catalyst for the reimagination of our futures. It serves as a platform to catapult our hopes, dreams, visions, and ideals. This, in turn, allows us to shape our own realities as African people through divine attraction and manifestation. AfroFuturism removes European patriarchal, masculinist, militaristic, and toxic racism from our future (Asante, 2014). Claiming ourselves as the agents of history is the first step to projecting ourselves as having something valuable to contribute to that future. The call in both AfroFuturism and Afrocentricity is for Africans to arise to assert their own agency in all matters of life, thus outwitting the tendency to regard themselves as marginal and spectators of a show that has defined them without their own input. Asante (1998, p. 8) contends: "By regaining our own (African) platforms, standing on our own cultural spaces, and believing that our way of viewing the universe is just as valid as any, we will achieve the kind of transformation that we need to participate fully in a multicultural society. However, without this kind of centeredness, we bring almost nothing to the multicultural table but a darker version of Whiteness." African people, by seizing the science-fiction platform, demonstrated their own ability to not merely occupy the back seat, rather they expressed their own creativities as agents in history to defy domination. Afrocentricity, and to a large extent AfroFuturism, creates what the ancient Egyptians referred to as a "*djed*" and the ancient Greeks as a "*stasis*," meaning, in both cases, a "strong place to stand" (Asante, 2007, p. 15). Afrocentrically speaking, when Africans use any platform to ground an analysis of any phenomenon within the rich African soil, they embark on revolutionary approaches and claim their power. What is also significant to accept is the fact that the predominant Eurocentric culture will not allow its slaves to leave its intellectual tradition without a fight. In order to reign victorious in this age-old battle of meaning and manifestation in resistance to marginalization, it is paramount to recognize the critical role of culture. AfroFuturism acknowledges the transformative potential of culture, while Afrocentric Futurism is methodologically grounded in Ancient African and contemporary diasporic African cultural traditions. Both approaches look ahead and attempt to transform reality. The critical distinction is perhaps the centrality of African culture, history, consciousness, and liberation, which are the cornerstones of Afrocentric Futurism. "AfroFuturism also has a redemptive quality. Exposure to the AfroFuturist perspective can psychologically free black youth who are trapped in the disabling mindset of urban dystopian milieu. Far too many vibrant and intelligent African Americans in the prime of life are being caught up in the subculture of gangs, violence, and drugs" (Rollins, 2015, p. 130).

This requires engaging AfroFuturism grounded on Afrocentricity. This combination represents an epistemic conceptualization that seeks to resist Eurocentric falsifications of African history, present realities, and potentialities. While Afrocentricity is not merely about denying a space for Europeans to narrate their intellectual framing, its emphasis is about contesting the right for Africans to narrate theirs in the spirit of democratizing knowledge. Numerous critics of Afrocentricity have advanced their agenda by misnaming Afrocentricity as "Afrocentrism" in an effort to discredit the work of the Afrocentrists, thus seeking to mitigate the discourse to sustain hegemony. White and Black Eurocentric scholars include Mary Lefkowitz (1996), Tunde Adeleke (2015), Yaacov Shavit (2001), Kieth Richburg (1996), and Michael E. Owens (2009), and many more critics represent the rejection of Afrocentricity without accepting the historical facts of African negation and do not see the significance of African agency. A portion of this empowering agency deals with naming and defining. In many instances in which scholars attempt to discuss Afrocentricity, they use a term popularized by critiques of the methodological approach—"Afrocentrism." The seminal *AfroFuturism 2.0* states:

> In many ways the search for cultural and personal meaning central to Afrocentrism can be linked to Baudrillard's ecstasy of the sign that obscures distinctions between the real and unreal, the simulated and the dissimulated. The ideal Africa articulated in Afrocentric signs is one in which to paraphrase Baudrillard, nostalgia is energized, in which "there is a proliferation of myths

of origin and signs of reality" (Baudrillard, 1983, p. 14). In Afrocentrism, African values and ideas have their origin in both the distant past and recent living history. (McLeod, 2016, p. 118)

This misnaming of "Afrocentricity" as "Afrocentrism" at times reflects an attempt to misdirect those who have not immersed themselves in the essence of what Afrocentricity really constitutes, and this is indicative of the ongoing ideological warfare to ensure the continuation of the subjugation of African people as objects of analysis, thus discouraging them from being their own agents in history. Maulana Karenga (2002, p. 46) also articulates the differences between "Afrocentricity" and the general media's use of "Afrocentrism" when he writes:

The term Afrocentrism appears more often in ideological discourse between Afrocentric advocates and critics especially in popular pieces on the subject. . . . [There is a] popular appropriation of the category by some of its advocates, critics and the media who use it for purposes which tend to define it as an ideological posture rather than an intellectual category. Its transformation from Afrocentricity to Afrocentrism is indicative of this. For the use of "ism," tend [sic] to suggest that it is seen as more of a political posture than a methodology or orientation in intellectual work.

However, despite the fear-based distorted descriptions of Afrocentric theory and methods, critics have not succeeded in their mission as avenues have been expanded in narrating Afrocentric tales. AfroFuturism has offered one such platform by taking over the technological devices to magnify the African stories.

The Loss of African Agency and the Implications for African Imaginations of the Future

Asante (2015) argues in one of his latest books, *African Pyramids of Knowledge: Kemet, Afrocentricity and Africology*, that the Eurocentric West is trapped, even in its best intentions, by its concentration on itself, its selfishness, its inability to draw a wider picture, and its unabashed drive for greed and materialism. The birth of the modern world system, which can best be described as Christian centric, patriarchal, capitalistic, Euro American, and colonial, is traceable to 1492 when it claimed that Christopher Columbus discovered the "New World" (Ndlovu-Gatsheni, 2013). The emergence of this world system gave birth to Eurocentrism as a guiding framework of thought that colonized how the world is seen, interpreted, and understood by others outside of the West. Perhaps as a way to organize our thoughts, it is important to provide a conceptual clarification on what fundamentally Eurocentrism means and entails. As defined by Samir Amin (2009, pp. 177–78), the idea of Eurocentrism is a modern construct that consists of a bundle of Western prejudices about other people. It is a prosaic form of ethnocentrism informed by a discursive terrain of racism, "chauvinism and xenophobia" underpinned by "ignorance and mistrust of others" used to confer on Europeans the right to judge and analyse others." Juliet Ucelli and Dennis O'Neil (1992, p. 35) also concur that "Eurocentrism" represents the deliberate distortion of the consciousness and self-knowledge of humanity by the insistence of the people of European descent that "all" valid, "universal" scientific knowledge, economic progress, political structures, and works of art flow "only" from their ancestors to the exclusion of the non-European others, in particular Africans.

George Joseph, Vasu Reddy, and Mary Searle-Chatterjee (1990, pp. 1–2) also pinpoint that the persistence of Eurocentrism has had the following effects on the non-European societies:

i. It has damaged non-European societies through the colonisation of their intellectuals.

ii. It has impoverished the academic disciplines themselves, which remain unaware of alternative sources of knowledge outside mainstream development.

iii. It functions, regardless of intention, to legitimize international systems of inequality.

In Afrocentricity's view, Eurocentrism has distorted African culture; de-Africanized the consciousness of Africans, and arrested their economic and cultural development, and it represents a potent threat to the cultural, social, economic, and political development of Africans. The Afrocentrists argue that the Eurocentric myth that the Greeks gave the world rational thought is historically inaccurate and that the construction of the Western notions of knowledge based on the Greek model are relatively recent, beginning with the European Renaissance (Asante, 1980). In the standard Western view, neither Africans, Chinese, nor Asians, in general, have rational thinking; only Europeans have the ability to construct rational thought. Their locus of enunciation in the argument they are advancing is itself self-serving as it inaugurates the paradigm of difference and epistemic racism and violence toward the humanity of others and their capacities. Thus, the Afrocentrists contend that the Eurocentric view has become an ethnocentric view, which elevates the European experience and downgrades all others. The critical challenge facing African scholars, poets, prophets, and scientists is to remove the Eurocentric lenses in their envisioning of the African future and wear their own to see properly. How do we envision the future of Africa when we are wearing defective lenses? There can be no authentic African future without African agency; such a future would require Africans to trust in their own abilities and be rooted within their historical and cultural setting.

The European voyagers of discovery, enlightenment, civilization, and salvation, during the expedition that started in the fifteenth century, were also voyagers of African impoverishment, dismemberment, and dislocation from an African perspective. The European idea that Africa was a part of the world saturated by subhumans with no history and culture, as pronounced by Hegel in 1800, was an attempt to question the very humanity of Africans. Based on their false pronouncement, Europeans justified their colonization mission, which masqueraded their insatiable lust for the mineral-rich continent. For this reason, no African future can be entrusted to the hands of any other people than Africans themselves. Afrocentric in practice, "AfroFuturism emerged as a means to understand the transformation of African peoples as they dealt with the oppressive forces of discrimination, and the complexities of modern urban life and postmodernity" (Anderson & Jennings, 2014, p. 35). Asante (2018) argues, "Africans are neither relics of race nor endlessly, to use a time frame, dominated people." African history does not begin with imperial domination, as this promotes reductionism in the understanding of Africa and advances Western propaganda. We are and have been free human beings advancing our own well-being despite our colonial encounters with Arabs and Europeans who pretended to be on the civilizational mission. There never were African slaves; there were only Africans who were enslaved (Asante, 2018).

The rise of modern Europe in the aftermath of 1492, which culminated with the African scramble during the 1884–85 Berlin Conference, marked the era of the loss of African agency (Ndlovu-Gatsheni, 2013). Within this racially driven system, Africans were rearticulated by the Western opinion makers as disabled beings without history and development. This articulation of non-Western subjectivities and being has been captured well by Ramon Grosfoguel (2007, p. 214): "We went from the sixteenth century characterization of 'people without writing' to eighteenth and nineteenth century characterization of 'people without history,' to the twentieth century characterization of 'people without development' and more recently, to the early twenty-first century of 'people without democracy.'" Against these malicious and dehumanizing descriptions by Europeans, Africans are quickly remembering a history that has been disremembered, ripped, and torn to shreds by the brutal hands of colonialists and enslavers with an aim to rewrite the future narratives free of fear. Asante (2018) contends that "we cannot enter the Afrocentric future on wagons of victimhood, hounded by the dogs of marginality, with our minds centered only on the past; we are not beggar people and out of the thorns and thickets of the past we must pick up fragrant flowers that enlightened and invigorated those futurists who created the cultural, technological and ethical platform upon which we build." The fundamental agenda in Afrocentric AfroFuturism is not necessarily to solely dwell in the past but rather use the past to raise victorious consciousness, which enables Africans to shape better futures.

The Significance of Asserting African Agency in the Pursuit of African Future

It is out of the great concern for African disenfranchisement and marginalization in the intellectual arena, as well as other spheres of life, that Asante (1980) "developed the theory of action and liberation known as Afrocentricity" (Mazama, 2014). In Asante's (2007, p. 41) view, "Africans have been negated in the system of White racial domination. This is not mere marginalization, but the obliteration of the presence, meaning, activities, or images of the African." Asante believes that it is only in the process of reassuming, in a most conscious manner, our sense of historical and cultural agency that we Africans can hope to put an end to our invisibility, stagnation, and helplessness.

"Afrocentricity is a frame of reference wherein phenomena are viewed from the perspective of the African person. The Afrocentric approach seeks in every situation the appropriate centrality of the African person" (Asante, 1991, p. 171). An agent must mean a human being who is capable of acting independently in his or her own interest. Agency itself is the ability to provide the psychological and cultural resources necessary for the advancement of human freedom (Asante, 2007). Similarly, AfroFuturism may be characterized as a program for recovering the histories of counterfutures created in a century hostile to Afro-diasporic projection and as a space within which the critical work of manufacturing tools capable of intervention within the current political dispensation may be undertaken (Eshun, 2003, p. 301).

Without our own agency, we remain under the tutelage of European agents as big brothers who direct the path to be merely followed. Thus, Black people exist in a show that defines us without our own input or contribution. For this reason, Black people have been rendered as objects in a European frame of reference and do not have a *djed* to stand on. Ndlovu-Gatsheni (2013) argues that decolonization must be deepened to deal with profound cultural, psychological, and epistemological issues. Without these processes taking place, the possibility of African people exercising extrastructural agency remains like a pie in the sky. Alondra Nelson explains: "Black creative life has too often been determined by this impulse to 'keep it real.' In order to be taken seriously, we have fostered and encouraged a long tradition of social realism in our cultural production. And we feared that to stop keeping things real was to lose the ability to recognize and protest the very real inequalities in the social world" (qtd. in Rambsy, 2013, p. 205–6). Artistic expression in AfroFuturism, therefore, claims a space for Africans to self-represent using speculative narratives, innovation, and engagements with science, machines, and technological devices to advance the Black speculative future. The truth is we are the future we want to have. It is only when African people represent themselves as their own agents that their aspirations will be attainable.

"African resurgence will never take place until Africans themselves champion a renaissance grounded in a new paradigm of dramatic narratives of victory" (Asante, 2015, p. 1). Our main challenge is to trust our own genius and be courageous to stand on our own platforms and make pronouncements about the future we want. However, for as long as those who have undermined our history and culture tell our own narratives, we shall continue to remain marginal. The necessary call is for Africans to dip the gourd into the eternal stream of African history and analyze every conceivable activity for its utility and application for present and future generations (Asante, 2015). We can do nothing less in recovering our historical stance toward the future. Just as people of Kemet (ancient Egypt) who lived along the banks of the Nile River took advantage of whatever situation was presented to them by the river flow, we also can learn from them and take charge of our circumstances

(Asante, 2015). As a cultural theory, "Afrocentricity is committed to the reclamation on ancient African classical civilizations as the place for interpreting and understanding the history of African people, narratives, myths, spirituality, and cosmogonies" (Monteiro-Ferreira, 2014, p. 3). The nexus between Afrocentricity and AfroFuturism has therefore offered Africans an avenue to present African history from a more informed point of view, which does not seek to subvert the achievements made by Africans in world civilization.

Until such time that Africans are able to narrate their tales as agents grounded in their own historical and cultural premises, they will continue to exist as marginal. Traditional AfroFuturism has been expressed as a response to White domination.

> AfroFuturism combines science fiction and fantasy to reexamine how the future is currently imagined, and to reconstruct future thinking with a deeper insight into the Black experience, especially as slavery forced Africans to confront an alien world surrounded by colonial technologies. AfroFuturism is born out of cruelty, and that cruelty of the White imagination was a necessary condition out of which the African diaspora had to reimagine its future. (Brooks, 2018, p. 101)

AfroFuturism grounded on the riches of Afrocentricity as a paradigm of liberation enables Africans to have a voice among others to contribute to their own imaginary futures. Afrocentric Futurism dares to imagine a world and a future absent of White domination or its residual impacts. Modernity has sought to reconstruct new identities for African people, which contributed to the loss of their agency and is a cause of African dislocation. Afrocentricity, in contrast, "seeks to obliterate the mental, physical, cultural and economic dislocation of African people by thrusting Africans as centered, healthy human beings in the context of African thought" (Asante, 2007, p. 120). After many years of the brutal acts perpetuated throughout the colonial history of both Arab and European incursions in Africa, the time for African liberation has come. The main challenge facing Africans globally is to trust their own knowledge, respect their own cultures, and refuse to be used as objects of others' imaginations. These are the elements required to illuminate a brilliant Afrocentric future. The time is forever!

REFERENCES

Abarry, A. S. (1990). Afrocentricity: Introduction. *Journal of Black Studies, 21*(2), 123–25.

Adebajo, A. (2010). *The Curse of Berlin: Africa after the Cold War.* University of KwaZulu-Natal.

Adeleke, T. (2015). Africa and Afrocentric Historicism: A Critique. *Advances in Historical Studies, 4*(3), 200–215. http://dx.doi.org/10.4236/ahs.2015.43016

Akbar, N. (1984). *From Miseducation to Education.* New Mind Productions.

Akua, C. (2020). Standards of Afrocentric Education for School Leaders and Teachers. *Journal of Black Studies, 51*(2), 107–27.

Amin, S. (2009). *Eurocentrism: Modernity, Religion, and Democracy: A Critique of Eurocentrism and Culturalism.* Monthly Review Press.

Anderson, R. (2016). AfroFuturism 2.0 & the Black Speculative Arts Movement: Notes on a Manifesto. *Obsidian, 42*(1–2), 228–36.

Anderson, R., & Jennings, J. (2014). Afrofuturism: The Digital Turn and the Visual Art of Kanye West. In J. Bailey (Ed.), *The Cultural Impact of Kanye West* (pp. 29–44). Springer.

Anderson, R., & Jones, C. E. (Eds.). (2016). *AfroFuturism 2.0: The Rise of Astro-Blackness.* Lexington Books.

Asante, M. K. (1980). *Afrocentricity: The Theory of Social Change* (Rev. ed.). Africa World Press.

Asante, M. K. (1988). *Afrocentricity* (revised ed.). Africa World Press.

Asante, M. K. (1990). *Kemet, Afrocentricity, and Knowledge.* Africa World Press.

Asante, M. K. (1991). The Afrocentric Idea in Education. *Journal of Negro Education, 60*(2), 170–80.

Asante, M. K. (1998). *The Afrocentric Idea* (Rev. and ex. ed.). Temple University Press.

Asante, M. K. (2007). *An Afrocentric Manifesto: Toward an African Renaissance.* Polity Press.

Asante, M. K. (2014). *Facing South to Africa: Towards an Afrocentric Orientation.* Lexington.

Asante, M. K. (2015). *African Pyramids of Knowledge: Kemet, Afrocentricity and Africology.* Universal Write Publications.

Asante, M. K. (2018, November 2–4). *Afrocentricity's AfroFuturism and the Countdown to the Future* [Conference presentation]. Berlin, Germany.

Asante, M. K., and Abarry, A. S. (1996). *African Intellectual Heritage: A Book of Sources.* Temple University Press.

Baldwin, J. A., & Hopkins, R. (1990). African-American and European-American Cultural Differences as Assessed by the Worldviews Paradigm: An Empirical Analysis. *Western Journal of Black Studies, 14*(1), 38–52.

Bell, Y. R., Bouie, C. L., & Baldwin, J. A. (1990). Afrocentric Cultural Consciousness and African-American Male-Female Relationships. *Journal of Black Studies, 21*(2), 162–89.

Ben-Jochannan, Y. (1971). Africa: Mother of Western Civilization. Alkebu-lan Books.

Boykin, A. W. (1983). The Academic Performance of Afro-American Children. In J. Spence (Ed.), *Achievement and Achievement Motives* (pp. 321–71). W. Freeman.

Boykin, A. W., & Toms, F. D. (1985). Black Child Socialization: A Conceptual Framework. In H. P. McAdoo & J. L. McAdoo (Eds.), *Black Children: Social, Educational, and Parental Environments* (pp. 33–51). SAGE.

Brooks, L. J. A. (2018). Cruelty and AfroFuturism. *Communication and Critical/Cultural Studies, 15*(1), 101–7.

Carruthers, J. H. (1999). *Intellectual Warfare.* Third World Press.

Césaire, A. (1955). *Discourse on Colonialism*. Monthly Review Press.

Dery, M. (1993). Black to the Future: Interviews with Samuel R. Delany, Greg Tate, and Tricia Rose. *South Atlantic Quarterly, 92*(4), 735–78.

Diop, C. A. (1991). *Civilization or Barbarism*. Chicago Review Press.

Dove, N. (1998). *Afrikan Mothers: Bearers of Culture, Makers of Social Change*. SUNY Press.

Dussel, E. (1993). Eurocentrism and Modernity (Introduction to the Frankfurt Lectures). *Boundary 2, 20*(3), 65–76.

Ekeh, P. (1983). *Colonialism and Social Structure: University of Ibadan Inaugural Lecture, 1980*. Ibadan University Press.

Eshun, K. (2003). Further Considerations of AfroFuturism. *CR: The New Centennial Review, 3*(2), 287–302.

Grosfoguel, R. (2007). The Epistemic Decolonial Turn: Beyond Political-Economy Paradigms. *Cultural Studies, 21*(2–3), 211–23.

Holbert, N., Dando, M., & Correa, I. (2020). AfroFuturism as Critical Constructionist Design: Building Futures from the Past and Present. *Learning, Media and Technology, 45*(4), 328–44.

Joseph, G. G., Reddy, V., & Searle-Chatterjee, M. (1990). Eurocentrism in the Social Sciences. *Race & Class, 31*(4), 1–26.

Karenga, M. (2001). *The Ethics of Reparations: Engaging the Holocaust of Enslavement*. N'COBRA. https://ncobra.org/resources/pdf/Karenga%20THE%20ETHICS%20OF%20 REPARATIONS.pdf

Karenga, M. (2002). *Introduction to Black Studies* (3rd ed). University of Sankore Press.

Kemp, G. (2018, October 28). *Black to the Future*. City Press. https://city-press.news24.com /Trending/Black-to-the-future-20181028-2

Lavender, I., III, & Yaszek, L. (2020). *Literary AfroFuturism in the Twenty-First Century*. Ohio State University Press.

Lefkowitz, M. (1996). *Not out of Africa: How Afrocentrism Became an Excuse to Teach Myth as History*. Basic Books.

Lewis, J. J. (2018, February 19). *AfroFuturism: Imagining an Afrocentric Future. Rejecting Eurocentric Dominance and Normalization*. ThoughtCo. https://www.thoughtco.com /AfroFuturism-definition-4137845

Mazama, A. (2014, June 27). *Afrocentricity and the Critical Question of African Agency*. Afrocentricity International. https://www.dyabukam.com/index.php/en/knowledge /philosophy/item/136-Afrocentricity

Mazrui, A. A. (2010). Preface: Black Berlin and the Curse of Fragmentation. From Bismarck to Barack. In A. Adebajo (Ed.), *The Curse of Berlin: Africa after the Cold War* (pp. v–xii). University of KwaZulu-Natal Press.

McLeod, K. (2016). Hip Hop Holograms: Tupac Shakur, Technological Immortality, and Time Travel. In R. Anderson & C. E. Jones (Eds.), *Afrofuturism 2.0: The Rise of Astro-Blackness* (pp. 109–24). Lexington Books.

Monteiro-Ferreira, A. (2014). *The Demise of the Inhumane: Afrocentricity, Modernism, and Postmodernism*. SUNY Press.

Ndlovu-Gatsheni, S. J. (2013). The Entrapment of Africa within the Global Colonial Matrices of Power: Eurocentrism, Coloniality, and Deimperialization in the Twenty-First Century. *Journal of Developing Societies, 29*(4), 331–53.

Ngugi wa Thiong'o. (1986). *Decolonising the Mind: The Politics of Language in African Literature*. James Currey.

Nobles, W. W. (2014). The Destruction of the African Mind, Shattered Consciousness, and Fractured Identity: Black Psychology and the Restoration of the African Psyche. In S. Cooper & K. Ratele (Eds.), *Psychology Serving Humanity: Proceedings of the 30th International Congress of Psychology, Vol. 1. Majority World Psychology* (pp. 87–104). Psychology Press.

Owens, M. E. (2009). *Yes, I Am Who I Am: A New Philosophy of Black Identity*. Yorkshire.

Rambsy, H., II (2013). Beyond Keeping It Real: OutKast, the Funk Connection, and AfroFuturism. *American Studies, 52*(4), 205–16.

Richburg, K. (1996). *Out of America: A Black Man Confronts Africa*. Basic Books.

Rollins, A. (2016). Afrofuturism and Our Old Ship of Zion. In R. Anderson & C. E. Jones (Eds.), *Afrofuturism 2.0: The Rise of Astro-Blackness* (pp. 127–47). Lexington Books.

Samatar, S. (2017). Toward a Planetary History of AfroFuturism. *Research in African Literatures, 48*(4), 175–91. https://doi.org/10.2979/reseafrilite.48.4.12

Schiele, J. H. (1991). Publication Productivity of African-American Social Work Faculty. *Journal of Social Work Education, 27*(2), 125–34.

Shavit, Y. (2001). *History in Black: African Americans in Search of Ancient Past*. Frank Cass.

Thomas, S. R. (2014). *Dark Matter: A Century of Speculative Fiction from the African Diaspora*. Hachette.

Ucelli, J., & O'Neil, D. (1992). Challenging Eurocentrism. *Forward Motion*, (1), 34–45.

van Veen, T. C. (2016). *Concepts of Cabralism: Amilcar Cabral and Africana Critical Theory*. Lexington Books.

4

BURY ME IN THE OCEAN
Erik Killmonger and Black Nationalism

John P. Craig

"Perhaps one of the biggest Afrofuturistic events of the decade, *Black Panther* set box office records as the highest-grossing film of 2018. . . . *Black Panther* tells the story of a fictional African country, Wakanda that is rich in a space metal called 'vibranium,' one of the world's strongest and most versatile metals" (McGee & White, 2021, p. 390). Just as this fictitious precious metal represents a most valuable commodity around the world, the Black Panther branch of the Marvel cinematic ecosystem has come to represent artistic gold for marketers of all types. There is no denying Marvel's *Black Panther* was a substantial financial and cultural success. The film inspired numerous think pieces, GIFs, and academic conferences. The fictional nation of Wakanda has a distinctive Afrocentric identity. Years after its release, "Wakanda forever" is still a collective chant found within African-descended communities worldwide.

Black Panther would go on to earn seven Academy Award nominations, including one for Best Picture, and win three Oscars. However, as mesmerizing as the film was, the standout character of *Black Panther* was, without a doubt, Erik Killmonger, portrayed brilliantly by Michael B. Jordan. Shortly after its release, *Black Panther* was heralded as an exemplar of AfroFuturism

going mainstream. The *New York Times* declared that "the film's most important distinction is that it is told from an Afrocentric point of view" (Harris,
2020, p. 279). This chapter explores and analyzes the ideas and goals of
Killmonger, why he was so popular among African-descended people, and,
ultimately, how his ideas could be harmful to the liberation of Africana communities (Speri, 2019). The erasure of African representation and agency
remains an ongoing challenge within the science-fiction world.

> Where science fiction capital erases race and Afrocentric points of view espe-
> cially in the professional industry of futures research, I [Lonny Avi Brooks]
> aim to restore them and re-categorize future scenarios by noting absences in
> Afrocentric values. Re-imagining the future with the rhetorical tools found
> in Afrocentric and Africology worldviews confirms a multiverse of possible
> identity futures held at once and interconnected and now heralded in the
> exponential algorithms of quantum computing. (Brooks, 2015, p. 150)

For many in the African American community, Killmonger represents
the goals of the great Black Nationalist thinkers of the past. What makes
Killmonger such an exciting and compelling character is, in many ways, his
representation of Black Power and a Black militancy often found in the writings of Marcus Garvey, Malcolm X, W. E. B. Du Bois, and Kwame Nkrumah.
In an era of rampant police shootings of unarmed African Americans and
the rise of White hate groups, how can African-descended people not be
enthralled by someone who advocates for Black empowerment and liberation
from institutions of White supremacy? Killmonger's desire to arm oppressed
Black people and unite the African continent is a noble goal, and for many,
he was the actual hero of the film, and T'Challa was the enemy. However,
Killmonger is not a compassionate man and has little value for human life. He
has become the very thing he despises and has the makings of a future dicta-
tor. It is easy to get swept up in his rhetoric of Black self-determination and
forget he is not the kind of man that should be in charge of a mighty nation.

By far, one of the most compelling and complex characters in the Marvel
Cinematic Universe is, without a doubt, Eric "Killmonger" Stevens, aka
N'Jadaka. The questions this character elicits during this film mirror real-
world discussions Black academics and activists have been having for over
a century. Killmonger, an exiled prince of Wakanda, grew up within the
traditional African American experience. The challenges of being a Black

male in the United States had shaped his worldview. Killmonger is Black, militant, and angry, and in the current cultural climate of African Americans being brutalized by law enforcement and incarcerated at enormous rates, Killmonger understands that, with vibranium, the playing field could be leveled for people of African descent throughout the world. The manifestation of Killmonger's frustrations being in line with the Black American radical tradition was intentional on the part of actor Michael B. Jordan. While preparing for the role, he drew inspiration from real-life figures, such as Malcolm X, Garvey, Huey P. Newton, Fred Hampton, and Tupac Shakur. Jordan discussed these inspirations and the pain he envisioned his character being formed by in an interview published in *Rolling Stone* magazine, where he states: "As an African American who has experienced systemic racial oppression in America consistently, I understood his rage, and how he could get to the point where he had to do what he had to do, by any means necessary" (Eells, 2018). Although expressed through the Killmonger character from a predominantly African American perspective, the theme of revolutionary resistance speaks to international paradigms of struggle through numerous overtones. "Although the story may have originated from the pages of a popular American comic series [the brainchild of European creatives], the tenor of its themes derives from, and speaks to, contentions about the nature of effectual tropes of processing and understanding the world as postcolonial" (Adélékè, 2020, p. 137).

A primary example of this anticolonizer stance Killmonger embodies is represented in the scene where Killmonger engages in the theft/reclamation of ancestral African artifacts, which had been secured through European conquest. In the scene:

> Erik Killmonger stops at the display case of a long-horned animal mask that is covered in the pale blue of vibranium, the highly prized, resilient material over which Wakanda enjoys a fiercely guarded monopoly. His eyes shining brightly with greed, Klaue asks, "You're not telling me that's vibranium, too?" and Killmonger dissembles the truth with a curt answer, "Nah, I'm just *feeling* it." The very brief, seemingly throwaway exchange is perhaps the most revealing allusion to postcolonial critique in the film. (Adélékè, 2020, p. 137)

The subjugation of peoples through the control and exploitation of their iconography is a consistent trope of colonization. The strategies related to these unfortunate realities resonate today in discussions on the proper place for Confederate statues and the celebration of Columbus Day as a holiday. A tactic of colonization has long been to divide and conquer, which is exemplified by the familial divisions that drive director and writer Ryan Coogler's epic cinematic narrative. These themes were expressed through actors Jordan and Chadwick Boseman, as they appeared to pull from the real-world representation of similar resistance as the challenges encountered by their respective characters. The most popular historical example perhaps appeared in the 1960s in the promoted tactical juxtaposition between Malcolm X and Martin Luther King Jr. Boseman states: "Those ideas, that conflict—I have been having that conversation almost my whole life, he says. But it's never actually happened on a stage where *you* can hear it. So the fact that we get to have that conversation, and you get to hear it—and have to *deal* with it? That's what makes this movie very different" (Eells, 2018).

Although they both bring up some challenging issues, there are differences between Killmonger in the comics and Killmonger in the movies. Killmonger, from the comics like his movie counterpart, was a Wakadian exile who grew up in the United States and was shaped by that experience. He eventually would return to Wakanda and try to steal the throne away from T'Challa. The story was personal, as Killmonger was exiled due to his father's failed coup against King T'Chaka. He had no choice but to leave with his father, and they would eventually end up in the United States. Movie producers made noticeable changes in order for the movie to have more dramatic tensions, such as being cousins, but the Black Nationalist politics were deemphasized. However, the movie Killmonger is much more complicated, which adds to the character's richness. In the film, he is Eric Stevens, who gets the name "Killmonger" based on the number of kills he racked up because of the Black Op missions he performed for the US military and the Central Intelligence Agency (CIA).

To understand Killmonger, one must understand his comic-book origin and how American comic books would eventually shape how the character was written and portrayed. "Like any work of art, *Black Panther* exists on at least three levels, the poesic or level of authorial intent, the textual level or what is actually there, and equally important is the reception level, which represents the social and semiotic interaction with the film's audience and the social world" (Washington, 2019, p. 1).

The American comic book originated from one-panel illustrations called comic strips that emerged in the late nineteenth century. *The Yellow Kid* is often viewed as the first comic strip, and it had the standard racist imagery of the time, mirroring the racist imagery of the southern minstrel shows. Black figures were often drawn to have exaggerated features, such as enormous red lips, large buttocks, or very dark skin. The Black characters were often sidekicks and spoke in stereotypical Black dialect. Characters such as Ebony White, the sidekick to the hero the Spirit, often played the loyal assistant to the noble White savior with no agency of his own. It would be decades before African American people had a character that attempted to break away from this racist imagery.

In his article, "Afros, Icons, and Spandex: A Brief History of the African American Superhero," Erick Hogan (2004) writes, "Lothar, Prince of the Seven Sons, was the forerunner of today's Black superhero. He was the first Black character to appear in a syndicated comic (the 'Mandrake the Magician' comic strip of the 30s) servitude." He goes on to say, "During the 50s, characterization of Blacks improved from the sidekicks and lackeys of the 30s and 40s. 'Waku, Prince of the Bantu' debuted in 1954. This marked the first time a Black character was featured as the lead in a comic" (Hogan, 2004).

In 1947, Orrin C. Evans would attempt to derail this racist imagery with the establishment of All Negro Comics. The company would only last one issue but featured two Black heroes, Ace Harlem and Lion Man. Ace Harlem was a sharp, intelligent detective who solved crimes in the Black community and protected Black people from evil. Lion Man was an African hero who used his intelligence and science to fight off evil threats. In the 1960s, as the civil rights movement and Black Power era shaped the American landscape, that impact was felt in the comic-book medium as well with the introduction of Lobo, a Black cowboy and former Buffalo soldier. It only lasted two issues, but he was the first Black character to lead a series. The sixties would see the creation of Black characters such as the Falcon, Black Panther, Joe "Robbie" Robertson, and a host of others (Jones, 2016, p. 52).

The 1970s saw a rise in Black superheroes due to the rise in popularity of Blaxploitation films. Adilifu Nama (2011), William Jones (2016), and Jeffery A. Brown (2016), in their texts, establish the stars of these Blaxploitation films as superheroes from Superfly and the Mack to Foxy Brown. These characters, albeit very problematic, were heroes in their own right, fighting against great evils and maintaining a strong sense of honor and integrity. The Black superhero construction was directly tied to these films and how they were created and embraced. Characters such as Misty Knight, Blade, Black Lightning, and

Black Goliath were directly tied to films and actors such as Pam Grier, Fred Williamson, and Jim Brown. In 1972, Marvel debuted Luke Cage, the first African American Marvel superhero, as a lead character. This character was created by Archie Godwin and George Tusk, neither of whom are Black nor have lived the Black experience. Cage had his own catchphrase, fought crime in Harlem, and spoke in jive, much like the characters seen in Blaxploitation films of that era. There were touches of progressiveness, but often these White creations relied on White ideas about Blackness. Nama (2011, p. 19) states in his text *Super Black: American Pop Culture and Black Superheroes*:

> Films such as *Sweet Sweetback's Baadasssss Song*, *Superfly* and *The Spook Who Sat by the Door* to name only a few, exemplified how blaxploitation cinema was often sexually gratuitous and bloody referendum on White authority. Of course, by showing Blacks killing, fighting, humiliating, loving and winning against Whites, many mediocre movies were able to make good economic sense. In the process, blaxploitation films increasingly relied on sensationalistic depictions of racial strife, wherein crazed and corrupt Whites appeared to live only to plot for the Black protagonist's death and by symbolic extension, Black peoples' defeat in the struggle for racial justice.

Within the comic books, Erik Killmonger is one of the Black Panther's most formidable foes. The capability and agency of Killmonger are expressed effectively through channeled rage and daring to envision a completely revolutionized world while implementing the strategies necessary to chase his dream of a new tomorrow. "These wills of imagination are affected by colonization and illustrated by the dichotomy between T'Challa and Killmonger" (Strong & Chaplin, 2019, p. 59).

Although not seen as the Black Panther's primary villain, Killmonger represents a severe internal threat that makes him a unique enemy and different from other foes such as Namor or Ulysses Klaw. Born N'Jadaka in Wakanda, Killmonger would grow up in the United States, having been kidnapped as a child by Ulysses Klaw after Klaw had killed his parents. Blaming the royal family for his parent's death, he vows to kill T'Challa and overthrow his monarchy. Eventually earning a PhD from MIT, he trained himself in numerous fighting styles and became a brilliant strategist and tactician. Over the years, he would continue to try and overthrow King T'Challa, failing each individual time. Eventually, he would be defeated for good, having been killed by

Monica Rambeau after he kidnapped her and T'Challa's sister, Shuri. Within the movies, his backstory was slightly altered to align itself closer to the story directors wanted to tell. In the film *Black Panther*, he is born N'Jadaka, son of Prince N'Jobu, nephew of King T'Chaka, and the cousin of Prince T'Challa. He is still a graduate of MIT but served in the US Navy, eventually becoming a Navy Seal. He would later be recruited by the CIA and worked in their Black ops division. His father would be executed by King T'Chaka for betraying Wakanda and selling vibranium illegally. His father, Prince N'Jobu, had fallen in love with a Black American woman and had been affected by seeing the treatment of African-descended people in the United States. These minor changes make the screen version much more complicated and gave the character new nuances to explore. This version also would influence the comics, as Marvel would release a Killmonger miniseries in which the character was much closer to the onscreen portrayal (Marvel, n.d.a).

Afrocentricity and Killmonger

An intriguing dynamic related to the character development of Killmonger involves his experientially influenced perspectives and geopolitical understandings as they relate to his chosen strategy and his assumed obligation to assist his marginalized peoples throughout the world. It has been theorized that this connection to his people, even above his ancestral connections, qualifies his Blackness to a more meaningful extent within the contemporary cultural and political context.

> Erik "Killmonger" Stevens is the only Black character in the film. His is the historically aware and historically burdened diasporic consciousness that assumes a necessary allegiance between Wakandans and the 2 billion other people in the world who, as Killmonger says, "look like them." Killmonger understands Blackness in terms of shared suffering and mutual obligation, and his understanding of Blackness has far more in common with the conceptions of Blackness that American audiences would recognize. (Williams, 2018, p. 28)

As stated earlier, in the era of Donald Trump and the rise of White supremacist hate groups, one can fully understand the logic of Killmonger wanting to use physical force to overthrow systems of White supremacy. With the police continuing to criminalize Blackness and the FBI keeping files on Black activists they have labeled "Black identity extremists," his method of using any means necessary falls in line with the ideas of Malcolm X. With Nazis marching down the streets of Virginia shouting racial epithets and White terrorists shooting up Black churches, how can one argue against his view of using offensive action to liberate African people? A line that he states often in the film and backed by his resume is he has learned from his enemies and knows how to beat them at their own game. In the face of these aggressive racist actions, African Americans are not wrong for feeling the need to arm themselves against White mob violence. The United States has a long history of terrorizing peaceful Black communities and destroying them for no reason at all. Shouldn't African American people remember the lessons that the massacres in Tulsa, Oklahoma, and Rosewood, Florida, taught them (Ecarma, 2020)? What is interesting is when there was a deep investigation into these "Black identity extremists," FBI Director Christopher Wray was forced to state that the Black Lives Matter (BLM) movement and other Black activists pose no terrorist threat. The FBI came to the conclusion that the biggest "home-grown" threat was from right-wing White extremist groups. Wray stated:

> "Within the domestic terrorism bucket, the category as a whole, racially motivated violent extremism is, I think, the biggest bucket within that larger group, within the racially motivated violent extremist bucket. . . . People ascribing to some kind of White supremacist-type ideologies is certainly the biggest chunk of that." The bureau chief went on to note that, when it comes to extremist violence in the US, 2019 was the deadliest year since 1995, when White supremacist Timothy McVeigh killed 168 people by bombing a federal building in Oklahoma City. (Ecarma, 2020)

"By contrast, when asked whether he was aware of 'any excessive violence' that could be attributed to Black Lives Matter, Wray said he could not think of a single example. He added that the FBI had seen cases of 'racially motivated' Black defendants who targeted law enforcement, but 'whether any of those cases involved some reference to Black Lives Matter, sitting here right now I can't recall one'" (Naylor, 2020).

This is another example of how the United States criminalizes Black people for demanding justice and equality. From Killmonger's point of view, the only way to seek justice against systemic oppression is to overthrow that system and replace it with something better.

In analyzing Killmonger, one must first understand he is an Afrocentric character, and to critique him as a character, one must do so from an Afrocentric perspective. This methodological analytical approach places African-descended people at the center of their lives and experiences. This is not to say Killmonger was the first Afrocentric character to be featured onscreen or that *Black Panther* was the first Afrocentric work of art; there have been many in films. What makes Jordan's performance notable is how relatable the character is to people of African descent. One may disagree with Killmonger's methods or how far he is willing to go for Black liberation, but most can identify with his anger; the only way to analyze Killmonger is through an Afrocentric lens. In his work "The Afrocentric Manifesto," Molefi Kete Asante (2007, p. 2) defines Afrocentricity "as a paradigmatic intellectual perspective that privileges African agency within the context of African history and culture trans-continentally and trans-generationally." This means that the quality of location is essential to any analysis involving African culture and behavior, whether literary or economic, political or cultural. The emphasis on perspective connects seamlessly with the concept of "AfroFuturism," opening a clear analytical and methodological pathway to Afrocentric Futurism. "Both an artistic aesthetic and a framework for critical theory, Afrofuturism combines elements of science-fiction, historical fiction, speculative fiction, fantasy, Afrocentricity and magic realism with non-western beliefs" (Womack, 2013, p. 9).

Killmonger seeks to be and is the hero in his own story, although there is a tragic ending. He is seeking the unification of the African continent and the empowerment of African people, which all Pan-Africanists advocate for. In his words, one can hear Garvey, Edward Blyden, and Martin Delaney, who all believed Africa was for the Africans. Garvey once stated:

> As four hundred million men, women and children worthy of the existence given [to] us by the Divine Creator, we are determined to solve our problems by redeeming our motherland Africa from the hands of alien exploiters and [to] found there a government, a nation of our own, strong enough to lend protection to the members of our race scattered all over the world and compel the respect of the nations and races of the Earth. (History Matters, n.d.)

In his text titled "Kwame Nkrumah and Pan African Consciousness: 1957–1966," Udida A. Undiyaundeye (2018, p. 2) writes, "race pride, racial unity, self-confidence, and economic independence formed the main themes of Garvey's preaching on the pages of the Negro World which was the organ of the Universal Negro Improvement Association (UNIA) and the street corners of Harlem." What is telling is, like Nkrumah, Killmonger sees Black people's suffering worldwide and is driven to do something about it. Undiyaundeye (2018, p. 2) further states: "By December 1935, Kwame Nkrumah had started his programme of study at Lincoln University. It was in the United States of America that Nkrumah came face to face with the sorry plight of the Blackman in America. The Blackman in America had given his all to the social, economic, and political development of the country, yet he was denied civil rights, intimidated, and despised."

Killmonger's ultimate goal was to achieve what Asante (2004, p. 25) describes as "victorious consciousness." The utilization of the transformative potential of energies resulting from painful experiences plays a major role in the African American experience.

> Contemporary African American myth contains the powerful suffering genre. Even in the most victorious myths, one frequently finds the suffering genre. Perhaps this is because victory, in a political sense, is often based upon suffering in the minds of African Americans. "How to turn the suffering genre into a positive, victorious consciousness occupies a whole Afrocentric literary school of thought." (Asante, 2004, p. 25)

Throughout the film, Killmonger acts within his agency and seeks power and a place in the world while remaining tragically centered in his pain, which at once fuels his ambition while problematizing his purpose. These ideas were thrust into the mass consciousness of viewers through the strategic and effective marketing of the film. The residual ramifications related to the global phenomena that has become *Black Panther* includes seeing more Afrocentric music, people, and literature in mainstream commercials, television shows, and social-media influences.

What is telling is throughout the movie Killmonger knows who he is and where he comes from. When he is in the throne room, meeting T'Challa for the first time, Shuri states his name is Erik Stevens, nicknamed Killmonger, a CIA Black op's operative, and he quickly corrects her. In his original

Wakandan tongue of Xhosa, he informs her that he is N'Jadaka, son of Prince N'Jobu. Killmonger, to a great degree, is meant to represent African American rage. Killmonger is a product of American racism and colonialism. He is a product of being forced to live in a society that devalues Black life, criminalizes Blackness, and ignores Black people's contributions. His anger and perpetual search for a balanced self and the assuredness of familial anchoring represents a precarious juxtaposition to the self-aware, ancestral-purpose-driven, culturally rooted protagonist T'Challa. "Killmonger is more angry than T'Challa, but this is understandable given their very different life experiences" (Thomas, 2021, p. 85).

A point of note was when the film *Black Panther* began, it included footage from the 1992 uprising in response to the verdict in the police brutality trial of African American motorist Rodney King. Another point that did not make it into the film but was one of the ideas in the script's writing was N'jobu's plan to break Killmonger's mother out of jail because she was an activist who had been wrongly imprisoned. It is also no coincidence that N'jobu and N'jdaka are in Oakland, California, the Black Panther Party's home. Among African Americans, the black panther has been a symbol of strength and power. The Lowndes County Freedom Organization, also known as the Black Panther Party, was a political party founded in Lowndes County, Alabama, by African Americans in 1965. During World War II, the 761st Tank Battalion was made up of African American soldiers for the US Army. Oakland played a pivotal role in the Black Power movement, being home to many Black militant organizations. Also, the 1980s and '90s were rife with police brutality, the cutting of social programs in the Black community, and a rise in conservative politics. The combination of these things would shape Killmonger's worldview. Added to that, he was the son of an African prince, which made him royalty (Lebron, 2018).

Killmonger knew who he was; he knew his real name was N'djaka, spoke Xhosa, the traditional Wakandan language, and was familiar with the Wakandan tradition. However, Killmonger was shaped by his experiences living a life as an African in America. Growing up in Oakland, he experienced what Malcolm X once called "the American nightmare." He saw the hypocrisy of the United States, how young Black boys and girls were harassed by the police daily, and how Blacks were paid less than their White counterparts for doing the same job. He experienced harassment by racist White militant groups and "liberal" suburban White Americans. He witnessed stories about

Black women being brutalized and sexually assaulted and receiving no justice. "If we understand AfroFuturism as a response to consistently racist
depictions of Blackness, then *Black Panther* presents a critical opportunity
to critique how the AfroFuturist tradition translates to the big screen for
mass audiences. Focusing on Killmonger reveals that Black US American
viewers are met with an origin story that leaves just as many real world questions unanswered as are imagined" (Harris, 2020, p. 280). In today's climate,
Killmonger's anger toward White racism and hypocrisy is as timely as ever.
For him to know there is an African nation, aware of these sufferings by Black
people and do nothing is something by which he could not abide. In the end,
the final fight scene shows a contest between T'Challa and Killmonger that
can only be interpreted one way; as Christopher Lebron (2018) writes in his
think piece, "in a world marked by racism, a man of African nobility must
fight his own blood relative whose goal is the global liberation of Blacks."

Killmonger's Black Nationalism

The character of Killmonger captured the audience with his ideas. Many
saw the ideals of Garvey, Malcolm X, Stokely Carmichael, and Bobby Seale
within him. Not only does his character stand up to oppression but advocates
armed resistance to White supremacy and White colonialism. In many ways,
people saw a hero that had gone too far and lived so long that he was able to
witness himself become a villain. What makes Killmonger such a compelling
character is his philosophical beliefs that resonate with Black audiences.
Wakanda is one of the most technologically advanced nations in the world.
They have the weapons and the means to prevent the enslavement of millions of Africans throughout the world, and they did nothing. "Killmonger
presents a different way in that he wants to use the technology and resources
of Wakanda to wage war against the colonizers" (Hodge, 2018, p. 1).

The people of Wakanda also appear to have been capable of preventing
Africa from being colonized by Europe, but they did not. Killmonger is correct in his anger with Wakanda sealing off their walls to the rest of the world.
He makes that evident when he meets T'Challa for the first time in the throne
room. He points out that over 2 billion people of African descent are spread
throughout the world, and their lives are a lot harder, while Wakanda has
the tools to liberate them all. Although many academics critique Killmonger

as a representation of the angry African American male criminal, he was a representation of unfiltered Black rage, built up because he grew up in a racist White supremacist society. Killmonger represents the palpable frustration of a branch of the human family in constant war with a toxic mix of racial exploitation and indifference. The contradictions, willful ignorance, and hypocrisy associated with racist ideologies in America produce a particular form of rage, which has been explored through literature and film by writers such as James Baldwin and cinematic creatives, including *Black Panther* producer Coogler. There are also several connections to political activism that flow through the provocative nature of the Killmonger character.

Within Killmonger, one can see the continuation of the legacy of Garvey and other great Pan-Africanist thinkers who sought to unite the continent of Africa under one national banner. Born in Jamaica, Garvey migrated to the United States and led one of the most massive Pan-Africanist movements in the African world's history. His founding of the Universal Negro Improvement Association (UNIA) would become a Pan-Africanist force, establishing chapters worldwide. Garvey would call for the Black man and woman to return home to their ancestors' land and rid themselves of a European mindset and practice. He called for Black people to support Black businesses and Black causes. From his worldview, all African-descended people were Africans and had a right to claim Africa as their home. He once stated:

> It is for me to inform you that the Universal Negro Improvement Association is an organization that seeks to unite, into one solid body, the four hundred million Negroes in the world. To link up the fifty million Negroes in the United States of America, with the twenty million Negroes of the West Indies, the forty million Negroes of South and Central America, with the two hundred and eighty million Negroes of Africa, for the purpose of bettering our industrial, commercial, educational, social, and political conditions. (History Matters, n.d.)

Killmonger was motivated by his worldview on the interconnectedness of humanity, which inspired his communal intentions for the usage of Wakandan resources. We can also see connections between the character's societal critiques and those of sociological pioneers such as W. E. B. Du Bois, who was extremely critical of White supremacy. Du Bois (2015, p. 93–94) states:

Daily the Negro is coming more and more to look upon law and justice, not as protecting safeguards, but as sources of humiliation and oppression. The laws are made by men who have little interest in him; they are executed by men who have no motive for treating the Black people with courtesy or consideration; and, finally, the accused law-breaker is tried, not by his peers, but too often by men who would rather punish ten innocent Negroes than let one guilty one escape.

Du Bois organized a series of Pan-Africanist conferences calling for the liberation of African-descended people throughout the world and the unification of the African continent. Eventually, Du Bois would leave the US to settle in Ghana, where he lived the remainder of his days. His teachings, combined with Garvey, would have a tremendous effect on Nkrumah, the future president of an independent Ghana. Nkrumah would take Pan-Africanism a step further, eventually offering African people across the globe citizenship to settle in Ghana. Be it symbolically or politically, it was a big step in the Pan-Africanist movement. For Killmonger, this was his political ideology as he sought to claim the throne of Wakanda. After winning the crown through ritual combat, his first order was to liberate African people worldwide. He said,

You know, where I'm from when Black folks started revolutions, they never had the firepower or resources to fight their oppressors. Where was Wakanda? Hmm? Yea all that ends today. We got spies embedded in every nation on Earth. Already in place. I know how colonizers think. So we're gonna use their own strategy against them. We're gonna send vibranium weapons out to our War Dogs. They'll arm oppressed people all over the world, so they can finally rise and kill those in power, and their children, and anyone else who takes their side. It's time they know the truth about us. We're warriors. The world's gonna start over, and this time we're on top. (Coogler & Cole, n.d.)

One exciting change from the comic book to the movie is that they made T'Challa and N'Jadaka first cousins. One can only assume the filmmakers made this transformation to add to the film's drama and to showcase to viewers how related characters with similar characteristics can be influenced by disparate upbringings. It was very controversial for T'Challa to work with the CIA's operative, but to no small degree, T'Challa did not have to live under the yoke of White supremacy. T'Challa grew up privileged in a society untouched by colonialism and European standards. In the comics and the movies, T'Challa grew up in royalty; his upbringing was the exact opposite of Killmonger. According to Marvel (n.d.b):

> Before becoming the Panther, T'Challa was simply the son of Wakanda's King T'Chaka, a previous Black Panther. T'Challa learned a great deal from inter-acting with T'Chaka while he was alive. He also has a very close relationship with his stepmother Ramonda, the mother of T'Challa's half-sister (and a Black Panther in her own right) Shuri. In his role as king, T'Challa has relied on his uncle S'Yan who filled the role of Black Panther before him, as well as his second-in-command W'Kabi and longtime bodyguard Zuri.

Having grown up this way, he would not view the CIA in the same light as an African-descended person who had not.

One of the most controversial aspects of the film was T'Challa working with CIA operative Everett K. Ross. Numerous think pieces emerged on why T'Challa would work with anyone from the CIA, given the problematic nature of the organization and its history in Africa. Killmonger's popularity intensified, eventually morphing into a hashtag on Twitter: #teamkillmonger. In the article "I Have a Problem with 'Black Panther,'" Russell Rickford (2018) states that Killmonger is a revolutionary, and his being portrayed as a sociopath is problematic. Within the article, he states that African descendants worldwide have sought to find repatriation to Africa. He writes: "For centuries, African Americans and other members of the African Diaspora have sought 'repatriation' to the Mother Continent. This yearning for reunification and restoration of kinship bonds is a byproduct of the historical experience of dispersal. Dispossessed and exploited throughout the globe, generations of Black folk have craved a land base where they might find security, prosperity, and power. Often, they have looked to Africa for such a foundation" (Rickford, 2018).

During the Cold War, he writes, the government sought to disrupt Africans and African Americans but still could not stop Pan-Africanism as an ideology, particularly during the Black Power era. He goes on: "But Black Americans never abandoned the effort to reclaim African ties. The objective inspired largely symbolic activities in the 1960s and '70s, including embracing African cultural garb, hairstyles, and names. However, it also helped revive a revolutionary consciousness, a belief that the process of decolonization could uproot western imperialism and liberate not only Africans but African Americans and other subjugated people" (Rickford, 2018).

The CIA has been involved in the politics of African nations, often siding with oppressive regimes to exploit African resources. The CIA assisted the Belgium government in the assassination of Patrice Lumumba and the installment of Joseph Mobutu. Nkrumah accused the agency of being involved in the coup that ousted him from power, and a declassified document shows they felt it was a fortuitous windfall for them because they felt he was undermining their interests in Africa. The CIA was involved in the 1970s civil war in Angola, in international politics in Sudan to have access to their oil, and in numerous other operations sanctioned by various US presidents. The most heinous time they got involved in African politics was the 1962 arrest of Nelson Mandela in South Africa. The CIA was involved in tipping off the apartheid government of his whereabouts, which led to his arrest and twenty-seven-year imprisonment (BBC News, 2016).

It should be a point of note that the CIA has had a long history of working with Hollywood films, as Lynn Stuart Parramore (2018) points out in her article titled "Why Does a White CIA Agent Play the Hero to Killmonger's Villain in 'Black Panther'?" In the article, she writes, "The agency, as Tricia Jenkins explains in her 2016 book 'The CIA in Hollywood,' has a long history of partnering with Tinsel Town, dating back to the 1950s. During the Cold War, movies helped win over foreign audiences, shape US foreign policy, and promote a cosy view of American life. The agency would often push for script adjustments, to make the United States look less racially divided" (Parramore, 2018). She continues:

A 1975–6 Senate panel chaired by Idaho Sen. Frank Church . . . investigated abuses by US intelligence agencies. The committee revealed that, among other things, the CIA and FBI had been spying on and harassing American civil rights leaders and anti-war protesters. In response, some Democrats, like Sen. Daniel Patrick Moynihan, went so far as to call for the abolition of the CIA. Congress demanded greater transparency and oversight of its spying operations. By the end of the Cold War, the agency needed an image makeover. So it hired Chase Brandon, a veteran secret operative, to help it get cozy with filmmakers, actors, and producers. CIA agents in the movies soon became heroes working for a highly moral organization desperately needed in the world (Parramore, 2018).

Was Killmonger Right?

So, the penetrating question about Killmonger being right comes down to a complicated answer of "yes" and "no." He is right in demanding Wakanda get involved in the world's politics and work to liberate oppressed Black communities. Wakanda is wrong for, what T'Challa calls, "turning your backs to the rest of the world." Wakanda should have gotten involved and prevented the enslavement of millions of Africans, the colonization of the African continent, and the establishment of White supremacist governments. For that, Killmonger has the right idea, but he falls short, like many revolutionaries. He starts with powerful ideas then falls prey to believing everything he does is right. He believes he is never wrong and cannot be challenged. By the end of the film, Killmonger does not come across as someone who wants to empower Black communities but rather as someone drunk on power. As Matt Wood (2018) writes, according to Sterling K. Brown, who plays N'Jobu in the film:

> He is a villain because, while his intentions, and N'Jobu's intentions for that fact, are honorable, they didn't necessarily go about it [in a way] that would actually bring about the change that they want" also adding "He wasn't trying to create a legacy. He was like, 'I want this for myself.' That's where the intention gets confused with personal ambition, but what he was able to illuminate . . . is that he is not without a point.

By the end of the film, Killmonger is bloodthirsty and has no compassion for human life or innocent life. One can only assume that, had he been victorious, he most likely would have gone down the road of African revolutionaries who evolve into brutal dictators. Killmonger's story is ultimately a tragedy about someone who has noble ideas that are, at some point, lost in a fit of spiraling anger, eventually leading to his undoing. However, it is telling that Killmonger delivers what many consider to be one of the most memorable lines of the film. He lays on the mountain, dying, and T'Challa suggests that they may be able to heal Killmonger's wounds. Killmonger then replies, "Why? So you can just lock me up? Nah. Just bury me in the ocean, with my ancestors that jumped from the ships . . .'cause they knew death was better than bondage" (Coogler & Cole, n.d.). The *Black Panther* film, generally, and the Killmonger character, specifically, embody the agency and innovative imagination that is foundational to the concept of Afrocentric Futurism. Killmonger believes that his destiny is to create a new, Black-led global empire (Lavan, 2018, p. 23). The cornerstone of the new world he longs for has been cast in his consciousness, polished by years of pain, and fortified in his heavy heart. Many Afrocentric Futurists share in the commitment to create a new United States of Africa and a liberated African diaspora and will not rest until African agency and innovation are manifested on every level of human and technological expression.

REFERENCES

Adéléké, A. (2020). Postcolonial Critique in Ryan Coogler's *Black Panther*. *Cambridge Journal of Postcolonial Literary Inquiry*, 7(2), 136–46. https://doi.org/10.1017/pli.2019.36

Asante, M. K. (2004). The Afrocentric Idea. In Ronald L. Jackson II (Ed.), *African American Communication & Identities: Essential Readings* (pp. 16–28). SAGE.

Asante, M. K. (2007). *The Afrocentric Manifesto*. Polity Press.

BBC News. (2016, May 17). *Four More Ways the CIA Has Meddled in Africa*. https://www.bbc.com/news/world-africa-36303327

Brooks, L. A. (2015) Playing a Minority Forecaster in Search of Afrofuturism: Where Am I in This Future, Stewart Brand? In R. Anderson & C. E. Jones (Eds.), *AfroFuturism 2.0: The Rise of Astro-Blackness* (pp. 149–65). Lexington Books.

Brown, J. A. (2016). *The Modern Superhero in Film and Television: Popular Genre and American Culture*. Routledge.

Coogler, R., & Cole, J. R. (n.d.). *Black Panther* [Script]. Internet Movie Script Database. https://www.imsdb.com/scripts/Black-Panther.html

Du Bois, W. E. B. (2015). *The Souls of Black Folk*. Oxford University Press.

Ecarma, C. (2020, September 17). The FBI Director Just Blew Up Team Trump's Anti-Antifa War Plan. *Vanity Fair*. https://www.vanityfair.com/news/2020/09/fbi-director-chris-wray-blew-up-trumps-anti-antifa-war-plan

Eells, J. (2018, February 18). The "Black Panther" Revolution: How Chadwick Boseman and Ryan Coogler Created the Most Radical Superhero Movie of All Time. *Rolling Stone*. https://www.rollingstone.com/tv-movies/tv-movie-features/the-black-panther-revolution-199536/

Harris, F. L. (2020). "Tell Me the Story of Home": AfroFuturism, Eric Killmonger, and Black American Malaise. *Review of Communication*, 20(3), 278–85.

History Matters. (n.d.). *"If You Believe the Negro Has a Soul": "Back to Africa" with Marcus Garvey*. http://historymatters.gmu.edu/d/5124/

Hodge, D. W. (2018). "Hi Auntie": A Paradox of Hip Hop Socio-Political Resistance in Killmonger. *Journal of Religion & Film*, 22(1), Article 43, 1–5. https://digitalcommons.unomaha.edu/cgi/viewcontent.cgi?article=1981&context=jrf

Hogan, E. (2004, February 5). *Afros, Icons, and Spandex: A Brief History of the African American Superhero*. CBR. https://www.cbr.com/issue-35-6/

Jones, W. (2016). *The Ex-Con, Voodoo Priest, Goddess, and the African King: A Social, Cultural, and Political Analysis of Four Black Comic Books Heroes*. Blue Artists.

Lavan, M. (2018). To Whom Does Wakanda Belong? *Journal of Pan African Studies*, *11*(9), 23–26.

Lebron, C. (2018, February 17). Black Panther Is Not the Movie We Deserve. *Boston Review.* https://www.bostonreview.net/articles/christopher-lebron-black-panther/

Marvel. (n.d.a). *Killmonger.* https://www.marvel.com/characters/erik-killmonger/in-comics

Marvel. (n.d.b). *T'Challa.* https://www.marvel.com/characters/Black-panther-t-challa/on-screen

McGee, E. O., & White, D. T. (2021). AfroFuturism: Reimaging STEM for Black Urban Learners. In H. R. Milner IV & K. Lomotey (Eds.), *Handbook of Urban Education* (pp. 384–96). Routledge.

Nama, A. (2011). *Super Black: American Pop Culture and Black Superheroes.* University of Texas Press.

Naylor, S. D. (2020, September 17). *Russia Working to Help Reelect President Trump, FBI Chief Says.* Yahoo News. https://news.yahoo.com/russia-working-to-help-reelect-president-trump-fbi-chief-says-214304310.html

Parramore, L. S. (2018, March 11). *Why Does a White CIA Agent Play the Hero to Killmonger's Villain in "Black Panther"?* NBC News. https://www.nbcnews.com/think/opinion/why-does-White-cia-agent-play-hero-killmonger-s-villain-ncna855401

Rickford, R. (2018, February 22). *I Have a Problem with "Black Panther."* Africa Is a Country. https://africasacountry.com/2018/02/i-have-a-problem-with-Black-panther

Speri, A. (2019, March 23). *Fear of a Black Homeland: The Strange Tale of the FBI's Fictional "Black Identity Extremism" Movement.* The Intercept. https://theintercept.com/2019/03/23/black-identity-extremist-fbi-domestic-terrorism/

Strong, M. T., & Chaplin, K. S. (2019). AfroFuturism and Black Panther. *Contexts*, *18*(2), 58–59. https://doi.org/10.1177/1536504219854725

Thomas, D. (2021). Killmonger and the Wretched of the Earth. In S. C. Howard (Ed.), *Why Wakanda Matters: What Black Panther Reveals About Psychology, Identity, and Communication* (pp. 59–70). BenBella Books.

Undiyaundeye, U. A. (2018). Kwame Nkrumah and Pan African Consciousness: 1957–1966. *Historical Research Letter, 44*, 1–10.

Washington, S. (2019). You Act like a Th'owed Away Child: *Black Panther*, Killmonger, and Pan-Africanist African American Identity. *Image & Text, 33*, 1–26. http://www.scielo.org.za/pdf/it/n33/06.pdf

Williams, D. (2018). Three Theses about *Black Panther*. *Africology: The Journal of Pan African Studies*, *11*(9), 27–30.

Womack, Y. L. (2013). *Afrofuturism: The World of Black Sci-Fi and Fantasy Culture.* Chicago Review Press.

Wood, M. (2018, March 11). *Why Black Panther's Killmonger Is Definitely a Villain, According to Sterling K. Brown.* Cinema Blend. https://www.cinemablend.com/news/2385641/why-black-panthers-killmonger-is-definitely-a-villain-according-to-sterling-k-brown

Part Two

TRANSFORMATIONS

5

DIRTY COMPUTER
An Afrocentric Analysis of
Janelle Monáe's Emotion Picture

Alonge O. Clarkson

Janelle Monáe has risen to fame due to her talent and ability to create works of art that address the state of African Americans. In *Dirty Computer* (2018), Monáe's third studio album, her lyricism is unique in that it tells a story of liberation, agency, and victory. The film *Janelle Monáe: Dirty Computer* (Donoho et al., 2018) is a visual depiction of the accompanying album. Upon watching this narrative film, dubbed an "emotion picture," it is evident that Monáe seeks to empower African Americans to define themselves as they please. An Africologist expectedly would recognize how the acts of defining and naming are critical to the desired self-determining functions of Afrocentricity. This chapter will explore the ways that Monáe aligns with African tradition throughout her visual and lyrical art. Additionally, this chapter will explore the ways *Dirty Computer* allows African-descended viewers the opportunity to transcend time and space as they consider what the future is and what it will look like for them to exist.

AfroFuturism

AfroFuturism is defined by Mark Dery (1994, p. 180) as "speculative fiction that treats African American themes and addresses African American concerns in the context of twentieth-century technoculture—and more, more generally, African American signification that appropriates images of technology and a prosthetically enhanced future." While Dery (1994, pp. 179–80) adds some context to the notion of "AfroFuturism," he concludes that this term was birthed out of "a conundrum: Why do so few African Americans write science fiction, a genre whose close encounters with the Other—the stranger in a strange land—would seem uniquely suited to the concerns of African American novelists?" The question is valid but does not consider the unwritten liberatory pursuits of African people and makes those pursuits appear reactive rather than proactively innate. "The concepts of AfroFuturism . . . make for an unrestricted tool to cross-examine the impacts of American history and the legacy of Black culture in the United States" (Barnes, 2020, p. 2).

The purpose and function of AfroFuturism have been to serve as a way for African people to envision themselves in a future where they may not have imagined they would be, given the circumstances they find themselves in in America. Nonetheless, historically, Africans have always envisioned themselves as people of the past, present, and future. It is evident in the term "*sankofa*," which means to "go back and fetch it." This translates to going back to the past for the tools and/or the lessons to bring into the future.

Reynaldo Anderson, a top AfroFuturist scholar, gives a more complete picture of AfroFuturism. Through endeavoring to uncover and connect foundational elements of Afrofuturism, located within the speculative arts movement, Anderson successfully establishes links to multiple tenants of Afrocentric theory found therein. These scholarly comparisons help to locate scholars more firmly within their understanding of the intersections and epistemological overlap of Afrocentric and Afrofuturistic schools of thought, which have given birth to Afrocentric futurism.

Because Africans are often othered and relegated to the periphery of thought and society, it is the Afrocentric scholars who center them, providing greater agency. Anderson (2016, p. 231) discusses the Black speculative arts (John Jennings coined this term in 2015) as an outgrowth of speculative fiction in an article titled, "Afrofuturism 2.0 & the Black Speculative Arts Movement: Notes on a Manifesto": "Black speculative art is a creative, aesthetic practice that integrates African diasporic or African metaphysics with science or technology and seeks to interpret, engage, design, or alter reality for the reimagination of the past, the contested present, and as a catalyst for the future."

It is through the creation of the movement and conference that this field of scholarship continues to grow and affirms the imaginations of those who desire to see a thriving African future. The pursuit of self-determination represents an ongoing struggle that requires awareness and resistance in all areas of existence. As a result, it is wise for African people to continuously be aware of spiritual, intellectual, and health-related attacks in order to exercise the agency required to secure a healthy and prosperous future.

Contemporary enemies often come in the form of bacteria and disease. The threats of viruses and pandemics affect Africans in the United States and globally. The Spanish flu, Ebola, SARS, HIV, and, ironically, the COVID-19 pandemic has destroyed approximately seven hundred eighty thousand families, many of the most impoverished. There are several unfortunate correlations between physical and societal scourges, which ravage marginalized communities disproportionately. Here we see how racism in education, healthcare, and beyond serves to stifle our collective future through the disregard and denial of our common humanity.

This reality manifested in America, as states continue to reopen schools during a pandemic in hopes that students will keep masks on, remain six feet from each other, and use hand sanitizer. Similar concerns of being left unprotected in a sick society are manifested in concerns about police brutality and a lack of affordable health care. These negative conditions thwart the fruition of AfroFuturism/Afrocentric Futurism. In fact, Molefi Asante's own statements about Afrocentricity leave no doubt about the ultimate goal of Afrocentricity, that is, the recovery of African freedom and creativity. The futuristic vision and mission that undergrid the collective mission of Afrocentric theory are predicated upon agency and freedom. How will a people denied knowledge of themselves and access to the benefits of being self-defining achieve liberation?

Jennifer Williams (2016, p. iii) interprets AfroFuturism as it intersects with gender to be an opportunity for "women to use their identity as a liberation technology—a spiritual, emotional, physical, and/or intellectual tool constructed and/or wielded by Africana agents. They wield their identity, like an instrument, and use it to emancipate Africana people from the physical and metaphoric chains that restrict them from reproducing their cultural imperatives." Therefore, it is important to acknowledge the complexities and intersections of Black women as they strive to imagine their future beyond skeptic opposition and the future generations that they will birth.

"Janelle Monâe explodes any notion that AfroFuturism is no more. If we define AfroFuturism as African American cultural production and political theory that imagine less constrained Black subjectivity in the future and that produce a profound critique of current social, racial, and economic orders, then there can be no doubt that Monâe stands at the center of a new form of AfroFuturism that she performs" (English & Kim, 2013, p. 217). It appears like Monâe is suggesting that the future is now. The fact that she has visually shown what it looks like to be in this White light space, owned, controlled, and operated by Europeans, is a depiction of the current-day America. Because African people understand time differently than the European Western world, it is quite possible that Monâe is alluding to the past plantation as well as the current ways the system of capitalism commodifies African people. Additionally, the election of Donald Trump and the nature of his politics, seeking to further marginalize Black and Brown communities, propels artists like Monâe to speak out and use their talent to provide a sense of hope. This hope messaged through Monâe's seamless merging of various artistic expressions as an entertainment icon contributes to multidimensional forms of healing.

Methodology

Afrocentricity

The use of Afrocentricity to ground this analysis is critical because it liberates African people from the mental, physical, and spiritual bondage that they are within in the system of racism, capitalism, and democracy that America provides as the only way to live. Afrocentricity positions African people squarely within the context of their own history, culture, and worldviews. The ability of African people to implement Afrocentric thought and theory has proven profoundly transformative for many who engage the theory. "Afrocentricity has become a valuable tool for the critique of domination, the assertion of place and subject location for the African person, and the reconstruction and presentation of African theories of communication" (Asante, 2018, p. 14). Resistance to this form of analytical empowerment has consistently been expressed through various attacks on African perceptions and people.

Historically, it was the work of the European to force the African to assume the role of servant, relegated to subhuman status. The African was robbed of their humanity, their identity of their previous livelihood, and the connection from whence they had come. Many Africans would forget their homeland due to generations of abuse and the mere fact that they came over on ships to a land that they had never known. Mental incarceration is still a symptom of colonialism because it causes confusion in the mind of the African person who believes that they can be European. While this mentality can be deliberate, it is often subconscious due to America's desire for assimilation and "melting-pot" mentality. It is often overlooked because it is disguised as something "different" from the original form of subjugation or enslavement that Africans continue to endure.

In an effort to achieve greater degrees of self-definition and self-determination, Afrocentricity emphasizes "the fundamental significance of agency for the unimpeded development of the individual combined with the fierce reinterpretation of the subject position as alien or resumed 'other' in hegemonic power structures [that] is shared characteristics of Janelle Monáe" (Aghoro, 2018, p. 330).

These powers that be in high places have long conspired to stifle the creativity, imagination, and life span of African Americans for centuries.

> Physically, many Africans were lynched, killed, and abused in unfathomable ways that left fear imprinted in the memories of those who had survived. The notion of being transported to an alien existence through abduction has been explored through AfroFuturist art and thought as it overlaps with tragic realities of the capture, transport, and enslavement of African people.
>
> As African Americans are the "descendants of alien abductees" sacrificed by the colonial west, Dery asserts, their captivity history has always inhibited a "sci-fi nightmare in which unseen but no less impassable force fields of intolerance frustrate their movements; official histories undo what has been done; and technology is too often brought to bear on Black bodies (branding, forced sterilization, the Tuskegee experiment, and tasers come readily to mind)." (Myungsung, 2017, p. 2)

It can be argued that the physical and cultural dislocations often create spiritual decentering and related internal conflicts.

When it comes to spirituality, initially, Africans were forbidden to practice their traditional religions. Europeans did not want Africans to practice Christianity until they realized that they could manipulate the scriptures of the Bible to control their minds and justify the inhumane treatment of those that they enslaved.

The importance of appreciating the power of being present while recognizing the reality of your own mortality was powerfully encapsulated within the words of the Odu Ifa. Often described as "the unwritten book" (Makinde, 1978, p. 305), the Odu Ifa merges time, spirit, and symbol in a manner that inspires great potential for the growth of Afrocentric Futurism. This is "a book of 16 volumes and about 256 chapters in the main-full of experience, wisdom, and a compendium of knowledge. In this book is found the deepest wisdom and philosophy of the Yoruba ethnic group" (Makinde, 1978, p. 305).

These African wisdom teachings can inspire the reader to recognize how African people need to be able to discuss their futures because our time on Earth is brief. As much as we would like to convince ourselves that the future is always later in life, we realize that every passing day is technically the future. The future is here, and much of our life is about what the future will hold. Asante (2018, p. 2) argues that Africa "woke with its visions firmly anchored to a speculative future grounded in the virtues of Maat can bring relief." As Africa begins to think about what a future would look like, drawing from examples of previous writers such as Octavia Butler and Rita Dove and of movies such as *Black Panther* (2018), the conclusion seems to be that the future must be built using the principles of *ma'at*. *Ma'at* means reciprocity, balance, order, and victory as defined by Maulana Karenga (2003) in *Maat, the Moral Ideal in Ancient Egypt: A Study in Classical African Ethics*. These principles are valued by African people throughout the diaspora, and the restoration of these principles will contribute to an African renaissance.

Locating a Text or Work of Art

The Afrocentric method of location is a tool that allows the viewer to determine and measure where the author or artist finds their ideological center. An artist and musician like Monáe is someone who speaks out against injustices in America, all while defining what it means to be an American herself. Given her background, education, and lived experiences, Monáe displays her knowledge of the unfair treatment of African people. Monáe strives to center African experiences within her works, therefore her location is Africa. I am advancing this notion because her entire work demonstrates an appreciation and knowledge of African history, but it still magnifies elements of the dominant American culture. As one explores the elements of language, attitude, and direction, the location must be considered to give context to the possibility of liberating African minds.

Examples of Monáe discussing what it means to be a woman is important because she also mentions "mother." She is challenging the American fabric and status quo of what it means to be a woman. Nah Dove (1998, p. 520) suggests, according to African womanist theory, that "the role of motherhood or mothering is not confined to mothers or women even in contemporary conditions." Dove articulates that a woman does not have to give birth to a child to be a mother. As with fictive kinships as well as African familial structures, it is not the nuclear family that determines a mother. Dove (1998, p. 521) also states, "In the European context, as Diop explains, the woman is considered little more than a burden that the man dragged behind him. Outside her function of child-bearing her role in nomadic society is nil. . . . Having a smaller economic value, it is she who must leave her clan to join that of her husband, contrary to the matriarchal custom which demands the opposite." Dove means that more value should be placed on matriarchal customs where there is value placed on the man who joins a woman's family and/or must pay a bride price to the woman's father to denote value. This is a metaphoric example of what is seen by those in charge of cleansing the dirty computers. They do not care what it will take to track down, capture, and clean the dirty computers and restore them to a more suitable representation of an "American."

Afrocentric Futurism

The study and implementation of the early ancient Kemetic technogenesis of pioneering, cutting edge, African cosmologies, creativity, and culture from an African/diasporic-centered perspective. This foundational historiography and worldview centers past, present, and future African expression, identity, evolution of thought, and civilization.

Nzuri Theory

This theory is used to analyze the meaning and aesthetics of Africa. Monáe's work is visually the perfect example of African aesthetic because she uses contrasting colors, artwork, Black bodies, and facial expressions to convey feeling and mood. It captures the audience and traps them into the song and the emotion picture in an enjoyable fashion.

Monáe also uses dance to drive the narrative of liberation, autonomy, and victory. "The Umfundalai technique is codified as much as a fluid and open-ended technique can be. The Umfundalai technique is a contemporary dance technique and draws on movements and dances from traditional dances to create a movement vocabulary that articulates the body and primes the dancer for particular expressive modes" (Glocke, 2011, p. 259). Kariamu Welsh's description of her dance technique gives context to the possibilities of the dances seen in *Dirty Computer*. The contrast between movement and stillness throughout the work serves as rebellion and not typical expressions. "The *ehe* principle recognizes the role of discovery and renewal in the process of artistic production (by individuals who are new and creative participants)" (McDougal, 2014, p. 70). The dancing within the work reaffirms Monáe's existence as well as the existence of the audience who internally roots for the protagonist.

Africana Theory

There are elements of other theories within Monáe's emotion picture, such as Black queer theory, critical race theory, and the womanist identity development model. "The womanist identity model is a conceptual framework for understanding the gender-related identity development of women across racial and ethnic groups" (McDougal, 2014, p. 77). This model is seen within Monáe's emotion picture because it serves as the "third stage, immersion-emersion . . . [when] women begin to idealize women while rejecting patriarchy . . . [and] develop positive conceptualizations of womanhood . . . [and] see affiliation with other women" (McDougal, 2014, p. 77). In *Africana Womanism: Reclaiming Ourselves*, Clenora Hudson-Weems (2019) expresses that womanism exhibits the qualities of being a self-namer, self-definer, genuine in sisterhood, whole, authentic, a role player, adaptable, and flexible.

Monáe and Her Work

The singer, actress, artist, and activist known to the world as Janelle Monáe is an African American woman, musical artist, and actress. "Monáe showed multiple talents at a young age, and her parents made sure that she had access to spaces that would develop her skills. During her childhood and adolescence, she performed in school musical productions such as *The Wiz*, wrote scripts and musicals, and performed in a singing duo" (Williams, 2016, p. 216). Monáe is also CEO of her label and a CoverGirl model.

> Janelle Monáe is a politically conscious singer/songwriter/producer from Kansas City, Kansas. She is notable for mixing multiple genres of Black music in her songs and wearing a wardrobe of predominately Black and White clothing. Science fiction is a prominent theme in her songs and music videos; she often sets her music videos in the future, and in her songs, she refers to concepts such as the apocalypse or time travel. (Williams, 2016, p. 7)

Monáe has two albums, *The ArchAndroid* (2010) and *The Electric Lady* (2013). Both these albums postulate Monáe as a technological woman. She is dually of the future and the present. Her development of these alter egos shows her growth toward self-defining despite the constant dehumanizing American landscape. "As a whole, AfroFuturism is a genre that allows artists, such as Janelle Monáe, to present new and innovative perspectives and pose questions that are not typically addressed in canonical works" (Gipson, 2016, p. 92).

As an actress, she stars in "the Oscar-winning *Moonlight* and the Oscar-nominated *Hidden Figures*, two hits led by Black casts. In both films, she tackles Black American stories as an act of resisting the rampant erasure of Black history and humanity. Monáe's *Dirty Computer* is that story but simultaneously serves as the story of African American women. Monáe has intentionally created art that is both inclusive and inspirational. She describes *Dirty Computer* as an album designed to empower the outcast, the bullied, the nonbinary, queer, gay, straight, and anyone still searching for their most authentic self. *Dirty Computer* pushes the definitions within her work to include men and not only people in America but worldwide.

The Metaphor of *Dirty Computer*

"Modern and contemporary African American writers employ science fiction in order to recast ideas on past, present, and future Black culture" (Kim, 2017, p. i). Throughout the emotion picture, the metaphor of a dirty computer is exemplified, both visually and lyrically. The metaphor of a dirty computer is a person who looks different, refuses to obey the laws of the society, or shows signs of resistance to the accepted status quo. Therefore, that computer does not have the correct content, according to those in power. Therefore, the computer must be cleaned, erasing everything that is on its hard drive. Historically, Africans within the diaspora have been described as dirty, implying their inferiority associated to skin color as well as indicating the supposed justification for the dehumanization. This is a complex position that African Americans find themselves in—the juxtaposition of being subhuman and alien at the same time. It is at such intersections of artistry and history where AfroFuturistic creatives redefine Black reality.

"There is a long rich Black music tradition to which AfroFuturism has been central. AfroFuturist musicians (from Sun Ra to Janelle Monáe) create post–civil rights worlds in which African Americans enjoy full social privilege and civil rights" (Murchison, 2018, p. 80). Monáe's previous artistic offerings have exemplified the struggle that she felt, expressed in her lyrics: "alien from outer space / The cybergirl without a face" (qtd. in Spanos, 2018). This desire for the dominant culture to control the narrative and delete memories of the past of African Americans contradicts the essence of AfroFuturism, which Monáe proves at the end of the story when she escapes.

Visual Aspects of Afrocentricity

The following songs exemplify visual aspects of Afrocentricity. On the surface, it can be described as Africanity, where the audience notices elements of African culture. However, the visuals combined with Monáe's lyrics and knowledge of African culture and White supremacy provide these songs with the ability to liberate and create a victorious consciousness for the listener.

"Take a Byte"

Monáe prefaces this song with an introduction of Jane 57821 (i.e., Monáe) encountering Mary Apple 53, a friend whom she remembers, who wants to bring her from darkness to light. This is a Christian spiritual reference, but also a reference to her Black body and the white rooms, men, and computers. Jane looks like an Egyptian woman in white with laser colors draining from her as she is "cleansed." Her wrist has an *mdw-ntr* image of a goddess.

"Django Jane"

Monáe as Django Jane is Black and proud. She is positioned in the center on "the throne" as a Black Panther Party member. This memory is more like a dream because it is so vivid with color with a forest-like ambiance. Django Jane is the leader of the group. She is wearing a crown-like hat, wearing a red, pink, and green suit, and gold jewelry. This contrasts with Monáe's frequent use of black and white in her previous videos.

"Way You Make Me Feel"

Jane's memory in "Way You Make Me Feel" is around who she loves. She cannot decide who she loves more, the guy or the girl. They both make her feel great. Each scene has vibrant colors—pink, red, and green. Jane is wearing a headpiece that resembles cowrie shells, yet it is silver to suggest something more Futuristic. Her dance moves are extensions of Prince and Michael Jackson.

"I Like That"

The colors of black and white contrasted on a red background give power to her memories. There are many Janes, sitting in a theater, perhaps representing her many sides but also the diversity of a Black woman's experience. There is a peacock and flamingoes with golden furniture. There are many hairstyles and braids. She is bathing in a white tub.

Lyrical Analysis

Monáe is an artist who understands the White supremacist culture that America thrives on. Her lyrics show that knowledge and her intentionality behind the lyrics juxtaposed to her inner responsibility to use her platform to promote change.

You told us we hold these truths to be self-evident
That all men and women are created equal
That they are endowed by their Creator with certain unalienable rights
Among these: life, liberty, and the, and the pursuit of happiness. (Monáe,
    2018b)

Visually, at the beginning of this video, Monáe is pulled over by the bionic
flying police. She and her friends must show their identification, which is
scanned and confirmed by the police. The "policebot" flies away, and Monáe
heads to the trunk to allow her other friends to come out from inside. The
dancing within this video portion is uniform/synchronized. The women
are wearing black, and at one point, they lift their arms high almost like
a Black Panther power fist. In the background, you can hear the "we hold
these truths to be self-evident . . . life, liberty, and the pursuit of happiness."
After this video, the memory is deleted by the cleaners, who are White men
in white suits behind a large screen that displays the memories of the dirty
computer that need to be deleted. These words and images show the defiance
of the system that Monáe seeks to create. She wants to be herself "young,
Black, wild, free and naked" (Monáe, 2018b). This is who she is and who
she desires to be. She wants to "break the rules . . . smell the trees" (Monáe,
2018b). Her desire is for freedom from gaze, from anything desiring to police
or silence her humanity. She does not want "another ruler. All of my friends
are kings . . . just let me live my life" (Monáe, 2018b). Monáe is alluding to
Donald Trump but also, even more broadly, to the system that seeks to rule
over Africans in America and those seeking the "American Dream." She is
boldly stating that she is not "America's nightmare," which means that she is
not a threat to America but rather an asset or the epitome of what America
stands for and should be.

I live my life in a magazine
I live my life on a TV screen
I live my life on birth control
I lost my mind to rock and roll. (Monáe, 2018e)

In "Screwed," Monáe's character is acknowledging the horrors of America
and/or the world while also identifying that while rebellion feels good to
the oppressed, it may come with consequences. Monáe (2018e) as an artist

lives her life in the public eye, and yet as a human, she is appalled by the "sirens calling / And the bombs are falling in the streets / We're all screwed." As Monáe (2018e) sings "You f*****' the world up now / We'll f*** it all back down / I, I don't care," she is concluding that things are so bad to the point that she could add to it, and it would not bother her. And in a jesting manner, she exclaims, "We'll put water in your guns / We'll do it all for fun" (Monáe, 2018e), meaning that when killing stops, happiness will arrive. This song is an anthem for those who are impoverished, striving to gain their own sense of autonomy, yet everything they do is not quite enough because there are the rich who control the narrative. This is the very reason why AfroFuturism imagines how life could flourish for African people.

> Pynk, like the inside of your . . . baby
> Pynk behind all of the doors . . . crazy
> Pynk is the truth you can't hide . . . maybe
> Pynk, like the folds of your brain . . . crazy. (Monáe, 2018d)

"PYNK" is a sexually suggestive song that Monáe makes fun and light-hearted with the playful beat, dance, and costume. The dancers in the video have custom-made "vagina pants" to drive home the pynk imagery. Monáe wears underwear that says "sex cells" on them, speaking to capitalism, specifically stem cells. Yet, the song seeks to normalize the idea that pink is only for girls or women. Williams's theory of women pushing boundaries of gender and liberation discussed earlier applies here; Monáe is reminding the audience that the insides of our bodies are pink, brains, eyelids, skin, especially our hearts. She is naming for herself what sexuality is, and she is showing her pride for the woman. This work describes a love that she wants to remember because if her hard drive is erased, those memories may "never come back" (Monáe, 2018d).

> Hold on, don't fight your war alone
> Hate all around you, don't have to face it on your own
> We will win this fight, let all souls be brave
> We'll find a way to heaven; we'll find a way. (Monáe, 2018a)

"Modern and contemporary African American writers employ science fiction in order to recast ideas on past, present, and future Black culture"

(Myungsung, 2017, p. i). The emotion picture ends with "Americans" playing with the credits. "Americans" is an anthem of victory. Monáe uses these lyrics to capture the history of the United States and how, nonetheless, she is proud to be an American. When she states "We'll find a way to heaven, we'll find a way" (Monáe, 2018a) it exemplifies her persistence in things working out for her good, despite the obstacles. Intersecting gender and race, Monáe says, "Hands go up, men go down, try my luck, stand my ground / Die in church, live in jail say her name, twice in hell" (Monáe, 2018a). These verses are powerful because they speak of police brutality cases of Trayvon Martin, Mike Brown, and Sandra Bland and the laws that failed to protect them. She speaks of church shootings and bombing that have claimed the lives of African Americans. In the verse, "Uncle Sam kissed a man, Jim Crow Jesus rose again," Uncle Sam is the patriotic figure who recruited men to war. As a kisser of men and comparing Jim Crow to Jesus is a contradiction or taboo in the mind of Americans. Yet, for some, these are the realities or experiences of people who have been deemed illegitimate or not worthy. The song is filled with sharp contrasts, yet they challenge the listener and audience to dig deeper to understand the reference. This song is not a feel-good song where the beat carries you to a peaceful place. It is a fast-moving song that gets the audience to move but also to think about its lyrics, even after the song has ended. The song challenges the listener to question the norms and symbols of patriotism to examine if they thrive on notions of inequality. After calling out much of America's issues, she states, "This is not my America" (Monáe, 2018a), repeated multiple times. Monáe states that she will not acknowledge the America that refuses to address issues of discrimination, yet she can still be an American. Here Monáe universalizes her stance to say that she will always be an American. Though she is correct in her conclusion, an Africologist would critique her position, challenging her to be content in her cultural center. It can be argued that she should feel content in her Blackness as an African woman in America.

Monáe's *Dirty Computer* allows her audience to visually see a story told from the perspective of an African American woman. It is approximately forty minutes of lived experiences that are complex and cannot be summed up by lyrics and/or solely a visual representation. Monáe was successful in this artistic expression because it is thought-provoking and adds to artwork that pushes the conversation toward liberation. What Monáe does is genius because she uses her talent and gifts to speak on the issues of the world not because she must, but because they are of importance as they impact her daily life. *Dirty Computer* is an Afrocentric expression of art because it centers Monáe's experiences, where she acts as an agent who achieves freedom from complete erasure within a White supremacist nation. Even with some memories being erased, the past has remained in the character Jane's mind. Lyrically, she challenges authority, physically, runs away from the system, and historically, reminds Africans in the diaspora from whence they have come.

> Janelle Monáe's music and videos digitize revolution by insisting on a his-toricized African American female presence in both highly technological and revolutionary roles. . . . The remixed histories of Monáe's songs and videos are the work of a "digital griot," a term coined by Adam J. Banks in *Digital Griots: African American Rhetoric in a Multimedia Age* (2011). The digital griot is an intervening figure who unites the past, present, and future, refuses the digital divide as a barrier to Black engagement with technology, and utilizes a specifically African American rhetoric. (Jones, 2018, p. 43)

Further Considerations

In the future, it is imperative that we continue the discussion of speculative arts and AfroFuturism as scholarship and as a pedagogical tool. It provides context that can "make connections to institutional and disciplinary struc-tures in education, the devaluing of historical knowledge, the importance of creativity and imagination in the classroom, and the transformative potential" (Ellis et al., 2018, p. 111). This means that AfroFuturism is meant to be engaged within the classroom because it centralizes the conversation on an African past, present, and future, giving vision to what is possible. Afrocentricity allows for that conversation to continue toward liberation, autonomy, and victory for African people.

REFERENCES

Aghoro, N. (2018). Agency in the AfroFuturist Ontologies of Erykah Badu and Janelle Monáe. *Open Cultural Studies*, 2(1), 330–40.

Anderson, R. (2016). Afrofuturism 2.0 & the Black Speculative Arts Movement: Notes on a Manifesto. *Obsidian*, 42(1–2), 228–36.

Anderson, R., & Jones, C. E. (Eds.). (2016). *AfroFuturism 2.0: The Rise of Astro-Blackness*. Lexington Books.

Asante, M. K. (2018). The Classical African Concept of Maat and Human Communication. In K. Langmia (Ed.), *Black/Africana Communication Theory* (pp. 11–23). Palgrave Macmillan.

Barnes, D. (2020). *AfroFuturism in Animation: Self Identity of African Americans in Cinematic Storytelling* [Master's thesis, University of Central Florida]. UCF STARS. https://stars.library.ucf.edu/cgi/viewcontent.cgi?article=1013&context=etd2020

Dery, M. (1994). Black to the Future: Interviews with Samuel R. Delany, Greg Tate, and Tricia Rose. In M. Dery (Ed.), *Flame Wars: The Discourse of Cyberculture* (pp. 179–222). Duke University Press.

Donoho, A., Duke, L., & Ferguson, A. (Directors). (2018). *Janelle Monáe: Dirty Computer* [Film]. Diktator; Wondaland.

Dove, N. (1998). African Womanism: An Afrocentric Theory. *Journal of Black Studies*, 28(5), 515–39.

Ellis, J., Martinek, J. D., & Donaldson, S. (2018). Understanding the Past, Imagining the Future: Teaching Speculative Fiction and Afrofuturism. *Transformations: The Journal of Inclusive Scholarship and Pedagogy*, 28(1), 111–22.

English, D. K., & Kim, A. (2013). Now We Want Our Funk Cut: Janelle Monáe's Neo-AfroFuturism. *American Studies*, 52(4), 217–30.

Gipson, G. D. (2016). Afrofuturism's Musical Princess Janelle Monáe. In R. Anderson & C. E. Jones (Eds.), *Afrofuturism 2.0: The Rise of Astro-Blackness* (pp. 91–107). Lexington Books.

Glocke, A. (2011). When the Past Dances into the Future: An Interview with African-Centered Dance Scholar, Dr. Kariamu Welsh. *Journal of Pan African Studies*, 4(6), 253–64.

Hudson-Weems, C. (2019). *Africana Womanism: Reclaiming Ourselves*. Routledge.

Jones, C. L. (2018). "Tryna Free Kansas City": The Revolutions of Janelle Monáe as Digital Griot. *Frontiers: A Journal of Women Studies*, 39(1), 42–72. https://doi.org/doi:10.5250/fronjwomestud.39.1.0042

Karenga, M. (2003). *Maat, the Moral Ideal in Ancient Egypt: A Study in Classical African Ethics*. Routledge.

Kim, M. (2017). *AfroFuturism, Science Fiction, and the Reinvention of African American Culture*. Arizona State University.

Makinde, O. (1978). Historical Foundations of Counseling in Africa. *Journal of Negro Education*, 47(3), 303–11.

McDougal, S., III (2014). *Research Methods in Africana Studies*. Peter Lang.

Monáe, J. (2018a). Americans [Song]. On *Dirty Computer*. Wonderland; Bad Boy; Atlantic.

Monáe, J. (2018b). Crazy, Classic Life [Song]. On *Dirty Computer*. Wondaland; Bad Boy; Atlantic.

Monáe, J. (2018c). I Like That [Song]. On *Dirty Computer*. Wondaland; Bad Boy; Atlantic.

Monáe, J. (2018d). PYNK [Song]. On *Dirty Computer*. Wondaland; Bad Boy; Atlantic.

Monáe, J. (2018e). Screwed [Song]. On *Dirty Computer*. Wondaland; Bad Boy; Atlantic.

Murchison, G. (2018). Let's Flip It! Quare Emancipations: Black Queer Traditions, Afrofuturisms, Janelle Monáe to Labelle. *Women and Music: A Journal of Gender and Culture, 22*, 79–90.

Myungsung, K. (2017). *Afrofuturism, Science Fiction, and the Reinvention of African American Culture* [Doctoral dissertation, Arizona State University]. ASU Electronic Theses and Dissertations. https://keep.lib.asu.edu/items/155710

Saigol, S. (2019). *Musical Activism: A Case Study of Janelle Monáe and Her Digitized Revolution of Love* [Master's thesis, Claremont Colleges]. Scholarship@Claremont. https://scholarship.claremont.edu/cmc_theses/2117

Spanos, B. (2018, April 26). Janelle Monae Frees Herself. *Rolling Stone*. https://www.rolling stone.com/music/music-features/janelle-monae-frees-herself-629204/

Williams, J. (2016). *The Audacity to Imagine Alternative Futures: An AfroFuturist Analysis of Sojourner Truth and Janelle Monae's Performances of Black Womanhood as Instruments of Liberation* [Doctoral dissertation, Temple University]. TU Libraries Repository. https://digital.library.temple.edu/digital/collection/p245801coll10/id/390887/

6

MESSAGE FOR THE PEOPLE PARTY
Hip-Hop and the Motherland in the Age of AfroFuturism

Kofi Kubatanna

The People Will Come

Mark Dery coined the term "Afro-futurism" in a 1994 set of interviews with Tricia Rose, Samuel R. Delany, and Greg Tate. The discussions were largely concerned not with music, the topic we are vitally interested in here, but with the relative absence of Black science fiction writers. . . . [T]he canon of AfroFuturist music—was essentially bound up, at least in its initial incarnation, with "sci-fi imagery, futurist themes, and technological innovation in the African diaspora." (Lewis, 2008, pp. 139–40)

However, the harsh realities of life for a diasporic or continental African often require a more specific historically and culturally contextualized analytical prescription for peace, progress, and liberation. To live as an African in this current world is to live in a world completely overwrought with the banality of capitalism, filled with vexation over Western hegemonic tomes, and with florid calls for the unity of all humanity. All of this marks the situation but without reparations for the ancestors and continued insidious educational policies that maintain the chime in the Hegelian belfry. Yet, with collective stability, determination, and power, we move toward victory.

> The Afrocentric vision of the future is predicated upon our ability to maintain a victorious consciousness despite the weight of the circumstances we work against. The first step is to properly delineate the self-perceptions of those rooted within the context of African tradition vs the eyes of the West. "AfroFuturist thinkers, such as Kodwo Eshun and Alondra Nelson, have indicated the overwhelming tendency of Western visions of Africa to indicate impending doom and disaster. The tendency has also been to disqualify Africa from claims of technological invention and innovation." (Hamilton, 2017, p. 18)

One of the most powerful mediums utilized to dispel the Western myths of Africa while internationalizing the diasporic experience has been the common vibrations manifested through hip-hop art and culture.

In this endeavor, I seek to advance an Africological approach totally encapsulated in Afrocentricity (Asante, 2003) as a means to properly identify the importance of a specific utterance of hip-hop. Erudite individuals have analyzed the impact of what some call "unconscious," "nonconscious," and "commercial" rap with the hope of locating a coherent message, only to advocate for a bibliophilic redress of poetic prerogative. Gangsta rap is assigned placement in the mentioned categories. This author feels many scholars tend to examine gangsta rap within individualized comfort zones. These zones are held in place by the need to embrace socially acceptable discourse and to advance reference points that fit into academic convenience. Michael Tillotson (2011, p. 156) sees this form of poetry as follows: "The explicit lyrics and communicative ideas of this genre are centered upon goals of individualistic and materialistic self-aggrandizement. This position is diametrically opposed to the early expositors of political or conscious rap who demanded attention to the abandonment and marginalization of the African American community located in post-industrial urban America." This assessment is centered on what is safely available for academics to formally and informally understand based on the need to place African agency into an acceptable elasticity. Does meaningful poetry require one to adhere to a mandated poetic format that is easily discernable to skilled scholars? The language of gangsta rap propels an agenda completely incongruent to those who seek to hear hymns of gentle remembrance, that use the same auditory imagery of the accessible group.

Certainly, there is a different message for a different audience and that audience fully understands the sender's dilemma—*crowd motivation*. There is consciousness in what is deemed by scholars as "nonconscious," "unconscious," or gangsta rap expression. Creators and consumers of hip-hop art and culture describe varying experiences of liberation within the process of each.

"Hip-hop is thus commonly linked with notions of escape and related concepts of fame and immortality. However, rap and hip-hop can also be understood in terms of Afrocentric concepts such as *nommo*—essentially a manifestation of the mystical power of words" (McLeod 2016, p. 115). Take an artist like Nipsey Hussle; he was a self-determined gangsta rapper, a self-professed Neighborhood Rollin 60s Crip (Williams, 2007) from Los Angeles, California, specifically Crenshaw Boulevard and Slauson Avenue. The messages he conveys through his poetry are not the glorification of gang life, but the reflection of the circumstances produced by self-hate. Nipsey Hussle (2018) states in a poem called "Status Symbol 3":

> Everything I said, I meant, I was never cappin'
> I was never scared to stand front line with MAC-10's
> Raise to shoot at Black men, never felt the satisfaction
> When I seen the game collapsin', guess they took the rules and whacked it
> Started movin' at a different frequency and got me livin' lavish
> All my partners steady passin', tryna wiggle through the madness
> Tryna fight this gravity every time, I swear I can feel it pull me backwards
> Puttin' thousands on they caskets, tryna pick the right reactions
> I appreciate the progress, but I'm so conflicted about the status.

Translation: Everything I said, I really meant it. I was never lying about anything I said. I was never afraid to represent my gang with a Military Armament Corporation Model 10 firearm (MAC-10). I was instructed at a young age by older gang members that I must shoot at rival gang members on sight; yet, I never got satisfaction from shooting people that look just like me. I witness my friends dying and saw how the rules that were instilled in me would not benefit me. I strive to not get pulled back into ignorance. I am still paying for burials. I am thankful that my life has changed yet want to remain humble.

This poet's birth name was Ermais Asghedom; he was the product of the union of an African American mother and an Eritrean father. Hussle was not a college graduate, and he never attended high school, yet he advocated for the economic empowerment of African people. He legally owned prime real estate in his own community, a successful clothing company, employed newly released felons, and owned the rights to all his music. Nipsey continually worked to establish gang unity amongst all the Black gangs in LA to prevent to prevent violence within the Black community. Sadly, Nipsey Hussle was shot on March 31, 2019, in front of his clothing store, while assisting a friend that needed clothing. Over ten thousand people attended his funeral. The Los Angeles City Council renamed the intersection where he died—Nipsey Hussle Square. When asked by Snoop Dogg in a 2013 interview what he was, Nipsey Hussle stated, "I am an African" (SnoopDoggTV, 2013). Can consciousness be invisible to the scholars looking for discourse that adhere to formatted lines of critique? I firmly believe so.

> For [hip-hop scholar, Alondra] Nelson and many others associated with AfroFuturism—a framework for thinking about the intersections of race and technology—black diasporic cultural traditions contain speculative narratives, innovation, and engagements with science, machines, and technological devices that deserve more of our attention if we are to fully appreciate the nature of those traditions. Music, for centuries now, has been one of the most consistently innovative sites in black creative life; thus, not surprisingly, thinkers interested in AfroFuturism and African American culture in general have viewed black music as a vital source of knowledge. . . . [T]he field has also been regularly populated by presumably accomplished leaders in the field interested in pushing and reshaping boundaries. (Rambsy, 2013, p. 206)

One of the most significant, cultural seismic shifts to occur in the world of hip-hop came with the popularization of gangsta rap (or what came to be known by that broad category).

Gangsta rap was designed to efficiently distribute a concise, vivid message to listeners on all Lexile levels. It is inaccurate to label the poetry, set to a rhythm, as unconscious. This represents a massive intellectual error. When one thinks of the words of Frantz Fanon (1963) in regard to the purposeful use of violence or the actions and deeds of Jean-Jacques Dessalines (Dubois, 2012), would they not fit perfectly within this poetic form?

On Record

Africans were kidnapped from their land, clans, and amniotic sac. There is not a metric formula available to calculate the impact of foreign invaders (e.g., Arabs, Portuguese, English, French, Spanish) and their heinous greed while performing their duty authorized by their god. When it comes to America; the year 1619 (Asante & Spivey, 2015; Kendi, 2016) establishes a need to delve into that significant time, as it relates to change in the form of social parity. Four hundred years of living within this capitalistic experiment called America have gone by without the slightest assistance in the way of regaining the wholeness of oneself. In fact, the task of the Western capitalist has always been to maximize profit and material assets, with a total disregard for human life. Ama Mazama (2002b) delivers truth in her edited volume *Afrocentric Paradigm*. The reason for this is that colonization was not simply an enterprise of economic exploitation and political control, as it was commonly held, but also an ongoing enterprise of conceptual distortion and invasion, leading to widespread confusion.

The founders of this calculated experiment were avid vessels for the pronouncement of "liberty"; they also were enslavers, rapists, Christians, and "enlightened intellectuals." Africans survived the founders' mission due to their remembrance of their ancestral ways, and the truth is the founders' offspring are still on that mission; the goals are global domination and the spread of American values, e.g., White supremacy, Western diet, White god. We live at a time when the forty-fifth president of the United States is a White, orange man, who actively spews vicious, White nationalist rhetoric daily. Their mission continues. While we live in a society calibrated for one group to essentially prosper economically, politically, militarily, and ultimately enjoy a White system indoctrinates, it does not educate; the US Constitution does not speak of educating the citizenry. Schools are charged with instilling knowledge into nascent thinkers, so the experiment will continue. Centered Africologists clearly understand the process and work to effectively correct the institutional cadence saturated in Greenwich chronology. In the text *Revolutionary Pedagogy* (2017), clarification of the hegemonic push is given: "It is not alarmist to say that education, as a system, has not always been our friend; indeed, the statistics of the condition of African American education suggest that education has systematically robbed Black children of their motivation, creativity, cultural identity, and assertiveness" (Asante, 2017, p. ix).

The dynamic discourse of Africans in America flows past the hegemonic canards, always gathering momentum and spreading, while delivering necessary appeals, declarations, manifestos, and affirmations. Gangsta rap informs society in a way that induces criticism and astonishment. The usage of certain language has a jarring effect on some, who question the need to use degrading language. According to Reiland Rabaka (2012, p. 222), "Let's be real here: a lot of rap is okay, more of it is good, but little of it is genuinely great or will one day be considered 'classic' music." His examination of rap music is wack, due to the need to influence, itemize, categorize, and explain utilizing a Western ethos of "classic." To whom and for what does his analysis serve? An opportunity for communal conferencing remains the basis for the poetic medium; the message enables a necessary evaluation of institutional intrusions. US politicians (e.g., Strom Thurmond, George Wallace, Thomas O'Neil Jr., George H. W. Bush, William J. Clinton, George W. Bush) have said and committed acts that greatly surpass any announcement from a gangsta poet reporting the findings in the community. Can the narrative be less explicit? Yes, but the goal of any MC is to first get your attention, whereby influence is stimulated to optimize the retention of thoughtful lyrics. A gangsta poet has no time for formal introductions or prefaces; they have one goal, and that is to properly impress the party people with their *wordplay*. The *word* restores the necessary balance, which is paramount in enabling the installation of collective resistance, within the walls of a system moving toward the goal of cognitive assimilation.

In the past, AfroFuturism was primarily regarded as a cultural mode of expression and philosophically as a form of aesthetics. However, contemporary AfroFuturism is maturing in the area of metaphysical components, such as cosmogony, cosmology, speculative philosophy, and philosophy of science. Currently, a dominant expression of AfroFuturism lies in its aesthetics. What is less understood is how AfroFuturism is related to the cultural production of hip-hop music, that is, how AfroFuturism is linked to the hip-hop culture that emerged during the decline of urban inner-city cores in the latter half of the twentieth century and its digital transition in the twenty-first century, especially in visual culture (Anderson & Jennings, 2014, p. 29).

In this sense, Afrocentric Futurism can be viewed as an evolution of AfroFuturism that utilizes foundational Afrocentric principles and perspectives, which proceeded the speculative term and ideology communicated by AfroFuturists.

Communication as an Afrocentric Futuristic Exit Strategy

Speaking to the people about the problems the people face alleviates the need to suppress the aggression caused by the policies enforced by White supremacy masked by men with the American flag on their lapels. The fantasy of tasteful discourse depends on what is deemed vulgar to the audience within listening range; it also requires the sincere need to find the truth in the message, to see the space that is being accessed. The ancestor Malcolm X, a man held in high regard in the gangsta community, gave a speech titled "Educate Our People in the Science of Politics," in which he states: "This is good to study because you see what makes him react. Nothing loving makes him react, nothing forgiving makes him react. The only time he reacts is when he knows you can hurt him, and when you let him know, you can hurt him, he has to think two or three times before he tries to hurt you" (Clark, 1992, p. 88). His words might be considered aggressively vulgar and fostering strategic violence toward those that did not understand the message. If spoken in today's media culture, these words would cause the speaker to be banned from popular social platforms due to implications of advancing direct change and concisely identifying a key community objective: liberation. The "he" and "him" serve one interest: America. They question the messages emitted but marvel at the impact of the messages. Then the argument is that the masses are misinformed, which explains why they embrace these messages. True, the masses of Africans living within the confines of the Americas are subject to miseducation (Woodson, 2023), so the message to inform must be disruptively coherent to relocate the thinker. The question is, What content is the consciousness developing in? The idea of a pristine evaluation of societal norms, which is void of profane critique, is like asking for a boxing match without the pugilist sweating, bleeding, or experiencing abdominal discomfort. For one to exist during sustained, institutional chaos and still possess the fortitude to alert the masses is a feat.

> This resilience has proved to be a cornerstone of futurist thought for African peoples throughout the Diaspora. The manner in which this victorious consciousness is expressed differs greatly dependent upon numerous factors including time and personal experience/perspective.
>
> As many similarities as there are among futurists, there are an equivalent amount of differences: stylistics, themes, utopian/dystopian results,

particularities, etc.... . This "AfroFuturism" came into prominence in the 1970s and has continued as a relatively popular aesthetic genre to the present day, inspiring a slew of critics to ponder what social conditions led to its rapid increase in popularity and production and what this futuristic bend means for Africana Studies and other fields of cultural studies. (Galli, 2009, p. 26)

The Afrocentric Future from the Academy to the Stars

We must make note of what Molefi Kete Asante (2003, p. 64) announces in his liberating text *Afrocentricity: The Theory of Social* Change: "There are two aspects of consciousness: (1) toward oppression and (2) toward victory. When a person is able to verbalize the condition of oppression, he exhibits the earliest consciousness of his oppression. This is the most elemental form of consciousness and is found in the speeches, poems, plays, and lives of a million people who parade as conscious individuals."

A poet by the name of Knowledge Reign Supreme Over Nearly Everyone, commonly called KRS-ONE, is recognized as being a magnificent, conscious forward-thinking, philosophical, hip-hop artist. "Analyzing and critiquing KRS-ONE's lyrics (and other similar artists) as an alternative text to traditional curricula have liberatory potential for educating all youth, regardless of race, ethnicity, and/or socioeconomic background, about African American culture, urban realities, marginalization and oppression" (Parmar, 2009, p. 3).

KRS-ONE notably advocated physical violence to address cognitive conflict. KRS-ONE is widely regarded as the consummate MC. An *MC* is responsible for effectively keeping the *party people* motivated to have a good time. The party people represent any and all people within a designated space that can hear, see, or feel the *word*. The word is always connected to a beat. At times, the beat will actually precede the word because the beat prepares the people to receive the word. The word has always been the fundamental reality for African people; it emerges in the African sense as being a formal signal of immediate transformation, for the word is a connective continuum to the Creator. Placement of ideas past, present, and future are housed in realities that unfold when generative speech is vaulted. Identifying the word is extremely important for those that understand the coding, signification, and breath of this poetry form. Identification allows for differentiation in the activation of clear images, which enable party people the ability to transport themselves from their current space and time to travel with the MC on a collective journey.

Asante (1998, p. 92) is correct when stating: "Let us look at this more closely. To understand the nature of African American communication, one must understand that *nommo* continues to permeate our existence. This is not to say that all or even most of us, given the situation, can immediately identify the transforming power of vocal expression." This is the point that is being missed by those researching hip-hop; they fail to identify and acknowledge the limitation of their approach due to their schooling. This perspective plays a role in critiques of certain aspects of AfroFuturism concerning its capacity to adequately address certain issues relevant to Black liberation within the context of methodology and modern technology.

Scholar Andre Brock (2020, p. 7) asserts, "AfroFuturism is a powerful framework for understanding Black engagement with technology, time, and space, but its literary mode of analysis renders it underpowered to examine Black engagement with today's digital technologies."

Hip-hop was created by Africans living in a borough called the Bronx; a place that KRS-ONE originates from. DJ Kool Herc (Clive Campbell), an African from Jamaica, lived in the Bronx and is credited as being the father of hip-hop due to his importation of a unique African diasporic musical format. Michael E. Veal (2007, p. 247) asserts, "The central stylistic difference, of course was that Jamaican musicians such as DJ Kool Herc, living and working in New York City, 'toasted' [rapped] over funk, soul, jazz, and rhythm-and-blues records instead of the reggae of their native country."

Hip-hop was a remedy to address the circumstances in the community of the South Bronx; it was a convergence of Africans formed in a matter that was tailored to navigate divisions within city blocks. A textbook does not possess the script for dilapidated housing, gang violence, incarceration, and schooling. Some forget this poetry set to a beat was born within *isfet*, where violence begot violence. Evelyn Gonzalez (2004, p. 120) informs: "Crime worsened when a new wave of youth gangs appeared in the South Bronx during the 1970s. With names such as the Savage Skulls, Cypress Bachelors, Black, Spanish Mafia, and the Reapers, these new groups attacked drug addicts and the pushers and asserted they were merely cleaning up the neighborhoods." The nature of the music resides in the removal of stress, just for a moment, to be better equipped to manage the daily routine of survival in urban aesthetics. Afrocentricity has been described by Asante as a means of regaining sanity. AfroFuturism involves the ability to transcend space and time through artistic creativity and speculative thought. Hip-hop, Afrocentricity, and AfroFuturism's intersections of relief and release serve as a veritable perfect storm for the methodological analytical winds of change that Afrocentric Futurism breathes into space.

When one explores the dynamic burst of hip-hop onto the landscape of Black America, the idea of environmental content must be included. Because the very nature of time and space and how that relates to circumstance affords the researcher the opportunity to see agency manifesting to address pervading *isfet*. The Bronx (or BX, as it is referred in the hip-hop community) went through a tremendous wave of disruption due to governmental malfeasance. The failures of the Carter administration maintained high unemployment, gasoline shortages, and a hostage crisis, all of which happened during one term (Krukones, 1985; Reston, 1980). This set the climate for a Hollywood C-level actor, who became a national spokesman for General Electric, as well as the thirty-third governor of California, to become the fortieth president of the United States of America. Ronald Wilson Reagan, a former Democrat, would usher in a new wave of Republican policies that permanently alter the lives of millions of Africans in America. There is no question amongst scholars of clear conscious that his visions for America produced changes in the urban landscape; major cities took on a new disastrous trajectory. Reagan was a politician steeped in the thought of restoring what he felt were American values. Those values did not consider the prosperity of Africans.

In Nelson George's (1998, p. 60) *Hip Hop America*, he evaluated the influence of the company man: "During the eight years of Reagan's presidency, the ripple effect of crack flowed through all the social science agencies of our country-welfare, childcare, Medicare, you name the area of concern and the crack's impact could be felt in it."

Reagan is mentioned in the history of hip-hop due to the conditions produced by his ideology of rewarding the wealthy with the goal of those folks generously forwarding their gains to their employees.

This music and culture—a safe space from the bloody gang runnings on the street—immigrated to the Bronx—a space so devastated by deindustrialization and governmental neglect that when Ronald Reagan visited in 1980, he declared that it looked like London after World War II. In the Bronx, the

Universal Zulu Nation, hip-hop's first institution and organization, literally emerged from a peace forged between racially divided, warring gangs.
(Chang, 2001, pp. 167–68)

Former President Reagan's idea of an economic plan centered on the
assumption that wealthy people make the right choices in society and the
poor can function perfectly well receiving figurative crumbs. An orchestrated
social experiment properly described Reagan's prosperity plan. The proposal
was an approach called "trickle-down economics." In a bizarre turn of events,
an entertainment personality made economic decisions that affected millions
of Africans living in America. The year 2016 is not an anomaly.

The 1980s were a time when entire Black communities were altered,
destroyed, and/or reprogrammed. All the while, the call for the criminaliza-
tion of communities afflicted by drug usage was heralded from Reagan's
pulpit. On September 14, 1986, Nancy and Ronald Reagan addressed the
American public about the issue of illegal drugs. Ronald had this to say:

Despite our best efforts, illegal cocaine is coming into our country at alarm-
ing levels, and 4 to 5 million people regularly use it. Five hundred thousand
Americans are hooked on heroin. One in twelve persons smokes marijuana
regularly. Regular drug use is even higher among the age group eighteen to
twenty-five—most likely just entering the workforce. Today, there's a new
epidemic: smokable cocaine, otherwise known as "crack." It is an explosively
destructive and often lethal substance, which is crushing its users. It is an
uncontrolled fire. . . . And drug abuse is not a so-called victimless crime.
Everyone's safety is at stake when drugs and excessive alcohol are used by
people on the highways or by those transporting our citizens or operating
industrial equipment. Drug abuse costs you and your fellow Americans at
least $60 billion a year. (Miller Center, n.d.)

Nancy followed with these words:

So, to my young friends out there: life can be great, but not when you can't see
it. So, open your eyes to life to see it in the vivid colors that God gave us as a
precious gift to His children, to enjoy life to the fullest, and to make it count.
Say "yes" to your life. And when it comes to drugs and alcohol, just say "no."
(Miller Center, n.d.)

These words were spoken while the presidential couple sat on a sofa, side by side, holding hands, both dressed in business attire. Nancy's slogan "just say 'no'" was pure Western hubris, like a line from a poorly written 1940s script; her words explained the ideological thrust of the jingoistic party, in all its simplicity. After this televised speech, Reagan would be completely exposed as a raconteur of covert lies while projecting an image of being a virtuous man who trusted his ignoble personnel; all of this took place less than two months later. The Paul Reveres of the age who carried messages of Reagan's role in government corruption prior to such revelations becoming common knowledge were often rappers.

The Man from Marinette, Wisconsin

Yes, blame it on Eugene Hasenfus, a former marine, who was flying a little low over the country of Nicaragua when his plane was shot down by Indigenous soldiers, called "Sandinistas." According to Noam Chomsky (2015, p. 122), "Sandinistas were spreading their 'revolution without borders' and advancing on Texas." The implied meaning in US terms is that they were socialists. These Nicaraguans were viewed by the Reagan administration as being "un-American," which is a problematic term because it advances the thought that everyone across the world should be American, pro-American, American like, or "friendly" to America; the same term denotes antidemocracy. So, to be "un-American" carries with it the weight of being an adversary, an evil regime, a person or persons dedicated to the unraveling of American imperialism also called American values. If we are talking about Western imperialism, we are talking about dichotomies: the Contras, a group also located in Nicaragua, were considered prodemocracy, which in the Western hemisphere means they are "okay" to do business with.

On October 5, 1986, Hausenfus was captured, interrogated, and showcased in front of mass-media outlets. The man from Wisconsin told it all: the nature of his mission and who his employers were. Reagan, the "just-say-'no'" advocate, was running an illegal criminal drug enterprise through the National Security Council and a covert shadow company, supervised by current and retired US military personnel. There was the other issue of arms sales to Iran for monetary gain, also happening simultaneously. A sitting US president and his comrades were selling arms to an identified un-American country, supplying funds and arms to antigovernment forces in another un-American country, and establishing a gateway for *Erythroxylum coca* to come to America (Webb, 1998). All of these activities violated at least one of the Boland Amendments, which were ratified by Congress (Colella, 1988; Hayes, 1988; Ricci, 1988). Out of fourteen US citizens charged, only one served any jail time (i.e., Thomas Clines). The remaining thirteen had their charges dismissed, vacated, received probation, or were pardoned. In what would be called the Iran-Contra scandal, American values continued to "trump" humanity. The events of the Iran-Contra fiasco were articulated in numerous rap songs. Artist Killer Mike dedicated an entire song, titled "Reagan," to the failings and corruption of the former president and the society that produced him. The song appeared on his 2012 album *RAP Music* in which he raps:

> But thanks to Reaganomics, prison turned to profits
> 'Cause free labor's the cornerstone of US economics
> 'Cause slavery was abolished, unless you are in prison
> You think I am [expletive], then read the 13th Amendment. (Killer Mike, 2012)

Afrocentric Futurism encourages the agency and freedom of culturally rooted expression, which helps to dispel lies and rebuff other attacks on African people through the communication of a self-defining and self-determining message.

PEACE

Hip-hop is approximately forty-five years old, according to oral history—still an extremely new communicative modality, but it possesses the educational structure that enables routes to consciousness. Is this a fortuitous manifestation? Establishing effective lines of collective dialogue has always been one of the agreeable objectives for Africans in America. Gangsta rap, unconscious rap, nonconscious rap, and commercial rap are titles that seek to locate the function of the message in order to predict what comes next. What is the listener thinking, and does the MC realize what she is doing? Can the DJ catch the beat at the right time? These are questions that primarily cross the mind when I think about my love for hip-hop. There is also a streak of rebelliousness that has traditionally rejected or worked to change the status quo into something more inclusive, relevant to the lives of the hip-hop generation, and less racially stratified. Themes of resistance and self-determination spawned or bolstered through hip-hop have ramifications throughout several aspects of society and human existence. One such byproduct of this creative genre has been a premium placed upon sincerity and accuracy in information presented as true to life or inspired by real events.

Due to this fact, many refused to be subjected to inaccurate information, attend failing schools, absorb inferior curricular lessons, and remain limited in mind, body, and spirit as a result. They created their own learning institutions via a microphone, turntables, and the community. Tricia Rose (2008, p. 216) announces in *The Hip Hop Wars*:

> In my own experience speaking to thousands of White students and fans of hip hop over fifteen years, I have found hip hop, and only hip hop, is the way most of these young people come to Black culture—and to Black people, for that matter: Yes, there is a highly informed core of young White fans who have a larger appreciation and understanding of Black culture and history, who critically engage with White privilege in their own lives and in society at large.

Her statement suggests the lack of proper K–16 institutional education for these students and a subjective research epistemology that labels proximity to imperturbable Whiteness as a measure of validation. This was never the objective for the MC; acceptance by one's community supersedes any and all outside accommodation. It takes community cooperation, self-determination, and insight gained from communal elders for any original MC to creatively thrive. It is a fact that millions of dollars are generated from an African discourse method, essentially created to maintain harmony in the community, bypassing learned oppression. Creative expression for any African that has been exposed to the toxicity of "King's English" mandates a salubrious understanding that liberation emanates from the center.

The agency filled, independent Futuristic thinkers will be key figures in the shaping of the Afrocentric Futuristic message they bring forth to the people. Kodwo Eshun describes the potential traps and distractions many artists are required to overcome to maximize certain levels of fame and potential that accompany transformative artistic capacity.

The African artist that researches this dimension will find a space for distinct kinds of anticipatory designs, projects of emulation, manipulation, parasitism. Interpellation into a bright corporate tomorrow by ads full of faces smiling at screens may become a bitter joke at the expense of multinational delusions. The artist might reassemble the predatory futures that insist the next years will be ones of unmitigated despair. AfroFuturism, then, is concerned with the possibilities for intervention within the dimension of the predictive, the projected, the proleptic, the envisioned, the virtual, the anticipatory and the future conditional. (Eshun, 2003, p. 293)

It is imperative for the artists, messenger, creative, Afrocentric-Futurist thinker/scholar, or simply human beings invested in African liberation worldwide, to recognize their power. Claim, own, and celebrate the future you design in your heart and mind and work to manifest in the physical world as a liberatory byproduct of Afrocentric Futuristic genius. This brilliance begins with the power of the word, is enhanced by the rhythm of the drum, and is grounded in the cultural, methodological underpinnings of Afrocentric Futuristic brilliance. Shine your message to the people, and let your light shine into the future through the powerful lens of the past, a reflection eternal, a message for the people.

REFERENCES

Anderson, R., & Jennings, J. (2014). AfroFuturism: The Digital Turn and the Visual Art of Kanye West. In J. Bailey (Ed.), *The Cultural Impact of Kanye West* (pp. 29–44). Palgrave Macmillan.

Asante, M. K. (1998). *The Afrocentric Idea*. Temple University Press.

Asante, M. K. (2003). *Afrocentricity: The Theory of Social Change* (Rev. and ex. ed.). African American Images.

Asante, M. K. (2017). *Revolutionary Pedagogy: Primer for Teachers of Black Children*. Universal Write Publications.

Asante, M. K., & Spivey, M.R. (2015). *African American Traditions: Portraits from African American History*. Sungai Books.

Chang, J. (2001). The Hip-Hop Generation Can Call For Peace. *Amerasia Journal, 28*(1), 167–71.

Chomsky, N. (2015). *Year 501: The Conquest Continues*. Pluto Press.

Clark, S. (Ed.). (1992). *February 1965: The Final Speeches. Malcolm X*. Betty Shabazz/ Pathfinder Press.

Colella, F. G. (1988). Beyond Institutional Competence: Congressional Efforts to Legislate United States Foreign Policy toward Nicaragua—The Boland Amendments. *Brooklyn Law Review, 54*(1), 131–70.

Dubois, L. (2012). Dessalines Toro d'Haïti. *William and Mary Quarterly*, *69*(3), 541–48.

Eshun, K. (2003). Further Considerations of AfroFuturism. *CR: The New Centennial Review*, *3*(2), 287–302.

Fanon, F. (1963). *The Wretched of the Earth*. Grove Press

Galli, C. (2009). Hip-Hop Futurism: Remixing AfroFuturism and the Hermeneutics of Identity [Honors project, Rhode Island College]. RIC Repository. https://digital commons.ric.edu/honors_projects/18/?utm_source=digitalcommons.ric.edu%2Fhonors _projects%2F18&utm_medium=PDF&utm_campaign=PDFCoverPages

George, N. (1998). *Hip Hop America*. Viking.

Gonzalez, E. (2004). *The Bronx*. Columbia University Press.

Hamilton, E. C. (2017). AfroFuturism and the Technologies of Survival. *African Arts*, *50*(4), 18–23.

Hayes, A. W. (1988). The Boland Amendments and Foreign Affairs Deference. *Columbia Law Review*, *88*(7), 1534–74.

Nipsey Hussle. (2018). Status Symbol 3 [Song]. On *Victory Lap*. Atlantic Records.

Kendi, I. X. (2016). *Stamped from the Beginning: The Definitive History of Racist Ideas in America*. Bold Type Books.

Killer Mike. (2012). Reagan [Song]. On *RAP Music*. Williams Street Records.

Krukones, M. G. (1985). The Campaign Promises of Jimmy Carter: Accomplishments and Failures. *Presidential Studies Quarterly*, *15*(1), 36–144.

Lewis, G. E. (2008). Foreword: After AfroFuturism. *Journal of the Society for American Music*, *2*(2), 139–53.

Mazama, A. (2002a). Afrocentricity and African Spirituality. *Journal of Black Studies*, *33*(2), 218–34.

Mazama, A. (Ed.). (2002b). *The Afrocentric Paradigm*. Africa World Press.

McLeod, K. (2016). Hip Hop Holograms: Tupac Shakur, Technological Immortality, and Time Travel. In R. Anderson & C. E. Jones (Eds.), *Afrofuturism 2.0: The Rise of Astro-Blackness* (pp. 109–24). Lexington Books.

Miller Center. (n.d.). September 14, 1986: Speech to the Nation on the Campaign against Drug Abuse [Audio]. https://millercenter.org/the-presidency/presidential-speeches /september-14-1986-speech-nation-campaign-against-drug-abuse

Parmar, P. (2009). *Knowledge Reigns Supreme: The Critical Pedagogy of Hip-Hop Artist KRS-ONE*. Brill.

Rabaka, R. (2012). Hip Hop's Amnesia: From Blues and the Black Women's Club Movement to Rap and the Hip Hop Movement. Lexington Books.

Rambsy, H., II. (2013). Beyond Keeping It Real: OutKast, the Funk Connection, and AfroFuturism. *American Studies*, *52*(4), 205–16.

Reston, J. (1980, February 6). Washington Carter's Successful Failures. *New York Times*, 27.

Ricci, A. (1988). The Iran-Contra Affair and the Boland Amendment: President Reagan Claims He Is above the Law. *Suffolk Transnational Law Journal*, *12*(1), 135–50.

Rose, T. (2008). *The Hip Hop Wars: What We Talk about When We Talk about Hip Hop— And Why It Matters*. BasicCivitas.

SnoopDoggTV. (2013, July 2). *Nipsey Hussle Takes a Victory Lap | GGN with SNOOP DOGG* [Video]. YouTube. https://www.youtube.com/watch?v=rui-Bjshh78

Tillotson, M. (2011). *Invisible Jim Crow, Contemporary Ideological Threats to the Internal Security of African Americans*. African World Press.

Veal, M. E. (2007). *Soundscapes and Shattered Songs in Jamaican Reggae*. Wesleyan University Press.

Webb, G. (1998). *Dark Alliance: The CIA, the Contras, and the Crack Cocaine Explosion*. Seven Stories Press.

Williams, S. (2007). *Blue Rage Black Redemption: A Memoir New York*. Simon & Schuster/ Damamli.

Woodson, C. G. (2023). *The Mis-Education of the Negro*. Penguin.

7

AFROFUTURISM AND AFRICAN PHILOSOPHY OF TIME
Analyzing AfroFuturism Utilizing African Cosmological Paradigms

Taharka Adé

The African world has for centuries dealt with relentless assaults on African epistemological foundations by way of European imperialism and hegemony. For Africans in America, in particular, and those throughout the diaspora, in general, a leading issue in regard to such assaults involves the contributions of Molefi Kete Asante (1998, p. 1), whose "work has increasingly constituted a radical critique of the Eurocentric ideology that masquerades as a universal view." This masquerade plays out in all sectors of life as Eurocentric ideology has dominated and remains hegemonic on both the native soil of the peoples in which such phenomena serve, as well among their once colonial and neocolonial subjects in many corners of the globe. Therefore, escaping the reach of Eurocentric epistemological foundations proves difficult. Further, and perhaps even more complicated within the historical social contexts of the geographically isolated, in the so-called "new-world" continent of North America, a masquerade of human cultural "universalism" exists, which is nothing more than invisible yet omnipresent systems of Eurocentric ethno-cultural norms, or European subjectivity (Asante, 1998), that operate as the standard by which individuals should think and behave. Such standards permeate all modes of people's activity. African Americans, a history of ancestors being forced into the bowels of ships, sold to the Americas, and enduring the pain of their progeny being culturally decentered by a geography, a people, and a culture foreign to African cosmology, have long since had to live on borrowed terms (Mazama, 2003).

This does not mean that we were irrevocably torn from our own cultural paradigms or that they have languished out of existence. However, there is a similar invisible phenomenon of African cultural dynamism and even political antiacculturation that exists among the African descendants of the Americas. Although, African cultural dynamism in the Americas continues the use of European "borrowed terms," this is, in many ways, an unconscious or unwitting concession. We see African cultural dynamism continue to play out in music, art, language, aesthetics, food, and, of course, literature. African people took African musicality and European notation to create art forms such as ragtime, jazz, blues, and even hip-hop (Floyd, 1995). We reimagined African folktales into our own folktale figures, such as Br'er Rabbit, Shine, John Henry, Stagger Lee, and High John the Conqueror (Asante, 1998).

However, the use of borrowed terms came with distortion. In the process of African musical survival in the Americas, spirituals, ragtime, blues, and jazz had to sacrifice aspects of African musicality (though could still exist in real form depending on the knowledge base or inherent understanding of the performer), and folktales such as Br'er Rabbit, which suffered from its isolation from African folktales such as that of Anansi, were appropriated and distorted by Whites for the purpose of minstrel entertainment (Floyd, 1995). Today, such cultural dynamism (distortions included) continues with the literary genre that is AfroFuturism. African and African American folklore and philosophy have always been central to African American literature, in general, and AfroFuturism, specifically. Ytasha Womack (2013, p. 21) makes this somewhat clear by discussing her experiences in college with other AfroFuturists, discovering the following: "But the logic in the cyclical equations this cadre of urban philosophers shared zigzagged from quantum physics to African philosophy to film aesthetics to economic theories to music theory and back."

In fact, Womack dealt with African philosophy quite a bit in her text *AfroFuturism* (2013). When speaking about her conversations with artist and curator Christine Kraemer, she reveals, "There's a tendency to view Africa for its cultural contributions in music and art, Kreamer told me, and a reluctance to understand the continent's long-standing contributions to science and our understanding of astronomy" (Womack, 2013, p. 91). Much later, she continues: "I shared that many AfroFuturists incorporate African mythology and spirituality in their work. The *African Cosmos* exhibit is a reminder that there is a legacy of weaving art, philosophy, and the realms of the sky from a Black and African perspective that predates the term afrofuturism and any newfound curiosity" (Womack, 2013, p. 91).

It is interesting that Womack makes sure to note within this passage that such artistic and literary phenomena predate the term "AfroFuturism" itself. AfroFuturism, again, utilizes borrowed terms, or borrowed epistemologies, that seem universal, however, it either stifles or distorts the African epistemological grounds. This is far removed from an individual psychologically located within his cultural reality simply choosing to borrow elements from other cultures in which to elevate their work. As aforementioned, the insidious nature of the Eurocentric masquerade is that it is a masquerade. It is a veil of European subjectivity that purports to be a corpus of universal human ideals. One should only question why AfroFuturism is regarded as such. No African people came up with this terminology. It was a term that bloomed from the mind of the White cultural critic Mark Dery. African Americans simply "borrowed" the term in order to describe this phenomenon within Black art. This is not to paint Dery in any malicious manner. He was simply operating from his own located reality as a White man in the Western world, who thought to blend the idea of African agency and science fiction as he saw it, a "-futurism" (Dery, 1994, p. 179). This etymology is being broken down in order to isolate the term and idea of "future" within the African context. As such, I seek to examine the African philosophical notions of time and how such cultural paradigms can better enrich AfroFuturism, as well as to serve to combat the Eurocentric masquerade by way of the restoration of African ways of knowing.

Deliberations on the meaning of time are largely a philosophical enterprise. Our understanding of the concept of time in African philosophy owes much to the scholarship of the late John S. Mbiti. Mbiti's pioneering work, *African Religions and Philosophy* (1969), devotes a whole chapter to the concept of time in African philosophy. There has been much praise and criticisms of Mbiti's contentions; regardless, what Mbiti attempted was not to draw parallels and logical relationships between African and European concepts of time, but to put forth a paradigmatic understanding of time based on African cultural paradigms. He set out to accomplish this task by investigating a set of East African languages (particularly the Bantu languages of Kikamba and Kikuyu) and discovered no Indigenous words for a distant future. In fact, according to Mbiti (1990), any notion of time that is to come would not extend outside the realm of two years. Mbiti (1990, p. 16) opens his explanation with this argument:

> The question of time is of little or no academic concern to African peoples in their traditional life. For them, time is simply a composition of events which have occurred, those which are taking place now and those which are inevitably or immediately to occur. What has not taken place or what has no likelihood of an immediate occurrence falls in the category of "No-time." What is certain to occur, or what falls within the rhythm of natural phenomena, is in the category of inevitable or potential time.

Given Mbiti's position on the African philosophy of time, how does this reconcile itself with our borrowed term "AfroFuturism"? Clearly African and European philosophical understandings of the temporal dimension vary greatly. While one can find some overlap in the philosophical tenets of each, such as having a concept of a present and a past, we begin to see that the notion of "future," at least in some Bantu languages, is tenuous. If we take Mbiti's construction at face value, this certainly constitutes a vast difference between African and European construction of reality in regard to time. Mbiti (1990, p. 17) himself submits that very contention as he continues:

> The most significant consequence of this is that, according to traditional concepts, time is a two-dimensional phenomenon, with a long past, a present and virtually no future. The linear concept of time in Western thought, with an indefinite past, present and infinite future, is practically foreign to African thinking. The future is virtually absent because events which lie in it have not taken place, they have not been realized and cannot, therefore, constitute time.

Mbiti's statement that time is two-dimensional is interesting. It seems that what he may be referring to as *dimensions* in African temporal reality could simply be "past" and "present." Even if so, it is not then entirely certain (as he never emphatically states) that Mbiti is implying a three-dimensional temporal reality (past, present, and future) for European philosophy. Though there's occasional discourse amongst theoretical physicists on multiple dimensions of time, Western civilization functionally considers time as one-dimensional and on a linear scale (Ani, 1994). Regardless, this becomes quite an interesting paradox. How is it then that today we consider an "Afrofuture" when the African concept of future remains elusive or even nonexistent? Also, if there exists no concept of future, how then do African people plan for what is to come? Mbiti (1990, p. 17, emphasis original) attempts to explain such as he continues:

> If, however, future events are certain to occur, *or if they fall within the inevi-*
> *table rhythm of nature*, they at best constitute only *potential time*, not actual
> time. What is taking place now no doubt unfolds the future, but once an event
> has taken place, it is no longer in the future but in the present and the past.
> Actual time is therefore what is present and what is past. It moves "backward"
> rather than "forward"; and people set their minds not on future things, but
> chiefly in what has taken place.

This last statement on time moving "backward," rather than "forward," is exemplary of African American tradition as we continue to formulate our own identities on our historical and even imagined pasts. Clearly, the past holds a sacred space in African diasporic reality, and this is thoroughly demonstrated in African American and general African diasporic literature. However, as Erik Steinskog (2018) points out in *AfroFuturism and Black Sound Studies*, Dery, despite the literary evidence to the contrary, hardly references the past in his definition of AfroFuturism. Dery (1994, p. 180) himself seems to submit to this as he states: "Speculative fiction that treats African-American themes and addresses African-American concerns in the context of twentieth-century technoculture—and, more generally, African-American signification that appropriates images of technology and a prosthetically enhanced future—might, for want of a better term, be called 'Afro-futurism.'"

Certainly, Dery references Black authors that themselves use the past as a vehicle for their stories, but he seems to find the past for African Americans to be, as he placed it, an "antinomy." "Can a community whose past has been deliberately rubbed out and whose energies have subsequently been consumed by the search for legible traces of its history, imagine possible futures?" (Dery, 1994, p. 180). There are two glaring issues with this line of questioning. The first is the suggestion of a "rubbing out" of the past. To be sure, the removal of African people from their geographical origins and centuries of forced enslavement in the Americas have broken the (for lack of a better term) purity of traditions and African epistemology, but that does not mean that our past, imagined or real, does not drive our literary traditions. In fact, one can argue that remembering and imagining the past, of a paradise lost, is the primary vehicle of African Americans' literary traditions. Dery (1994) even goes on to mention AfroFuturist fictions such as Milestone Media's *Icon*—a comic in which the initial setting is the antebellum South—and pioneers such as Samuel Delaney and Octavia Butler, whose works are steeped with the reimagining and refashioning of the African American and African past.

The second issue with this question is the very contradiction he places forth. He labels the genre "AfroFuturism" because, according to him, there was a lack of a better term (Dery, 1994, p. 180). However, he bases the coining of the term not on the cultural, intellectual, and philosophical foundations of his subject pieces, but on what he foresaw as "signification that appropriates images of technology and a prosthetically enhanced future." The idea that such images are "appropriated" suggests that science fiction and general technoculture aren't African American culture to begin with. The argument here is not to show that African Americans, either wittingly or unwittingly, have contributed to (and our aesthetics and culture exploited within) the very formation of science fiction and technoculture—though there are a number of scholarships proving this to be true (Lavender, 2011).

However, what Dery is perhaps unconsciously unraveling is that, even with that truth, the paradigmatic cultural basis for science fiction and technoculture has been that of Europeans. He seems to have at least an inherent understanding of this as he writes, "Furthermore, isn't the unreal estate of the future already owned by the technocrats, futurologists, streamliners, and set designers—White to a man—who have engineered our collective fantasies?" (Dery, 1994, p. 180). The significance of such an assertion is that it becomes a primary example of the aforementioned Eurocentric masquerade. The choice of wording such as "unreal estate" cleverly addresses the idea of uncharted intellectual territory that the explorer is destined to shape and form in the image of their cultural and epistemological foundations. After it is fully explored, a propaganda campaign is then employed that permanently instills in the minds of that and future generations dogmatic definitions, aesthetics, and ideologies (and even counterideologies). Interestingly, there has been at least one that has accused Dery of doing just the same with his "discovery" of AfroFuturism. Another White cultural critic and theologian, Marika Rose (2014, emphasis original), seemed to be reminded of colonial explorers such as Henry Morton Stanley—who, while often appointing *native* guides in order to get him into the hinterlands of the continent, violently and reprehensibly "explored" Africa and paved the way for absolute colonial conquest—when she penned the article, "The Uncomfortable Origins of 'AfroFuturism'":

> Dery, a White guy, is positioning himself as a bold *explorer* into a largely unknown region populated by people of colour. A voyage into the heart of darkness, if you will. This "largely unexplored" region is so unknown, so previously unthought, that Dery must appoint as his native guides an author and literary critic (Delany), a musician, producer and cultural critic (Tate) and a Professor of Africana Studies who is "currently at work on a book on rap music and the politics of Black cultural practice."

Nevertheless, in Dery's view, and arguably in the view of many, any attempt at scripting a "future" reality is grounded by a certain cultural ethos, one which Dery admits is White. Put another way, had Europeans not so forcefully and violently upended (as well as appropriated) African epistemology and supposing transcultural relations between Africans and Europeans persisted, Africans would have been free to approach (or even not approach) the European concept of "future" on their own terms. The aesthetics and ethos of a paradigmatically "African future" would perhaps vary greatly from the current confines of science fiction or even AfroFuturism itself.

Afrocentricity's foundational premise, that Africans be agents and not subjects in their own historical realities, does not exclude that which is fictional (Asante, 1998). Further, the restoration of African cosmology and cultural ethos is the driving force behind the Afrocentric paradigm (Mazama, 2003). Thus, Afrocentrists see it as an imperative that all modes of activity African people engage in must be grounded by African cultural paradigms, which largely means an investigation and reutilization of the cosmologies of the African past. This thinking is in itself paradigmatically African. One exemplifier is the Akan notion of *sankofa*, meaning "*se wo were fi na wosan kofa a yenki*" or "it is not wrong to go back and fetch what you forgot," which fosters respect for past tradition in order to promote unity in the present.

However, any notion of a people's history is inherently elusive as there are many factors that may influence any one individual's perspective on the past they or others have lived. This is true not only for Africans but all other peoples of the world. Written histories are often subjective, influenced by the experiences of the writer and the political leanings of those who commissioned the writing. Objectivity is a concept typically advanced by Western academia, which many Afrocentric scholars believe has no basis in reality. This becomes even more complicated in contemporary times when historical investigation is not from written or oral sources yet from archaeological material culture (Connah, 2016).

Oral histories and oral traditions among African people are not only subject to the same issues as written histories, but the traditions themselves may include purposeful distortions or reimagining of the past to suit contemporary conditions (Salm, 2000). This, however, doesn't make the past any less real or meaningful to the cultures from which the history was produced. Examples of such include, for Africa, the mythical tales of Menelik I or, for Europeans, the mythical tales of Charlamagne. Both figures, though shrouded in myth, have irrevocably influenced the course of history in Africa and Europe respectively. Thus, the absence of, distortion of, and inability to fully reclaim history have never stopped humanity, and particularly African people, from using the past, partially constructed or partially imagined, in order to shape present realities. In fact, it is often within the realm of imagination in which old realities may once again be restored anew and new realities are challenged.

With this in mind, Mbiti's (1990, p. 17) revelation on the African philosophy of time becomes more salient: "actual time is therefore what is present and what is past. It moves 'backward' rather than 'forward'; and people set their minds, not on future things, but chiefly in what has taken place." However, what do Mbiti's critics have to say about his generalization of time in African philosophy based on East African Bantu languages? The Akan philosopher Kwame Gyekye (1995, p. 171) argues, in his seminal text *African Philosophical Thought*, that while Mbiti is perhaps right to say that "in African communities the reckoning of time is done in connection with events," he goes on to explain that: "It is not events that compose time; it is not events that generate the awareness of the existence of time. If that were the case, all talk about the future in Akan language and thought would be nonsense. Rather, it is time, conceived as objectively existing, within which such events and changes take place and which makes possible the dating of such events." Gyekye (1995, p. 172) concedes: "It may well be that there is no expression for the distant future and hence the concept of a distant future does not exist in the thought of East African peoples. However, my objection is to Mbiti's generalization of a concept derived from just two local African languages to the whole of the African peoples." Gyekye (1995, p. 70) finds an issue with Mbiti's assertion that, in African philosophy, there exists only two temporal dimensions and bases his disagreement by offering, among several other examples, the fact that the Akan conception of the supreme deity, Onyame, "dwells in an infinite time," which "gives the lie to the supposition, made by Mbiti, that Africans do not have a concept of a long or infinite future, for surely a concept of an eternal, infinite being implies a concept of an infinite time. If there were no concept of an infinite time the infinite being would be limited by time, and he would no longer be infinite."

He also concludes in his critique of Mbiti that if time were the key factor in understanding African philosophy, then arguably West Africans and East Africans must be different in most or all of their philosophical doctrines. This is a point he suggests is "probably not the case," while also arguing, "despite the fact that East African peoples, according to Mbiti, hold a two-dimensional conception of time and the Akans (and possibly other people in Africa) hold a three-dimensional conception of time, there are certainly some philosophical doctrines common to all of them" (Gyekye, 1995, p. 177).

Here we have two of Africa's greatest intellectuals from opposite sides of the continent disagreeing on the African philosophical notion of time. Gyekye, as you've read, is not accusing Mbiti of gross generalizations of African culture. In fact, he accuses Western philosophers of doing the opposite as it pertains to African cultures: "The exaggerated diversity of African cultures is, to my mind, a consequence of the European invention of Africa" (Gyekye, 1995, p. xxiv). Nevertheless, would then the late Gyekye, if asked to investigate and give commentary on AfroFuturism, not find an issue with the idea of an Afrofuture? Perhaps not. However, Gyekye (1995, p. 37) would clearly have issues with the notion of the future defined by Europeans juxtaposed with that defined by Africans as he states that his position on African philosophy is "suggested by a knowledge of the history of philosophy in other cultures of the world. Acquaintance with that history shows the difficulty of basing African philosophy purely on the Western tradition of philosophy."

This transcontinental debate between Mbiti and Gyekye is poignant for Africans in the Americas given the geographical locations of their philosophical paradigms. It is known that the Portuguese transported Africans from the Swahili coast and other regions of southeast Africa toward the Caribbean and Brazil. It is also known that the Portuguese, the British, and later Americans transported Africans from the so-called Gold Coast region and surrounding areas (which includes the land of the Akan) down toward southern Africa, particularly Angola, to the Caribbean, South America, and North America. African people brought their culture, customs, language, spirituality, and philosophies along with them, much of which still remains in witting and unwitting vestige as aforementioned or, more accurately, in a witting or unwitting continuity of the dynamism of African culture.

Using the scholarship of Mbiti and Gyekye, if we look toward some examples among the peoples of the three cultural-geographic zones between East Africa, West Africa, and the Afro-Americas, we find, naturally, much correlation as it relates to the philosophy of time. I will provide two examples. Mbiti (1990, p. 19) states, among people in Africa:

> The rising of the sun is an event which is recognized by the whole community . . . when a person says that he will meet another at sunrise, it does not matter whether the meeting place takes at 5 a.m. or 7 a.m., so long as it is during the general period of sunrise . . . for the people concerned, time is meaningful at the point of the event and not at the mathematical moment.

Mbiti (1990, p. 19) expresses this as he lambasts Europeans for considering Africans late and lazy (a concept also known as "African time"). Nevertheless, this concept is eerily similar to the concept of "colored people's time," or "CP time," in the Americas. "CP time" is a borrowed term itself and, of course, derogatory when applied externally. However, within group, it provides as much understanding as what Mbiti describes. In Geyeke's (1995, p. 70) case, one of the Akan terms for Onyame, "*tetekwaframua*" or "he who endures from ancient times and forever," has similarity with the African American proverb, "God is good all the time, and all the time God is good." For African Americans, to say "all the time" evokes just as much eternal and infinite regard for a deity as it does for time. These are but two examples of social activity and the use and dynamism of social idioms, respectively. However, such phenomena are also littered throughout the literature on AfroFuturism.

AfroFuturism is now understood as a diasporic African phenomenon (Womack, 2013). As mentioned before, revisiting or reimagining the past is a central theme in AfroFuturist literature. It is also arguably a central theme in both continental African (as you have read) and African American philosophy. Marimba Ani (1994, p. 60), African American scholar and author of the seminal text *Yurugu*, joins the debate as she states:

> Indeed, it is the European lineal conception that is one dimensional. This is one of Mbiti's most obvious errors. Past, present, and future are meaningful only as relationships in a lineal sequence, necessarily unidimensional. They do not represent three dimensions. In the African conception, sacred, cyclical time gives meaning to ordinary, lineal time. The circle/sphere adds dimension to the line as it envelops it. The sphere is multidimensional, and it is curved. Sacred time is not "past" because it is not part of a lineal construct. The ancestors live in the present, and the future lives in us. Sacred time is eternal and therefore it has the ability to join past, present, and future in one space of supreme valuation.

Ani's assertion of cyclical time is also championed by another Akan philosopher, Joseph Adjaye (1994, p. 73), as he critiques the philosophies of both Mbiti and Gyekye: "Akan time perceptions are at one and the same time linear and cyclical. . . . [I]t is clear that the Akan do not see this linear perception of history as conflicting with the view of time as being cyclical from the present to the future and back to the present, which becomes the past of tomorrow." Others, such as the philosopher John Parratt, critique Mbiti on his notion of linear time, in agreement with Ani's assertion of African time being cyclical. But Parratt (1977, p. 117) also gives some credence to Mbiti's notion of African philosophy of time being a focus on the past: "cyclic or periodic time is clearly grounded in the past, for it attempts to recreate, within present time, the benefits of a mythical or bygone time. It is thus backward-looking." Another philosopher, Newel S. Booth Jr. (1975, p. 81), relates, "I think Mbiti might have made it clearer than he does that it is not 'time' that moves into the past, but events."

This is in alignment with Parratt's notion of "backward-looking," as, of course, it is not time itself but the people who look to recreate or reimagine past events. However, in a critique more aligned with Gyekye and Ani, African philosopher Kibujjo Kalumba (2005, p. 11) contends, "if traditional

Africans believe that potential time extends infinitely into the future, then it is contradictory to say that they cannot conceive of a distant future beyond two years from now." One can argue that, though philosophical contentions vary, what many of these philosophers are arguing between cyclical notions of time and dimensional notions shares more or less the same ethos. They all seem to agree that African people recreate the past or past events in the present in ways that shape the so-called future. Interestingly, this is stated very poignantly by Greg Tate in the interview he did for Dery's (1994, p. 211) article "Black to the Future": "you can be backward-looking and forward-thinking at the same time."

If we follow the literary genealogy and now submit to the cyclical notion of time and events for African philosophy, then we find we are actually in good company with a corpus of AfroFuturist scholarship. Media theorist tobias c. van Veen (2016, p. 81, emphasis added), while dubiously referring to "Afrocentricity" as "Afrocentrism" (perhaps simply displaying his lack of understanding of the two), states, "'revisioning' the past is part of Afrocentrism's arsenal of historical reconstruction just as it is a strategy of AfroFuturism," later continuing, "at stake is a recovery of past *cycles of futurity*." In *Bodyminds Reimagined: (Dis)ability, Race, and Gender in Black Women's Speculative Fiction*, Black women's studies professor Sami Schalk (2018, p. 110, emphasis added), discussing the work of Walidah Imarisha and adrienne maree brown's *Octavia's Brood* (2015), relates, "imagination, representations, and the real world influence each other *cyclically*. As authors and activists imagine better futures . . . they open up for us new ways of being in the world that may not yet exist, but could." In Dery's (1994, p. 211, emphasis added) "Black to the Future," Greg Tate informs us, "ancient time and things to come coexist, which is simultaneously a very African, mythic, *cyclical* way of looking at time."

This last line on past and future coexisting is quite interesting as it draws us back to Ani's (1994, p. 60) notion that, "time is eternal and therefore it has the ability to join past, present, and future in one space of supreme valuation." Also in "Introduction: Future Texts," paradigmatic AfroFuturist Alondra Nelson (2002, p. 1) makes note of Ishmael Reed's version of this coexistence: "The 'anachronism' that is an element of much of Reed's work is used to express a unique perspective on time and tradition . . . 'putting disparate elements into the same time, making them run in the same time, together.'" She also makes a comparison with artist Fatimah Tuggar: "Tuggar employs digital photomontage to construct a collision of time, place, and culture in a manner reminiscent of Ishmael Reed's synchronicity" (Nelson, 2002, p. 8). This too could relate us back to Mbiti's (1990, p. 17) notion that to speak of any notion of future is to speak of events that "fall within the inevitable rhythm of nature," as one must look to the past to understand in the present day that the rhythm of nature brings about both an inevitable and cyclical future. It is Womack (2013, p. 153, emphasis added), in her seminal text *AfroFuturism*, that we should credit for illuminating the significance of the African philosophy of cyclical time in a number of ways:

> There's something about African American culture in particular that dictates that all cultural hallmarks and personal evolutions are recast in a historical lineage. Whether it's the concept of prophesy and speaking into the future or tropes of the past shadowing the present, whether by need or by narrative, many speak as if the *future, past, and present are one*. The threads that bind can be as divergent as a tersely worded tweet, musical chord, fiery speech, ancient Kemetic symbol, Bible quote, starry night, or string theory, but there's an idea that the power of thought, word, and the imagination can somehow transcend time. Just as the right words and actions can speak the future into existence, the same can recast the past, too. This *cyclical nature of time* and the contemplation of it all is a favorite theme and conversation point for AfroFuturists.

Much later in the text, Womack (2013, p. 154) quotes Rasheedah Philips of the nonprofit AfroFuturist Affair: "The main thing with me doing AfroFuturism is helping to look at time as a cycle and use that and the past for change. How can I use those cycles in a way that is more powerful for me to change my future?" Finally, Womack (2013, p. 158) quotes musician Shawn Wallace: "As African Americans and Blacks in the diaspora, we think cyclically . . . we view time cyclically. We usually return to something in the past to interpret it." Clearly, this should paint a detailed enough picture to understand that though we exist on borrowed terms, whether wittingly or unwittingly, African philosophy prevails. However, it is important to note, as aforementioned, that our cultural property is one that is often at risk of exploitation and being robbed of our agency due to the hegemonic nature of Eurocentricity. Perhaps much of our own cognitive hiatus (Mazama, 2018) contributes to this, as, for what we have seen, African philosophy is foundational to the genre. However, while we may have, in many ways, since defined what the term means for us, the absence of agency to coin our own terms for our own phenomena based on our own intellectual paradigms is evident. Further, as stated by AfroFuturist scholar and professor Isiah Lavender III (2011, p. 38), given the field of AfroFuturism, one very agreeable perspective becomes clear: "AfroFuturism is its own aesthetic register that 'merely' borrows from the [science-fiction] tradition . . . to explore Black life—past, present, and future." He further elucidates, "AfroFuturism is separate and distinct from [science fiction], not synonymous with it" (Lavender, 2011, p. 38).

With such revelation, what does this mean for the "borrowed term" AfroFuturism itself? We now know through Gyekye's critique of Mbiti that perhaps an Afrofuture is not completely in conflict with African philosophy. However, now we may find ourselves entrapped by the Eurocentric philosophy of temporal linearity. How do we reconcile this within our identities as AfroFuturists and our art as AfroFuturism? If we submit to the philosophical variant stemming from Adjaye, "it is clear that the Akan do not see this linear perception of history as conflicting with the view of time as being cyclical," can it serve as our answer? Or, in the spirit of Ani, do we revamp this genre with a new moniker more indicative of the heavy emphasis on cyclical time found throughout AfroFuturist literature and scholarship? Nevertheless, clearly, we see that AfroFuturism isn't unaffected by the Eurocentric masquerade, and to rescue it from the Eurocentric entrapments of such contentions as that of Dery and others, continually revisiting African and African diasporic paradigms becomes a necessity. As the Afrocentric scholar Mazama (2018, p. 35) has so eloquently informed us, "We must saturate ourselves with Africa so that [it] occupies our mental space as much as possible . . . constantly learning about African culture and history, in order to become even more familiar with our historical trajectories and worldview."

REFERENCES

Adjaye, J. K. (1994). *Time in the Black Experience*. Greenwood Press.
Ani, M. (1994). *Yurugu: An African-Centered Critique of European Cultural Thought and Behaviour*. Africa World Press.
Asante, M. K. (1998). *The Afrocentric Idea* (rev. and ex. Ed.). Temple University Press.
Booth, N. S. (1975). Time and Change in African Traditional Thought. *Journal of Religion in Africa*, 7(2), 81–91. https://doi.org/10.1163/157006675x00058
Connah, G. (2016). *African Civilizations: An Archaeological Perspective*. Cambridge University Press.

Dery, M. (1994). Black to the Future: Interviews with Samuel R. Delany, Greg Tate, and Tricia Rose. In M. Dery (Ed.), *Flame Wars: The Discourse of Cyberculture* (pp. 179–222). Duke University Press.

Floyd, S. A. (1995). *The Power of Black Music: Interpreting Its History from Africa to the United States*. Oxford University Press.

Gyekye, K. (1995). *African Philosophical Thought: The Akan Conceptual Scheme*. Temple University Press.

Kalumba, K. M. (2005). A New Analysis of Mbiti's "The Concept of Time." *Philosophia Africana*, 8(1), 11–19. https://doi.org/10.5840/philafricana20058111

Lavender, I. (2011). *Race in American Science Fiction*. Indiana University Press.

Mazama, A. (Ed.). (2003). *The Afrocentric Paradigm*. Africa World Press.

Mazama, A. (2018). Cognitive Hiatus and the White Validation Syndrome: An Afrocentric Analysis. In K. Langmia (Ed.), *Black/Africana Communication Theory* (pp. 25–38). Palgrave Macmillan. https://doi.org/10.1007/978-3-319-75447-5_3

Mbiti, J. S. (1990). *African Religions & Philosophy* (2nd ed). Heinemann. (Original work published 1969).

Nelson, A. (2002). Introduction: Future Texts. *Social Text*, 20(2), 1–15. https://doi.org/10.1215/01642472-20-2_71-1

Parratt, J. (1977). Time in Traditional African Thought. *Religion*, 7(2), 117–26. https://doi.org/10.1016/0048-721x(77)90019-7

Rose, M. (2014, November 20). *The Uncomfortable Origins of "AfroFuturism."* An und für sich. https://web.archive.org/save/https://itself.blog/2014/11/18/the-uncomfortable-origins-of-AfroFuturism/

Salm, S. (2000). Written and Oral Literature. In T. Falola (Ed.), *Africa* (Vol. 2, pp. 285–300). Carolina Academic Press.

Schalk, S. (2018). *Bodyminds Reimagined: (Dis)Ability, Race, and Gender in Black Women's Speculative Fiction*. Duke University Press.

Steinskog, E. (2018). *AfroFuturism and Black Sound Studies: Culture, Technology, and Things to Come*. Springer.

Womack, Y. (2013). *AfroFuturism: The World of Black Sci-Fi and Fantasy Culture*. Lawrence Hill Books.

8

AFROCENTRICITY'S AFROFUTURISM AND THE COUNT UP TO THE FUTURE

Molefi Kete Asante

A brilliant Yoruban philosopher has provided the world with a powerful gift of insight and relevance in the form of the Odu Ifa. This religious, spiritually inspired text of the Yoruba consists of sixteen primary chapters used by grand priests (Iyanifas and Babalawos) to decipher and disseminate divine messages for the purposes of guidance and inspiration.

Afrocentricity provides cartography that allows us to anticipate the future without shock because we are grounded in the markers from the past even while we consume the present. There is no riddle here; there is only the steady pace of a people creating, recreating, and procreating toward the future where social, political, cultural, and restorative justice, that is, *ma'at*, reigns supreme.

The great fear that grips racists and fascists who know that the deep past of *Homo sapiens* rests in Africa is that all the elements of the future are in Africa's womb; indeed, however they protest, they are also the children, though often wayward, of Africa itself. What is the irrational fear of immigrants in Europe, Australia, and America among those who have often dismissed the First Nations upon their own arrival? Terror is the belief that others like themselves will replace them. At one level, it is a cultural fear, and, at another, it is ontological, but it is justified as economic. At the core of irrational racism's hatred is a tightly held existential fear that creates automatic resistance. As Cronus Ampora sings of hope to hold back the forces of the evil magician, it becomes increasingly apparent that Africa *woke* with its visions firmly anchored to a speculative future grounded in the virtues of *ma'at*, which can bring relief. *Ma'at* was the original human vision of order, balance, harmony, righteousness, justice, truth, and reciprocity. When the earliest Nile valley philosophers contemplated the cycle of life and death, they saw that the eternal struggle on all levels was chaos. Thus, how to hold back chaos, to keep it at bay, and to protect the community from being engulfed in it were the aspects of the fundamental quest for the future, the beginning of an Afrocentric response to our realities and possibilities. They named this concept "*ma'at*" and represented it as a female with a feather in her hair. Maulana Karenga (2004) sees *ma'at* as the very door to the future of the world because it is the accumulation of wisdom, as a concept, from thousands of years of human thinking about how to overcome chaos. It sits, therefore, at the beginning of African thought as an organizing concept into the thickets of human futures.

Those nations and peoples who are willing to engage in the future will find rewards in **woke** Africa where the consciousness of being is discernible. For example, China has seen the future, and it is based upon the minerals of Africa. Zambia has seen the future, and it is being colonized by China. Airports are being built by China at a fast clip throughout the continent. The small country of Togo has a very functional airport recently erected by the Chinese. The facility is beautiful, extremely comfortable, and demonstrates the Chinese mode of hospitality with young, beautiful ladies welcoming you to the country, holding multicolored pieces of African fabric designed in Africa and produced in China.

Ascent

What is anticipated is for someone to claim that since Aimé Césaire, Leopold Senghor, Wole Soyinka, Chinua Achebe, Cheikh Anta Diop, W. E. B. Du Bois, Frantz Fanon, and Amilcar Cabral, a new cadre of thinkers has been discovered in faraway places in our imagination. We are heirs to Rita Dove, Octavia Butler, Toni Morrison, and Maya Angelou who sat in the highchairs at the table of

Richard Wright, Gwendolyn Brooks, James Baldwin, and Ralph Ellison. This conclusion is informed by an understanding of the many strands of this complex polyrhythmic dance to the future (R. Anderson & Jennings, 2014).

In fact, the work that has happened throughout the world in regard to Afrocentricity and Futurism, whether in conferences such as those held in Berlin, New York, London, Philadelphia, and Harare, has demonstrated agency as a part of AfroFuturism (Eshun, 2003). The moral aesthetics of Afrocentricity is that it situates Africans within the center of the African narratives of place, time, and space, hence demonstrating that the dislocation of Africans from the center of their own history is a form of intellectual and cultural terrorism that is a constant attack on the African's concept of self and the idea of time (Asante, 2014). There are some things that are not AfroFuturism and not Afrocentricity; there are avenues that challenge us to deconceptualize, degenerate, destroy, abandon decision, and therefore promote a future that is anti-African. These avenues must be avoided since the objective, at the very base, is to define parameters of a growing field of study that covers a sense of agency with an eye toward an ascendance toward the light of the future.

Intervolutions

To approach the future, one must be clear about meanings and intentions, and this means that there must be an unlocking, unfurling, and uncoiling of the future by understanding the past and the present. There is no "Black secret technology" as there is no "White or Asian secret technology"; Afrocentric scholars are all asserting agencies in an effort to create humans with the modality to listen to many voices and to hear a multiplicity of sounds. There are, however, thousands of mythologies bearing the weight of the future on imaginative shoulders. One does not see ankhs in hairstyles without recognizing that the ankh is the most famous of all personal African icons. Like *Sankofa*, it has become a part of the repertoire of many conscious Africans. In fact, the technological marvels of the pyramids of Nubia and Kemet, the *tekenu* of Waset, and the *hawelti* of Axum are monumental examples of the principle of permanence where a meme stretches from one era to another. The inclination, as Afrocentric AfroFuturists, is to assert what is known and to challenge what is not known in the realm of the technical because it is only in this action that revolution is made, that is, human possibilities are extended.

Johannesburg, New York, Paris, Dallas, Lagos, Shanghai, San Francisco, Berlin, Cape Town, and Barcelona are the same cities, but we all have different histories and cultures underneath the *faux* similarities of buildings, subway systems, parks, and stadia; indeed, the new religion is already sport, and the football or baseball stadium in an American city is a defining aspect of its contemporary narrative. People travel by plane to visit these monuments for creativity and leisure as they did in the pilgrimages to Oshogbo, Ile-Ife, and Lourdes. These new cathedrals of leisure are much like the old ones where people go to watch the sacramental offering of oneself or someone else's self to the cross. In the stadia, we see the defeat of our enemies and feel the presence of our own faux god.

Reynaldo Anderson, in my judgment, understands the coiled nature of AfroFuturism and has been able to trace its origin and mesh it with his understanding of Afrocentricity as a theory that supports the recentering of Africans from the marginalities inherent in many European constructions of reality and the future. In effect, he has uncoiled Mark Dery's use of the term "AfroFuturism" by showing its connection to Afrocentricity (Black Scholar, 2018). Like James Stewart (1976; 2004), Abdul Alkalimat and Kate Williams (2001), and Kodwo Eshun (2003), Anderson has advanced the attachment of technology to the imagination in a chrono-political and chrono-historical manner that allows for the full unfurling of AfroFuturism as a speculative intervention that could never have happened without Afrocentricity because it was the concept of African agency that allowed us to think about the future on African terms.

Culture

All serious discourses around AfroFuturism must be based on the philosophical soil of African culture; otherwise, there can be no real African renaissance nor any useful future. Anderson has become one of the leading voices announcing the agency of African people in the assertion of the future. What this means is that you cannot have a future for Africans if Africans no longer exist. In *AfroFuturism 2.0: The Rise of Astro-Blackness*, Anderson and Charles E. Jones (2016) stake out a new periphery in the field of Futurism.

In response to a question about the difference between Black speculative arts and AfroFuturism, Anderson (2016, p. 231) says:

Unveiling Visions: The Alchemy of the Black Imagination . . . established its [the Black speculative arts movement's] existence. Black speculative art is a creative, aesthetic practice that integrates African diasporic or African metaphysics with science or technology and seeks to interpret, engage, design, or alter reality for the re-imagination of the past, the contested present, and as a catalyst for the future. Moreover, this manifesto explores the question, "What is the responsibility of the Black artist in the 21st century?"

The one quarrelsome part of Dery's (1994a, p. 182) notion of "AfroFuturism" that is difficult to agree with is when he says that "concepts and constructs of time have always been central to the historical subjugation of Black lives." Our history is not simply four or five hundred years of resistance to the imperial domination of White racism, which if we speak of relics, is a relic that is still being shelved for a different world. We are and have been free human beings, resisting and refusing domination from the very beginning of our encounters with Arabs and Europeans. It is important to consistently reiterate that European plunderers did not take slaves out of Africa but rather human beings who were kidnapped, who became prisoners of war and were later subjugated through a system of enslavement throughout the diaspora.

Thus, it is necessary to bank this philosophy deep in the imaginative soil of Africa. Africans are the world, and Africans are the future of this contemporary civilization should it continue without the existential threat posed by ruthless laissez-faire capitalism or ruthless social capitalism. The future may be, despite the wailing wolf of liberalism, a radical social democracy in most of the world. There are areas of the world where the lingering illnesses of the colonial inheritances of the past two centuries will have to be stamped out completely by technological transformation. They can no longer hang on to their comfort pillows of racism, sexism, patriarchy, and classism (Nelson, 2002; Stewart, 2004). AfroFuturism, through a long cultural lens, offers hope that an assertion of *ma'at*ic culture might show us how to heal the wounds of a broken compact with each other.

One could declare that the multiculturalism of the West and the ethnopluralism of the past are completely bankrupt, but the episodic eruption of Trumpian demagoguery, as explained in my book *The American Demagogue: Donald Trump in the Presidency of the United States of America* (Asante, 2018), convinced me that these ideas are not bankrupt and, so long as declared vanquished, will not be recognized by their insidious will to worm their way into the imagination of the future. Therefore, as vigilant as society may be in protecting the present, humanity must be equally attentive to the memes that constitute the groundwork for a turbulent future. Racism, anti-Semitism, sexism, homophobia, and anti-immigrant reactions are of the same woven fabric that conceals underneath, in the subterranean arena, the tattered clothes of impoverished minds.

Vile currents of economic injustice still have the possibility of stealing our future, that is, accelerating the bad tendencies of geo-hegemonic domination that we see in the present. The example of the Congo War, the biggest clash over resources in our generation, is a telling point. In every aspect, this war is more prophetic than the Afghan War and the Syrian War or the Saudi-Yemen War because the Congo War is an international war to control the resources of the future. The others are bound up in ideological and religious struggles to control narratives of the past, while the Congo War is preeminently about the future.

There is a boldness to Anderson's formulation of a radical AfroFuturism that challenges the geo-racial, self-absorbed legion of devourers of their own children. If a society cannot protect its own children from the monstrous irrationalities of fascism, racism, and masochistic patriarchy, it is bound to destroy its own future. Every radical movement must begin with the decisive break with the past and the enthroning of a provocative agency that asserts a firmness that postmodernism rejects. Just as Africans rise from the ashes of five hundred years of European colonization and enslavement to define a reality based on the memes of classical Africa, we are told that this is a nonconditional for postmodernism. Then one must reject this idea that fluidity trumps location from a centered position within a historical narrative. Africans cannot be future oriented if Africans cannot conceive of themselves as subjects and agents responsible for freedom. To be human is to be able to create, but this does not constitute *goodness* in the sense that one is above others. To be human is goodness enough, as the Akan people say in Ghana, that is, to be good is to be human, and to be human is to be good.

Truth Telling

How will the children know that they are not gods if the fathers falsely promote fratricidal wars where only the survivors operate as tellers of narratives? And if they think they are gods, then they are truly being set up for utter death because the future quite certainly will rob them of that delusion. A question that haunts thoughts of the future, especially in the case of African people exerting and asserting agency, is, Who speaks for the dead, the glorious dead, whose sacrifices on the altars of manic oppression trail off into faint memories? Advanced Western civilization as constructed and promoted by demagogues on the illusions of a world free of people who have color represents a dangerous set of ideologies. These false promises could stunt the ethical, social, and cultural health of any people who propagate the values of this construction. In our own country, the cult of nationalism, literally in Donald Trump's mind, White nationalism, is a phenomenon used for political domination over the masses of people who feel powerless in their own societies. We must be done with the Neanderthalian notion of society based on fear, moral weakness, and dishonesty.

African people are quickly rejoining a history that has been disjointed, ripped, and torn to shreds by the brutal hands of colonialism and enslavement in order to write a future free of fear and threats. We cannot enter the future on the wagons of victimhood, hounded by the dogs of marginality, with our minds centered only on the past; we are not beggar people, and out of the thorns and thickets of the past, we must pick the fragrant flowers that enlightened and invigorated those Futurists who created the cultural, technological, and ethical platform upon which we build today.

There is no equal historical time, and there will not be any equal future time. As Aunt Aurelia said, when in her dementia, she had traveled far into the future and returned to be with me in conversation. "I have been there to see the other side. You know those people over there; you know out there are the same people as the ones who are here. There is bad there, and there is good there, just like here and now: there is good, and there is bad."

Speculation

Waiting for the future is not possible because it will come anyway. When we say "the future" it is almost like we know precisely and exactly when that will be. If we wait for it, when will we see it, and what will it look like if it does not look like us? What is the future if we are not in it? How can we determine what the future will contain?

There are, to be sure, conditions for transitions; but even then, one cannot be sure that people will be absolutely cognizant of either those conditions or the time of the transition to the future. Just like in the old days and in the present, the new society, even the radical Afrofuture, will have the potential for good actions or bad actions. In every case, human beings will have to intervene, and much of the intervention will be as speculation in the arts, comics, aesthetics, physicality, science, and drone technology, just to name a few areas where there will be changes.

Speculation is different from hope, but it is not prophecy either; it is a focused attempt to qualify and quantify the future based on what we know today. The source of speculation is our current contemplation of the past augmented by our knowledge of mythology, ethics, technology, and aesthetics. This necessary combination for speculation could be referred to as "meta" to indicate that it is beyond the theological idea of hope. "Meta" engages us at the individual and collective levels. Individuals are surely agents of change if they are conscious of the meta combination. A collective—as in a group, community, synagogue, church, mosque, school, club, or corporation—may engage meta in order to effect change.

One of the burdens of any future, Afrofuture or any other type of future, is the hefty existential question, Will humans be around to witness the future? If there are no *Homo sapiens* to witness the future, will it exist? We are confronted with numerous existential threats, some human-made and some naturally waiting in the future, that may intervene with human existence. Scientific estimates suggests that 99 percent of all the species that have lived on the Earth since its origin 5 billion years ago are no longer here. They are gone forever. What gives humans the idea that we will survive and that the future will see us flourish even when the level of risk is greater today than it has ever been? I am not so sure as others are that we will be saved by our inventive technology or our moral compass; it may very well be the cause of our disappearance since humans already have enough nuclear bombs to utterly destroy, in the biblical sense, every living creature on the Earth. Crazy, power-driven humans with macho spirits seeking to test their testosterone-fueled wills may bring us not just to the brink but across the threshold to human elimination as a species.

There are many threats that are not considered because thinking about them reduces our chance to experience the possibilities of a future. The Earth, our planet, exists in a shooting arena where it is believed gamma rays, at least once, obliterated life on Earth 400 million years ago! Who is to say what time it is now? As recent as 2008, there was a burst of gamma rays that hit the Earth; such rays can paralyze the entire ecosystem and bring about an end to everything we know.

Universe

The universe is estimated to be 15 billion years old. The Earth is 5 billion years old. Hominins started appearing around 7 million years ago. *Homo sapiens* first appeared about three hundred thousand years ago. Our species has not been here a long time, and there is no guarantee that we will be here another three hundred thousand years.

Consider that our entire solar system orbits a black hole twenty-seven thousand light-years away. Black holes are made by the collapse of stars. If our sun, which is a star, collapses, then it would swallow everything; it would be the end of time. Of course, the eventuality of a star collapsing does not have to be our sun; it could be a wandering black hole, like the one observed in 2001 moving through the universe as a remnant left over from a supernova. These events are totally unpredictable and do not appear on any human's time scale.

More immediate may be the end of the future from an asteroid, like the ten-kilometer one that wiped out 65 percent of life 65 million years ago and killed all the dinosaurs that had lived on the Earth for 75 million years. This is precisely why scientists now track asteroids, but a greater danger may even be comets because they are larger than asteroids and travel twice the speed.

As dangerous as threats from space are, they are not the most dangerous, although it is true that they can pose an end to human life. Scientists actually know that some of the most significant threats to the future are homegrown from our own planet.

The volcanic threat, with danger emerging from the interior of the Earth, may be the most extreme danger humans face. Volcanoes can appear in many places, and we know the visible ones that give us signals of their activities, but a massive volcanic explosion is the one threat that nearly destroyed *Homo sapiens* about seventy-five thousand years ago. The explosion in Sumatra's Mount Toba caused the Earth to change, and our ancestors in Africa felt the Earth grow cooler because it froze at the equator and caused a mighty volcanic ice storm.

Most Earth scientists predict that there will be an explosion in Wyoming at Yellowstone, a constantly active volcano that is forty miles wide, eighty long, and two miles deep into the Earth, containing one of the largest magma beds in the world. Like most volcanoes, Yellowstone has no predictable cycle, but it erupted six hundred thousand years ago, before *Homo sapiens* appeared on the Earth.

The future could also be endangered, or, at least, hostile extraterrestrial forces could endanger *Homo sapiens*. They could come from our solar system or one of the 100 billion stars in our galaxy, the Milky Way, not to mention others that exist in the universe. Their technologies may be far superior to ours. Of course, if we are the only intelligent life in the universe, then there may be no threats, but this is highly unlikely. Such beings, if they exist, may be extremely hostile and aggressive, such as those large ships of White men approaching the Arawaks in the Caribbean, and three generations later, not one Arawak was left.

Perhaps closer to us as threats to our existential reality are microbes, viruses, and bacteria that have proven to be more hostile than any threat so far to humanity. Our scientists are always looking out for pandemics, like COVID-19, Ebola, SARS, HIV, and the flu. Humans have not forgotten that the flu wiped out 80 million people at the top of the twentieth century. "World War I claimed an estimated 16 million lives. The influenza epidemic that swept the world in 1918 killed an estimated 50 million people. One fifth of the world's population was attacked by this deadly virus. Within months, it had killed more people than any other illness in recorded history" (National Archives, n.d.). The 1918 epidemic killed more people than the first international European war. In fact, it was called the Spanish flu, and it far exceeded the war's death toll. Flu vaccines have been used to prevent the spread of the flu, but nothing seems to wipe it out. In fact, viruses abound that can replicate patterns using our own cells. Now that we have some experience with COVID-19 in this contemporary era, we understand that our futures are complicated by its aggressive tendencies to deny humans the right to exist.

Protecting ourselves from our own destructive tendencies that have caused humans to create nuclear bombs that have the potential, like COVID, to also destroy the human future is necessary. I visited Hiroshima and went to the museum dedicated to the American attack on Japan and came away shaking with awe at the fact that supposedly reasonable humans went so crazy that they dropped atomic bombs on Japanese cities. It unleashed a crime of inhuman proportions; it is like the difference between throwing stones and using machine guns.

Possibility

It is essential that AfroFuturists indicate what future we propose and not leave speculation to those who have screwed up the atmosphere, the water, and the soil by advancing predatory capitalist schemes that have changed the climate of the world and endangered our present and our future (Ferreira, 2013; Karenga, 2011). It is unwise to wait for some mad politician or mad scientist to assume the authority to hold the future hostage. Humanity must all reject the disquiet that can erupt in a world that does not imagine a future because someone or a collective of people seek to steal it. In the United States, it is estimated that Trump dismantled nearly 80 percent of the progressive agenda rules, enacted provisions, and regulations set in motion during Barack Obama's eight-year presidency. Was this the unbearable truth of a latent racism within the society? (Tal, n.d.). Trump's blitz took down laws and regulations protecting health care, water purity, natural habitats for animals, air quality, food-production quality, and gun safety. Those who followed him down this path took the ostrich's position despite the inevitability of danger to human beings.

Black or African cultural expressions—especially with a strong ethical base, as in Charles Fuller's plays about sexual assault in the US military or Okwui Okpokwasili's emphasis on how the Western world sights African bodies, experiences, contemporary interactions, and futures—have continued to evolve. I speculate that these issues and other issues of color, gender, class, and sexual orientation will be rolled into the African political imagination in ways that will produce more Hatshepsut-like women leaders in Ethiopia and Liberia and political cabinets that are 50 percent female in Ethiopia, Rwanda, and South Africa. In a way, Okpokwasili has put the Black capital that is spoken of in AfroFuturistic circles on stage.

It is impossible to dream of a future or *the* future without imagination, and in so many of us, imperial capitalism and centralized statism have murdered the imagination. The trauma brought about by the death of imagination blurs the consciousness of the future and imprisons us in the unacceptable presence, where we battle the demons that occupy the highest political, social, and economic spaces. Our materialism has run over to our acceptance of the ownership of all forms of property, even to the creation of other people as property to be owned, controlled, and thrown away when we no longer can find a use for them.

Yet we are propositioned, as any people are positioned, to tackle the cultural, intellectual, gender, and ideological issues of the future (Barr 2008; Hendrix et. al, l984; Stewart, 1976; Womack 2013). Our proposition as Black people arrives on the backs of our ancestors who squatted in the cotton fields to gain a little rest after hoeing all day. I am the child of the hoers who chopped cotton in the thickest jungles of the American South, hitting the Earth as they chopped with the hoe as a definitive statement that we were here to live. This was the empire that the Whites created in the Americas and the Caribbean. We were and are till this day victims of economic, political, spiritual, and ethical warfare as pawns in the old cycle of *Homo sapiens*-Neanderthalian antagonisms where the soul of the time, the *geist*, is conflicted with itself because we are all *more* human and less *unhuman* as we become more harmonious with each other.

Encounter

Boaventura de Sousa Santos speaks of the end of the cognitive empire. Uncertain of a cognitive empire, it is possible that there have been some political states here and there that have expressed their willingness to be realms of cognition. Even Trump wrapped himself up in the theme of his great brainpower. Of course, his irrationality was on display for all to see.

It seems that de Sousa Santos is convinced that Europe has reached a point of which there is less efficacy and efficiency in its projection of superior claims, while numerous authors of the Afrocentric school predicted this fact long ago. Cheikh Anta Diop (1976), Ana Monteiro Ferreira (2013), Ibram X. Kendi (2017), Théophile Obenga (2004), and Michael Tillotson (2013), for example, are worth mentioning. Therefore, de Sousa Santos's genius comes in pointing to the "south" for possible ways to revive Europe's drive. This may not be about assisting or strengthening the south, but rather about the reinvigorating of the north by appropriating some of the strengths of those who have resisted racism, imperialism, ruthless capitalism, and planned economies with equal fervor.

It is a victory of sorts to have a European writer admit the failure of Europe to usher in a peace based on justice. There is bankruptcy in a culture that can only think of, as Tillotson would say, ways of reducing the agency of those considered different by virtue of color, creed, gender, or culture. There is, however, also insatiable greed in the need to rob the south of its resilience against aggression and use that strength to steel Europe against the inevitable attacks on the defining structures of domination.

There is no question in my mind that the Tasmanians of Australia have a lot to teach the Whites who invaded their land and then claimed that "Australia is a young country" when in fact the Blacks have been in that place for fifty thousand years. What is it that forces the person who has no shame to summon the will to look the truth in the eyes and then lie with impunity? Are the lies of Trump any different than the lies of the opinion makers, church leaders, corporation elites, and generals regarding the origin of civilization in Australia?

But it is no different than South Africa where the Whites made up a narrative of power for occupation of someone else's land by saying that the Whites came to the country about the same time as they met the Blacks migrating from the north. This was always a lie, and it was told with such regularity—written in the texts and preached from the pulpits—that Whites believed it, and some Blacks had begun to believe it before they controlled the government. Now with researchers free to explore and view the historical realities of South Africa, they have had to write a different story. Africans occupied the entire continent for thousands of years before the coming of the Whites in the seventeenth century. Why would Africans leave an entire region untouched in their migration from the east and the south? Why would Africans leave southeast and southern Africa empty of humanity until Jan van Riebeeck came in 1652?

We are condemned to find our way through the thickets of time to arrive at the savannas of a new future. African nations are entangled in bilateral relationships that deny them the possibility of continental unity. I decry the fact that there is no political or ideological engine driving the African train; there are only individual and nationalistic desires for advantage.

If it is true, as I believe the record shows, that Zambia received billions from China and cannot pay its annual repayment fee, then there is trouble looming for the African future, despite all progressive advances of AfroFuturism. Why would Zambia make such a deal without some cooperative relationship with another African nation? No small African economies can withstand the power of the United States, China, the United Kingdom, or Germany. They are most vulnerable to the assaults on their economies because of the limited nature of their Afrocentric consciousness; they fail to see that what is in the best interest of continental unity is in their best interest. Afrocentricity is a guide for all types of Futuristic thinking (King, 1992; Little et al., 2001). One asks, as several African scholars questioned in 2020, Did Ghana's government sell the W. E. B. Du Bois Memorial Centre for Pan African Culture to Americans? The question is more important in many ways than the answer because the question poses issues of weakness, that is, economic and visionary weaknesses, that endangers AfroFuturism.

Image

Imagery is ahead of action because societies are stuck with bureaucracies of crass unimaginative types who do not see that actions are possible to make better futures. People are called visionaries as if they can see farther than others when actually what they are able to do is to overcome the obstacles that confront their imaginations. They have a particular kind of courage that allows them to manifest their images in concrete ways. The founders of giant African industries like Dangote, Adenuga, and Motsepe are called visionaries, but it may be that they had a particularly advantageous perch from which to view the coming era. There are many such stories. I can cite what happened to M. K. O. Abiola and William R. Spivey, two individual Africans who happened to be in the proper place when inquiries about the future came to them, and they both responded positively.

Who is to define what imagination is Futuristic in African senses? How can the best Afrofutures be ensured? What models do we have in the incubators at this time? What levers of power can be exploited at this time? To experience the creation of futures by the very theories that we hold about our social reality, Africa cannot have a future that is African without African assertions, without African agency. Afrocentricity remains the dominant philosophical paradigm to advance the role of African agency, urging Africans to interrogate our own histories, experiences, and possibilities (Everett, 2002). Africans can look only to European and Asian philosophers if they do not know their own. If I know my own, I can explore others as well, thus giving me a heads-up on what to expect from the futures proposed by others (Asante, 2014). Without that advantage, Black people are locked in a closet without lights and without a key to open the door to freedom and remain unable to assert themselves.

It has been observed that whatever theories we have about astronomy do not affect the stars, the moon, or the planets. However, social scientists often theorize, and their theories become the world we live in. As AfroFuturists, we may not have the capacity to affect everything that will happen in the future, but we can and we do set the platform from which the divers into the deep space of our imagination can leap.

Of course, as we have done in questions of culture, we may have to rethink the idea of ethno-futures or plural futures when we mean Afrofutures, Sinofutures, Gulf futures, etc., while leaving Europe. I no longer live in a world where Europe is kept out of the circle as if it is above the circle of ethnicities. Europe is itself full of ethnicities. It is like speaking of multiculturalism without including Europeans, or it is like speaking of Indigenous people without thinking that all people, who are not invaders, are Indigenous. As an Afrocentrist, I like Europe inside the circle but never above it. I like European cultures to be considered alongside other cultures but never outside of human culture. In the past, Europe has put itself outside of human culture by imposing itself as universal. All impositions must be challenged as the first line of ethical value. This is not just a personal cachet, but one that is applicable to all forms of bilateral and collective interactions.

Here is the gist of this remark: AfroFuturism removes European patriarchal, masculinist, militaristic, and toxic racism from our future. We urge, of course, our European friends to do the same so that we bring forth into the world a kind of *ma'atic* spirit that pursues peace, harmony, consensus, justice, and reciprocity. What we preserve for the future are the best ideals of ourselves; there is no interest on the part of Afrocentrists or AfroFuturists to preserve into the future the worst examples of our own histories. Like Butler (1988) has demonstrated in order for us to face the future, we must, of course, turn to the past. To be sure, there will be clashes, debates, discourse provocations, and ethnic tensions in the future as there are now in the present because all humans will not be engaged in this process of projected preservation of the best elements. There will be those who will take a Trumpian attitude that they should be only for themselves.

There is a real danger that nationalism can destroy the possibility of coop-erative futures. Afrocentrists do not want a racist future of any color, and we detest those who seek to intrude into our speculative future with dangerous imaginations of the obliteration of those with whom they disagree. Therefore, one must reject all terms of *subalternity, postcolonialism,* and *thirdness* as Afrocentrists have, over the last decades, rejected *culturally deprived, under-privileged minorities* and *marginality.*

Toward AfroFuturism

AfroFuturism must mean that people of African descent can project the best ideals and values of a multiplicity of mythological-historical narratives into a speculative space to create a techno-aesthetic ethic based on the best qualities of African people. Such a conception is different from what Dery (1994b) may have intended in his edited book *Flame Wars: The Discourse of Cyberculture.* In fact, Dery's "Black to the Future" (1994a) famously inter-viewed Sam Delany, Greg Tate, and Tricia Rose, all on the cutting edge of the new Black thought of the 1990s. There can be no Afrofuture without an assertion of African agency, the fundamental element in Afrocentricity. Claiming oneself as an agent of history is the first step to projecting oneself as having something worthy for the future. When Georg Wilhelm Friedrich Hegel wrote, in 1827, that "Africa was no part of history," he was expressing his racism as a part of his concept of Africans as having no agency for his-torical consciousness. One of the reasons that Afrocentricity has threatened the patriarchy more than many other ideologies is because it asserts African agency by insisting that there is nothing more critical for African people than their own historical experiences. Without those narratives being centered in projections, African people are nothing more than marginal to other futures.

Time is important because of the cosmic and terrestrial activities that exist within certain chronotopes. Human activity has no impact on the cosmic activities that are constant in the universe. Even if all humans disappear, it would mean very little to the cosmos that has been here 15 billion years to our mere three hundred thousand as *Homo sapiens.* Even the Earth, our terra firma, is 5 billion years old and would hardly miss us if we should disappear. Perhaps it would revert to a purer atmosphere, with less destruction of the coral reefs, and less melting of the snows in the north and south poles.

Neither terminology nor chronology can be dismissed in the Afrofuture as I understand it. There is no transatlantic slave trade, and there is no trans-Sahara slave trade; there is a European slave trade and an Arab slave trade, both loaded with historical time and future projections. In the interest of clarity, the platform that we are preparing for a speculative future based on the realities of history must use language that frees us from the past totalitar-ian constructs of White racial domination. Therefore, I have often warned that Africans can be easily trapped in the language of our captivity. There is no "Black Atlantic" because this trope has neither practical nor philosophical possibilities for our freedom or our future. To divorce Africans living in the United States and the United Kingdom from Africans on the continent is to criminalize families, genealogies, and ancestors and to desacralize common experiences at the hands of enslavers and colonizers.

Modern technology has allowed people to more effectively transcend challenges related to time and distance. Some think it is only a matter of time, not of hardware or software, but of active time, before we are able to advance ourselves. The future envisions not thinking machines but autom-atons or humanoids that will be hominin in every respect except sexual reproduction. They will, of course, be programmed to reproduce themselves. All humanoids will disappoint us; they will come looking like us, but they will always be binary creatures. If we should make it as humanoids into the future, human beings will have independent ways of dealing with ambiguity and hypothetical situations.

It is true that, when one thinks they are describing thought when they are actually describing the processes of selecting and tabulating data, they are really silencing thought because selection is not choice in the sense of reasoned thought. Thinking and writing means that something is allowed to reveal itself after reflection. Now, what this means is that we cannot allow ourselves to be deluded by technology or the technical, and we should not fool ourselves into believing that we will make the rules for the future.

Any periodization of time is a part of the false history of the world. When we say precolonial and postcolonial or premodern, modern, and postmodern, we are really expressing a political vision that negates African agency and distorts time. I reject terms like *precolonial, postcolonial*, and *postmodern* because they are handed to us like universal realities when, in fact, they are nothing more than European particularities. They make no sense to me. One cannot connect one's future to a European universalism that allows neither space nor time for Africa or Asia. We are not merely linked to dislocation from Europe or alienation from Europe, as if Europe is the central pole; we are disengaged from Africa, and that is why we are constantly producing intellectuals such as Paul Gilroy or Stuart Hall or Henry Louis Gates, for example. They are in crisis about the future because they have reached for a Europe that seeks to make them in its own image. Afrocentrists believe it is possible to have many futures and that the legitimacy of the African future is just as valid as any other.

How relevant is a periodization that privileges patriarchy and White racial domination? (Asante, 2007). Is this something of an obsession with the modern Western world? Do these periods work for Africans and Asians? What is the diachronic understanding of the future? What was the language of the future in African languages? As you can see, I have more questions than I have answers. For Marx, prehistory is anything in the West that preceded the socialist revolution that was predicted by him, that is, to say, prophesied. There is only gloom and fog before the opening of the revolution, and then when Afrocentricity is realized by a critical mass, history begins again. The trauma of the imagination is the death of dreams and the impossibility of seeing yourself in the future. Imperial capitalism and centralized statism both destroy the future and hand us the dirty rags of the impoverishment of our souls. Our experiences should have propositioned us for a future bursting with freedom (Conyers & McKnight, 2005).

I am not looking for a future without identities because such a world is impossible regardless of how much Western society seeks to wipe out those who are different. Pittsburgh's murder of Jews at Squirrel Hill is not dissimilar from all the hate-filled killings that come with the despising of human beings. Afrocentricity seeks to recenter Africans in the midst of our own narratives, not rewrite the narratives of Europe or Asia in our image. I see the future through the eyes of the Yoruba philosophers who proclaimed "*K'a wò'wajú ojo lo titi*" (Let us give continuous attention to the future).

REFERENCES

Alkalimat, A., & Williams, K. (2001). Social Capital and Cyberpower in the African American Community. In Dave Eagle et al. (Eds.), *Community Informatics: Shaping Computer-Mediated Social Networks* (pp. 177–204). Routledge.

Anderson, R. (2016). AfroFuturism 2.0 & the Black Speculative Arts Movement: Notes on a Manifesto. *Obsidian*, 42(1–2), 228–36.

Anderson, R., & Jennings, J. (2014). AfroFuturism: The Digital Turn and the Visual Art of Kanye West. In J. Bailey (Ed.), *The Cultural Impact of Kanye West* (pp. 29–44). Palgrave.

Anderson, R., & Jones, C. E. (2016). Introduction: The Rise of Astro-Blackness. In R. Anderson & C. E. Jones (Eds.), *Afrofuturism 2.0: The Rise of Astro-Blackness* (pp. vii–xviii). Lexington.

Asante, M. K. (2007). *The Painful Demise of Eurocentrism*. Africa World Press.

Asante, M. K. (2014). *Facing South to Africa: Essays toward an Afrocentric Orientation*. Lexington.

Asante, M. K. (2018). *The American Demagogue: Donald Trump in the Presidency of the United States of America*. Universal Write Publications.

Barr, M. S. (2008). *Afro-Future Females: Black Writers Chart Science Fiction's Newest New-Wave Trajectory*. Ohio State University Press.

Black Scholar. (2018, March 13). *On Black Panther, Afrofuturism, and Astroblackness: A Conversation with Reynaldo Anderson*. https://www.theblackscholar.org/on-black-panther-afrofuturism-and-astroblackness-a-conversation-with-reynaldo-anderson/

Butler, O. E. (1988). *Kindred*. Beacon. (Original work published 1979).

Conyers, J., & McKnight, E. (2005). African-Centricity and Techno-Scientific Education: A Twenty-First Century Polemic. *International Journal of Africana Studies: Journal of the National Council for Black Studies, 11*, 122–31.

Dery, M. (1994a). Black to the Future: Interviews with Samuel R. Delany, Greg Tate, and Tricia Rose. In M. Dery (Ed.), *Flame Wars: The Discourse of Cyberculture* (pp. 179–222). Duke University Press.

Dery, M. (Ed.). (1994b). *Flame Wars: The Discourse of Cyberculture*. Duke University Press.

Diop, C. A. (1976). *L'antiquité africaine par l'image*. Université de Dakar.

Eshun, K. (2003). Further Considerations of AfroFuturism. *CR: The New Centennial Review, 3*(2), 287–302.

Everett, A. (2002). "The Revolution Will Be Digitized: Afrocentricity and the Digital Public Sphere. *Social Text, 20*(2), 125–46.

Ferreira, A. M. (2013). *The Demise of the Inhuman*. SUNY Press.

Hendrix, M., Bracy, J. H., Davis, J. A., & Herron, W. M. (1984). Computers and Black Studies: Toward the Cognitive Revolution. *Journal of Negro Education, 53*(3), 341–50.

Karenga, M. (2004). *Maat: The Moral Ideal in Ancient Egypt. A Study in Classical African Ethics*. Routledge.

Kendi, I. X. (2017, February 22). A History of Race and Racism in America, in 24 Chapters. *New York Times*. https://www.nytimes.com/2017/02/22/books/review/a-history-of-race-and-racism-in-america-in-24-chapters.html

Karenga, M. (2011). *Introduction to Black Studies*. University of Sankore Press.

King, W. M. (1992). The Importance of Black Studies for Science and Technology Policy. *Phylon, 49*(1–2), 23–32.

Little, W. A., Leonard, C., & Crosby, E. (2001). Black Studies and Africana Studies Curriculum Model in the United States [Pamphlet]. In N. Norment (Ed.), *The African American Studies Reader* (p. 691–712). Carolina Academic Press. (Original work published 1981).

National Archives and Records Administration. (n.d.). *The Deadly Virus: The Influenza Epidemic of 1918*. https://www.archives.gov/exhibits/influenza-epidemic/

Nelson, A. (2002). Introduction: Future Texts. *Social Text, 20*(2), 1–15.

Obenga, T. (2004). Egypt: Ancient History of African Philosophy. In K. Wiredu (Ed.), *A Companion to African Philosophy* (pp. 31–49). Blackwell.

Stewart, J. B. (1976). Black Studies and Black People in the Future. *Black Books Bulletin*, 4(2), 20–25.

Stewart, J. B. (2004). Science, Technology, and Liberation: Foundations for a Black/Africana-Science Technology and Society (STS) Partnership. In J. B. Stewart (Ed.), *Flight: In Search of Vision* (pp. 277–304). Africa World Press.

Tal, K. (n.d.). *The Unbearable Whiteness of Being: African American Critical Theory and Cyberculture*. Kali Tal, PhD. Retrieved March 21, 2023, from https://kalital.com/the-unbearable-whiteness-of-being-african-american-critical-theory-and-cybercultur/

Tillotson, M. (2013). *Invisible Jim Crow*. Africa World Press.

Womack, Y. (2013). *AfroFuturism: The World of Black Sci-Fi and Fantasy Culture*. Chicago Review Press.

9

AFRICAN DIASPORIC CONSCIOUSNESS
The Historical and Psychological
Impact of the Haitian Revolution

Ifetayo M. Flannery

Citizen,

You are not ignorant that there exist in the United States of America, several hundred thousand individuals of African blood, who, on account of the dark hue of their complexions, are objects of all the prejudice and prepossession that can arise from difference in colour. . . . I have replied in a favourable manner, explaining all the advantages that our constitution has taken care to assure to those of our brothers who come from other parts of the globe and establish themselves among us. . . . Already have we seen arrive in our ports, several of these children of Africa, who have come from the United States, and have fixed themselves here . . . happy at being delivered from the degrading yoke of prejudice.

—PRESIDENT BOYER OF HAYTI, "Instructions to the Citizen," 1824

The triumph of Haiti securing their freedom from the institution of European slavery was felt as a triumph for African people throughout the diaspora. This relatively small island generated a wave of dialogue across the diaspora and particularly among African Americans. African Americans had already been in a constant siege against enslavement and oppression in America through a series of actions and reactions for over a century. The knowledge of Haiti's revolution and open-border policy to any Africans willing to come and settle as citizens spurred organizing efforts and interest in African American communities. Prior to the revolution, African Americans, particularly in the port cities of Boston, New York, Baltimore, and Philadelphia, had an established circuit of information and contact with Haiti by way of African American sailors, enslaved Africans who arrived with their masters during the revolution, and wealthy independent African Americans who visited and worked abroad in trade and mercantilism (Bolster, 1997). In fact, sailors of African descent constituted almost 20 percent of seamen, including Africans who had escaped slavery as "runaways." These sailors "were well traveled and multilingual—a skill useful for fostering links between otherwise discrete black communities" (Bolster, 1997, p. 40). Haiti's emigration project represented an enormous power and potential for relationships between African diasporic communities. The significance of this intradiasporic initiative has perhaps been undervalued or underresearched because it implies such a potent self-determining capacity through international connections that enslaved or oppressed groups are not assumed to readily exercise. Moreover, the extension of citizenship by Haiti to any and all Africans desiring to withdraw from European domination exhibits an unfamiliar level of African agency to world observers both then and now.

Nonetheless, this chapter is not intended to function as historiography of the Haitian Revolution. I support an Afrocentric analysis of the significance and impact of the Haitian Revolution to Haiti and to African Americans, particularly located in Philadelphia, as a model of optimal *African diasporic consciousness* and African world expansion. "Africa" is located both cognitively and geopolitically in early diasporic world history through the successful Haitian Revolution. The Haitian national design for incorporative relations with other African diasporic communities suggests Haiti's intent to not only secure the freedom and longevity of Haitian natives but also to secure the African world's presence in territory that had long been considered the Western world. I offer an alternative reading and analysis of the Haitian Revolution's significance for the benefit of cultural, historical, and psychological African restoration.

This chapter evaluates the significance of the relationship between Haiti and free Africans of Philadelphia following the Haitian Revolution. In evaluating this historical moment and cross-national exchange, I intend to service the underlying inquiry of what the significance of the African diaspora is to Africans in the diaspora from an Afrocentric perspective. This case study supports the following three points:

1. There is evidence of an existing sense of linked fate and linked ancestry between Africans in the diaspora, particularly expressed as African diasporic consciousness.
2. Haitian and African American diasporic communities were aiming to design a large-scale, multi-ethnic cultural location that would extend the presence of Africa in the diaspora through African leadership and legal autonomy.
3. The Haitian emigration project represents an advanced model of *home* construction in the diaspora, having established both cognitive and geopolitical sovereignty.

Haiti's relationship with free Africans of Philadelphia is also represented as optimal *African diasporic consciousness* because agency, support, and circumstance aligned to propel the existing consciousness into direct action, which ultimately shifted hegemonic European world domination.

African Foundations

Proper orientation and perspective resolve philosophical inconsistencies. Hence, orientation and perspective are fundamental to scholarship in Africology. To understand my contribution to the utility of the African-diaspora framework and this chapter development, specifically, one must first consider that I am working from the perspective that Africans in the diaspora have not gone from being slaves to being free; we have gone from being free to enslaved and thus have been fighting to return home ever since. Before Africans in the diaspora were permanently linked to the history of slavery, they were the Ashanti, the Yoruba, and the Fon, for example (Tsehloane, 1994). As stated by Michael Tillotson (2016), "Africana scholars must establish chronological authenticity." How do we understand what we know, and where do we begin our own narratives? My research establishes a reorientation to a historic world event that holds contemporary cultural and psychological value to African communities.

First, it is understood that "free" Blacks existed in slave societies during the antebellum period and prominently so in Saint Domingue and Philadelphia. However, as history has substantiated, these "free" Blacks never held the free status of Whites. "Free" Blacks often functioned as potential slaves under tenuous probationary good behavior. In many slave societies, the behavior of "free" Blacks was constantly regulated and renegotiated by state authorities (Landers, 2010). From this perspective, the rationale for the protracted struggle of Haitians and "free" Africans of Philadelphia to establish independence in solidarity is better understood. There is a necessary critique of Eurocentric definitions and identity constructions of African people that negate their historical and contemporary responses to the endemic wilderness. Persistent in the deep structure of African culture is the communal orientation to identity and survival. It was not uncommon for African people during the antebellum period to recognize that there was no such thing as a "free" African living in an African slave community (Hunt, 1988). Therefore, the clash of social organization between displaced Africans and European colonizers was established well before the Haitian Revolution erupted.

> The Haitian Revolution is said to have begun on August 22, 1791 when thousands of slaves crudely armed with stolen weapons, various tools and torches, overran and destroyed most of the plantations and besieged the towns of Northern Saint Domingue, the most prosperous European colony in the world at that time. Actually, this well planned, sustained offensive was the culmination of nearly three centuries of periodic Black rebellions against the European settlers who imported kidnapped Africans to supply their labor needs. (Carruthers, 1985, p. 9)

Prior to the revolution and even before France took the Western part of the island from Spain in the seventeenth century, the only free Africans who lived in great numbers were the Maroons. The Maroons lived outside of the colonial slave structure, and because of their position, they endured the most consistent struggle with European settlers in Haiti, beginning as early as 1522. "[Their] social structure was organized to reflect the same type of divisions common to indigenous African civilization. Thus, generations of free Africans were born and died in these communities never having been enslaved" (Carruthers, 1985, p. 11). At the foundation of the Haitian Revolution, which is regarded as a unique phenomenon, was the conventional African quality of Haiti that proceeded its revolution.

Even among the unfree population of Haiti's Africans, there existed subversion to the slave order for generations. Enslaved Africans were known to play sick, steal valuables, and kill their masters. Most importantly, many of the enslaved Africans were in constant communication with the Maroons to practice their religion—Vodun, have meetings, and participate in cultural celebrations. According to Jacob Carruthers (1985, p. 18), "The defection of the slaves individually and in groups was so common that a full labor force was the exception on most plantations." We know rebellion and revolt were frequent in Haiti for an extended period prior to the culminating revolution because the Black Codes of Louis XIV were established in 1685 to temper African revolt through provisionary manumission for certain Africans. By the first quarter of the eighteenth century, repressive and brutal attacks by Whites on Maroon communities had intensified. With some acknowledgment of retreat in 1786, the colony offered a treaty recognizing the freedom and territory of one of the Bahoruco Maroon communities. This was just five years before the revolution swelled. Following 1786, however, conflicts between different classes of Africans and European settlers continued in correlation to the American independence movement from Britain and the French Revolution of 1789 (James, 1963). African Americans were likewise facing stark contradictions in the newly liberated America, which continued to exile them. Instability was shaking the Western world order everywhere.

Agency, Support, and Circumstance

There existed a high level of overlapping agency, support, and circumstance for African people during eighteenth-century American and Caribbean life, which facilitated direct collective action. In Philadelphia, the Free Society of Africans was developed by formally enslaved Africans who had purchased their manumission. Richard Allen was a founder of this organization and later purchased the land where he would found the first African Methodist Episcopal (AME) church, Mother Bethel. Allen had frequently experienced being asked to leave worship services by White patrons while renting a White

space known as St. George's. He soon after vowed to establish an autonomous space for African American services and communing. With the African
American community of Philadelphia, Allen raised enough funds to establish
Mother Bethel with intentional support and agency from the community
to exist on their own terms. The opening of the church as an organized
body under the leadership of Allen marked the year the Haitian Revolution
formally began, in 1791. In Philadelphia, Mother Bethel was the only autonomous African worship center at the time, and within a few years, the congregation served nearly 90 percent of the African population in Philadelphia,
both enslaved and "free." Allen became a notable figure in the Philadelphian
African community. Mother Bethel supported its community in many ways,
especially being politically active in the neighboring African residences.
Leaders of the church were also founders of the Freed Black Society, which
became the primary source of outreach for the Philadelphian community
during the 1793 yellow-fever outbreak in the city (Carey, 1793).

Philadelphia was a popular port-city designation for people of African
descent. Between 1780 and 1820, the size of the African community of
Philadelphia grew twelve times its initial population to 12,110 from 1,100. This
population inflation was due to many factors, including the arrival of Saint
Domingue refugees, formally enslaved Africans traveling north through the
underground railroad, the migratory impacts of being drawn to prominent
African American leadership in Philadelphia, and the news of greater job
prospects in Philadelphia (Du Bois, 1996). Mother Bethel was the centralized
venue for affairs to accommodate the growing population. Lectures, speeches,
abolition meetings, organizational social committees, and other agency-
enhancing activities frequently took place at Mother Bethel with the support
of Allen and the congregation. Among the most famous members of their
congregation were those from Philadelphia's African elite, including James
Forten, Paul Cuffe, and the Haitian representative for African American
emigration Prince Saunders (Newman, 2008). As a major port city and des-
tination for African Americans escaping slavery, Philadelphia was growing
in size, representation, and impact for African people near and abroad.

Simultaneously, the significance of Philadelphia in the context of the
broader American national and international politics lends irony to the
agency, support, and consequence aiding African-diasporic direct action.
The American Declaration of Independence from Great Britain was signed
on July 4, 1776, in Philadelphia, Pennsylvania. Philadelphia has represented,

both then and now, the cornerstone for the European American revolution, constitution writing, the Bill of Rights, and a philosophy of liberty, which held some influence on the French Revolution (Holton, 2007).

The international connections between Philadelphia and France and between France and Haiti are revealed in more ways than one. In early America, the residency of the president of the United States was located in the area of Philadelphia currently known as "Old City"—the same district of Philadelphia that was considered the "Black" side of town and home to Mother Bethel AME church. During the American struggle for independence, Benjamin Franklin was dispatched from Philadelphia to Paris by Congress as a representative of the American government. He was instrumental in persuading the French government to send 1,500 men from Saint Domingue to the immediate assistance of the American mainland. Franklin's impression of the French facilitated the alliance of the French to America during its defeat of British colonial rule. However, the French Revolution, beginning in 1789, affected all three segments of Saint Domingue society; the Whites, the Africans, and the biracial descendants from the aforementioned groups. The conflict in France and between segments of Saint Domingue was of great consequence to Africans in Saint Domingue, who took direct action during this European state of chaos to incite what became the Haitian Revolution.

Before European Americans could swallow their own liberty anthem, they became critically concerned about the security of slavery for themselves and their French allies. Not surprisingly, soon after in 1793, President George Washington, a devout slave owner who lived in Philadelphia, signed the Fugitive Slave Act. The Fugitive Slave Act completely destabilized the veneer of a "free North" for African Americans. The law provided "legal return of runaway slaves to their owners" (United States, 2013). As stated earlier, the status of "free" Africans in slave societies would always remain negotiated to protect the greater interest of slavery. African Americans who would have been considered "free" in Philadelphia and other Northern territories were now subject to slavery if they fit the description of a "runaway" or were simply kidnapped twice over into slavery by bounty hunters. In fact, in 1805, one year after the Haitian Revolution, Allen was kidnapped by White bounty hunters in front of his church and was accused of being a runaway slave. This was at a time when Allen could be considered the most famous and influential African American in Philadelphia. As the story is remembered, Allen was only saved from a return to slavery because the mayor of the city happened to be walking by the church during the kidnapping and ordered the bounty hunters to release him (Meaders, 1995). While the Fugitive Slave Act of 1793 strengthened the protection of slavery in America constitutionally, it simultaneously prevented Haitian refugees from entering and settling in northern American communities. Neither free nor enslaved Africans could be safe in the northern American territories under the Fugitive Slave Act, particularly entering from a foreign community and network.

African revolution was to be annihilated everywhere. When the Haitian Revolution erupted in 1791, President Washington urged the United States to render every possible aid to France to help resist the "lamentable . . . unfortunate insurrection of the Negros in Hispanola"(Horne, 2015, p. 7). The Euro-American interest in the demise of the Haitian Revolution resulted in the $15-million deal of 1803 between America and France, known as the Louisiana Purchase. With the Louisiana Purchase, Napoleon attempted to recapture Haiti but was weakened when his armies in Europe were defeated by the British; the neighboring colonial power France had betrayed them by assisting American independence (Fleming, 2003). The diasporic influence of the Haitian Revolution could not be quarantined from African Americans. In the backyard of the president's estate, African Americans in Philadelphia and down the east coast were ardently engaged in abolition campaigns and "slave rebellion" (L. Du Bois, 2012).

For example, in 1800, just nine years after the onslaught of the Haitian Revolution, Gabriel Prosser, an enslaved African in Virginia, led one of America's most remembered and feared "slave revolts." He had been inspired by the Haitian Revolution and used their slogan of "liberty or death" to encourage over one thousand enslaved African Americans to take up arms against White slavers in Virginia (Dass, 2010). The stretch of African agency crossed states and oceans alike. *African diasporic consciousness* was peaking as a result of the alignment of African agency, support, and circumstance. African agency was asserted in the immediate will to act and organize by both African Americans and Haitians on their own behalf toward freedom on their own terms. Also considering the Maroon communities of Haiti and the significance of the AME church in Philadelphia, African agency to direct action was employed without the aid and oversight of Europeans. Africans in the diaspora were the leaders of their own pursuits during this radical era of world history. The support of these communities was driven internally as well, and these communities would soon support each other cross-nationally to build one large free African republic. The circumstance was the weakness and limitation of European philosophical hypocrisy and free-labor dependency, which ultimately led to the hemorrhaging of British, French, and European American power networks. Everything at the surface was beginning to reveal what was underneath. *Under the pressure of the eighteenth century was the presence of Africa in diaspora bubbling over and stretching its arms beyond the capacity of the impeding and unforgivable Western wilderness.*

The Relationship

As a case study, the relationship between Haiti and free Africans of Philadelphia following the Haitian Revolution in tandem with the most significant aspect of this relationship, the cultural interpretation of it, surrender evidence to the expansion of Africa in diaspora. The end of the Haitian Revolution in 1804 marked the beginning of new development and planning for Haiti and the African communities abroad, who were curious about the face of freedom. The Haitian Revolution was bloody and necessary but left the African population in Haiti fatigued and sizably less dense. Meanwhile, African Americans were still under hostile oppression in the United States and were running out of alternatives and optimism in multicultural relationships. The leaders of Haiti and the African community of Philadelphia had urgent mutual interests. With a series of "slave" insurrections spurring all over the country, the American media propaganda about Haiti was dark and discouraging. Nonetheless, the Philadelphian community, in particular, had already established communication with Haiti, and their contact and relationship with Haiti intensified. Because of their sense of linked fate through African diasporic consciousness, African Americans would form an Auxiliary Society for Promoting the Emigration of Free People of Color to Haiti by June of 1824 (Nash, 1998). The vast majority of African American leaders supported the Haitian Revolution; most of these same leaders rejected the mission of the American Colonization Society (ACS; Moses, 1996). One can infer from these efforts that escape at any cost was not the goal of African Americans. They had a sophisticated and intentional approach to facilitating a relationship with an African diasporic community—a community they had built trust with and had a common interest with on their own terms. African Americans were uncertain of their fate in Liberia, being the location of interest for the ACS. The ACS was primarily composed of conservative and untrustworthy Europeans who expressed willingness to pay for "free" Africans in the North to relocate them to the homeland. With the initial proposition, some African Americans left. However, it is estimated that while the ACS had many more years of existence and more resources than the Haitian emigration project, between 1820 and 1831, they were only able to emigrate about three thousand African Americans. By the mid-1830s, negative reports from African American emigrants on the economic conditions of Liberia led to the decline of new recruits for emigration through the ACS (Burin, 2005). Comparatively, in less than one year, between 1824 and 1825, as many as six thousand African Americans pursued emigration to Haiti (Mackenzie, 1830).

What Haiti Had to Offer Was Something Different

Unlike European revolutions that sought "individual liberties and freedom," Haiti was seeking to build a Black nation, an independent African republic that would defend the collective identity of their people. This type of public consciousness and sovereignty was unparalleled even among many Maroon communities. Haiti had defeated the dominant European powers, including the French, Spanish, and American armies, and was prepared to open its borders to all African people in the diaspora who sought refuge. This was an attractive force to African Americans who identified with the struggle of Haitians, who desired a free and safe community among other people of African descent, and who had yet to experience belonging to a nation and land.

At the end of the successful Haitian Revolution, Jean-Jacques Dessalines declared "liberty or death!" as he tore the white from the French tricolor flag (Ardouin, 1853). In 1804, Dessalines determined the act of independence should be written and the first order of restoring the island to a new state should be to change its name to the name recognized by its first inhabitants; the new nation would be Haiti. In African cultural tradition, naming is an act of self-determination and destiny. Naming is held in high regard and identifies the legacy of a person or place (Ugwueze, 2011). The first order of business for Haiti was thus to strip away the tarnish of being colonized under another country's identity and to institute a new cultural memory that would make the African inhabitants the natives rather than slaves.

The second order of business was to draft a declaration of independence. The grievance of the African natives against France was considered important, as was the emphasis on triumph. On January 1, 1804, Dessalines delivered the independence-day speech to the newly liberated Haiti. He began,

> Citizens, it isn't enough to have expelled from your country the barbarians who have bloodied it for two centuries. . . . We must finally live independently or die! . . . What do we have in common with this people of executioners? We dare to be free; dare to be so by and for ourselves. . . . Natives of Haiti . . . in fighting for your liberty I worked for my own happiness. . . . Take the vow to live free and independent and to prefer death to anyone who wants to place you again under the yoke. (Ardouin, 1853, p. 5)

The independence declaration identified the enemy of the nation and the natives. The enslavers were barbarians and had nothing in common with the African natives now instituting freedom forever. Dessalines underscored the agency of the people by declaring that the nation reached freedom for itself by itself. Significant to the formation of the first free African nation in the Western hemisphere was the intentional unification of the people around the preservation of "freedom" and not nationality. This remained relevant later when Haiti decided to open its borders to other African diasporic communities who held a common ideal and common enemy. Moreover, becoming a Haitian citizen nested in being a person of African descent who identified with Africa as a unifying principle. Following the independence declaration, the men and women of Haiti took a vow that connected them as a race of African people with a destined future and distinct motherland (Ardouin, 1853). This vow embodied African diasporic consciousness in its awareness of the African self, collective consciousness, and orientation to the homeland. Furthermore, Haiti represented the first African state in the diaspora that independently evoked cognitive and geopolitical sovereignty.

In the first draft of the Haitian constitution written in 1801, article three states, "There cannot exist slaves on this territory, servitude is therein forever abolished" (Marxist Internet Archive, n.d.). This constitution was already more advanced and progressive than the British, French, or American constitutions. Freedom would no longer have to be a negotiated status; it was an inevitable right in the new African republic. When it was revised in 1805, a preliminary declaration was added. Of specific interest are the following:

1. The people inhabiting the island formally called St. Domingo, hereby agree to form themselves into a free state sovereign and independent of any other power in the universe, under the name of the empire of Hayti.

2. Slavery is forever abolished.

3. The citizens of Hayti are brothers at home; equality in the eyes of the law is incontestably acknowledged, and there cannot exists any titles, advantages, or privileges, other than those necessarily resulting from the consideration and reward of services rendered to liberty and independence.

10. Fathers and mothers are not permitted to disinherit their children.

12. No white man of whatever nation he may be shall put his foot on this territory with the title of master or proprietor, neither shall he in the future acquire any property therein.

14. All acception [*sic*] of colour among the children of one and the same family, of whom the chief magistrate is the father, being necessarily to cease, the Haytians shall hence forward be known only by the generic appellation of Blacks. (Dessalines, 2013, p. 50)

The morals and intent of the Haitian government demonstrate the ultimate type of marronage, collective consciousness, orientation to Africa by linked fate to the progeny of Africa, and a commitment to community sustainability through family and principles of democratic rule. The national identity does not rest in conflict with African ethnic difference. Instead, it openly distinguishes difference as that between Whites (Europeans) and Blacks (Africans). All persons identifying as "Black" are thus naturalized, familiar, and welcomed. This was the most liberatory and self-determined construction of *home* for diasporic African people who had entered the "New World"—the world which publicly denied their existence and utility as an African world person. No longer did African people have to stand idle to European acknowledgment and happiness. The significance of the Haitian Revolution to Haitians and African Americans was its construction of home through a broad orientation to all Africans in diaspora without prejudice for being children of Africa, as children who can always be natively at home.

In the earlier part of the year 1818, Haitian diplomat Saunders wrote and delivered a "proclamation" to the kingdom of Haiti. Following in the footsteps of the late Dessalines, he began by asserting that Haitians proclaim to be free or die. Second, he offered a critique of France. He wrote:

In 1814 we were menaced with an unjust aggression; the French, instead of enjoying like other nations the advantages and sweets of that peace which they had just obtained of the High Allies, instead of applying themselves like them to healing the evils of war, instead of making some amends for their cruelties and injuries to us, by a conduct more humane and diametrically opposite . . . [they] disturb us in the peaceful enjoyments of our rights. . . . We have replied to their new outrages with the firmness and energy that characterizes us, and thus we will ever repel all unjust pretentions. (Saunders, 1818, p. 141)

The critique of France and continued acknowledgment of the French as a present enemy, even fourteen years after the independence victory, laid the foundation for the Haitian people to prepare for the proposed emigration plan. Saunders continued by stating that the plan for Haitian progress would profit from African American emigration, which was said to increase the population, happiness, and commerce. Saunders expressed that African Americans were skillful artists and professors. He proclaimed, "they will experience the utmost toleration: difference of nation and religion will be no ground of exclusion: we shall pay respect to merit and talents alone" (Saunders, 1818, p. 144). This portion of the proclamation prepared the palate of the Haitians to receive the national plan that was underway for the emigration of African Americans. The latter part of this most important speech would encourage Haitians to recognize they had made world history and to be in celebration of their great accomplishments. This message was necessary considering the continued nuisance of European infiltration and the laborious rebuilding of the nation. A few months later, on December 11, 1818, Saunders visited Philadelphia and delivered a speech with an alternative approach to encourage the interest of aspiring African American emigrants. Saunders was an African American scholar and diplomat who devoted his life to serving the interests of African Americans in independent Haiti under the direction of Emperor Henri Christophe. In 1818, Saunders wrote *A Memoir Presented to the American Convention for Promoting the Abolition of Slavery, and Improving the Condition of the African Race.*

This historical document written by Saunders was used to appeal to the African American community by making a gentle persuasion, focusing on how beautiful Haiti could be to potential emigrants and what Haiti has to offer interested families. Saunders suggested that African Americans would be "blessed" for serving the island and that Philadelphians would be most appropriate as representatives of the first city to abolish slavery. Saunders was most skillful in his empathy for African Americans' subjection to slavery and to their religious Christian piety. He wrote:

> And if those who consider the poor . . . are authorized to look for the favour of providence; with how much more full an assurance may those who have delivered their fellow beings from the inhuman grasp of the unprincipled kidnapper, or saved them from dragging out a miserable existence, amidst the thralldoms of the most abject slavery; with what confident expectation of becoming the recipients of that inconceivably glorious recompence of reward, which God has prepared for those who love and obey him, may such persons anticipate the period when Christ shall reappear, to make up his jewels. (Saunders, 1818, p. 8)

Saunders ends his benevolent appeal to African Americans of Philadelphia by exploring the potential for a great international relationship between free people of color in America and Haiti and English philanthropists who were financial supporters of abolition (Saunders, 1818). Saunders was a genius diplomat who carefully studied his audiences and delivered eloquently in anticipation of the successful transformation of two ethnic communities into one nation. He appealed to the cultural sensibilities and experiences of African Americans to ensure that Haiti was a deliverer for African people and that both parties would be in the highest favor of God if they worked together. His appeal to the African Americans in Philadelphia and to the Haitian citizens at home reflected the mutual desire of both Haitians and African Americans to pursue a growing relationship for the benefit of both parties.

In a few years' time, after some organizing and planning in both Philadelphia and Haiti, President Jean-Pierre Boyer made a more aggressive attempt within the districts of Haiti to secure land and agricultural profit for emigrating African Americans. In 1824, President Boyer wrote *Correspondence Relative to the Emigration to Haiti, of the Free People of Colour in the United States Together with the Instructions to the Agent.* The agent to receive this notice and organize efforts for emigration had been a falsified parishioner, Loring D. Dewey. Dewey was a White man who held membership in the American Colonization Society. Without consent from his organization, he wrote President Boyer, inquiring about what detailed plan would be employed to emigrate African Americans. He presented himself as a deep sympathizer for the African people in America who had experienced such discrimination and who would be happier in their relocation to Haiti (Boyer, 1824a). Dewey had previously expressed his intent to contact the president of Haiti regarding emigration to his organization. Not surprisingly, the ACS was not supportive of his efforts. The Euro-Americans within the ACS had no interest in Haiti because they had no control or ability to own anything in Haiti. Moreover, for France and the United States of America, Haiti represented an enemy and thus would always represent a lack of common interest. Dewey's break with the ACS draws attention to the fact that the end goal for Haiti and the ACS was actually the same. Both wanted to facilitate the emigration of "free" African Americans to a new nation for perceived benefits. What is of greater significance then is the identification of what relationships represented communal linked fate and orientation to Africa. The ACS did not recognize Haiti as a community that would ensure their fate, nor did they align with a cultural responsibility to Africa. Dewey had become withdrawn from the political struggles of the ACS and joined the Society for the Emigration of Free People of Color to Haiti as a board of directors' member (Library Company of Philadelphia, 2011).

Unsuspecting any foul play, President Boyer responded to Dewey's inquiries. Dewey had outlined a series of questions regarding Haiti's coverage of the expense to transport African Americans, their access to land and animals, tolerance of religion, and whether the emigrants could exist as a United States colony with its own laws. Dewey closed with:

> There are many Whites who truly lament their [African American] unhappy lot, mourn over their wrongs, and would gladly do anything to redress them; but they find that such is their degradation, and public opinion towards the coloured people, that it is next to impossible to elevate them . . . and to benefit them in this country . . . I speak of the mass. . . . These benevolent men, therefore, are looking for an asylum for these injured sons of Africa, in some other country. (Dewey, 1824, p. 5)

Dewey reflected his ideological positioning in his attempt to fake concern while expressing interest in African Americans remaining colonial property to the United States. He did not believe African Americans could assimilate into the American fabric. They would be "next to impossible to elevate"—this is White liberal talk for the belief that African Americans can never reach a quality of citizenry and equality in America. Furthermore, his affiliation with African Americans only allowed him to see them as property, hence their inability to live alongside Euro-Americans and inability to live without the supervision of the United States from abroad. Ultimately, Dewey's emigration plan looked vastly different from African American organizers and Haitian leadership.

President Boyer responded to Dewey immediately, on May 24, 1824. He wrote:

> In reply to that you addressed tome of the 4th of March, preceding, on the subject of emigration to Hayti of a portion of the children of Africa who are in the United States, I now announce to you that I send to you . . . the agent, the citizen Granville. . . . He is the bearer of my particular instructions, and will communicate them to you. . . . I shall then, Sir, only entreat you to make every effort to forward the success of the great object, we both have in view. You cannot better serve the cause of humanity, since those of our brethren, who drag out in the United States a painful and degrading existence, will become, on arriving to Hayti, citizens of the Republic, and can there labour with security and advantage to themselves and children. (Boyer, 1824a, p. 13)

President Boyer sent his agent, J. Granville, to handle further emigration plans directly with the leadership of African Americans in Philadelphia. He rejected Dewey's interest in holding a colony in Haiti. These sentiments were powerfully echoed "as Haiti's Secretary General Balthazar Iginac assured Black New Yorkers in the early 1800s, under 'The constitution of the Haytian republic, all Indians, Africans and their descendants born in the colonies or elsewhere who shall hereafter reside in this republic shall be [treated] as Haytians'" (Ferrer, 2012, p. 43). The emigrants would no longer be American and thus will not be regarded under different legal applications; the emigrants would immediately become Haitians and function accordingly. He outlined instructions for African Americans, which were sent personally through Granville. The instructions offered a detailed contract containing fourteen separate articles to address the expectations, land allocations, laws, process, and procedure for emigration, and notice of immediate citizenship as a Haitian upon entering the country.

On June 17, 1824, Granville arrived in Philadelphia and was welcomed into Allen's church, Mother Bethel, to report on the instructions and facilitation of the voluntary emigration of all African Americans expressing interest in relocation to Haiti. Granville addressed the African American contingent as "citizens" and reported:

> You are not ignorant that there exist in the United States of America, several hundred thousand individuals of African blood, who, on account of the dark hue of their complexion, are objects of all the prejudice . . . numerous communications were addressed to me [Boyer]. . . . To these inquiries . . . I have replied in a favourable manner, explaining the advantages that our constitution has taken care to assure to those of our brothers who come from other parts of the globe and establish themselves among us. Already we have seen arrive in our ports, several of these children of Africa, who have come from the United States . . . happy at being delivered from the degrading yoke of prejudice. (Boyer, 1824b, p. 18)

The concerns and assurances of President Boyer were met with a great reception within the African American communities near and far. Mother Bethel was respected for being the first independent African institution in Philadelphia, respect that was extended to Allen. The common pursuit of self-determination and agency for African people strengthened the trust between these diasporic communities and led to rapid direct action.

On June 29, 1824, Allen hosted a convention at his home for a number of African Americans to discuss the emigration plan to Haiti. Allen was chosen as chair of the governing body, and on July 6, the secretary of the Auxiliary Committee for the Emigration of People of Color to the Island of Haiti issued a press statement on the planned meeting at Mother Bethel. Allen chaired the meeting, and the correspondence between Dewey and President Boyer of Haiti were discussed. The plan was accepted and approved unanimously. In less than two years afterwards, more than six thousand African Americans emigrated to Haiti. African agency, support, and circumstance had aligned to produce optimal African diasporic consciousness and collective action in establishing a multiethnic cultural location and to solidify a design for a cognitive and geopolitical *home* design in the diaspora.

The Impact

There are four key indicators of the unique significance of this case study in the context of African diasporic history and relations. First, the self-sustained, intradiasporic relationship between free and enslaved African populations in Haiti and in the United States during the eighteenth and nineteenth centuries was so endemic that it led to the reorganizing of the European "New World" order. Slavery was not just abolished, it was defeated. The Haitian Revolution marked the beginning of the end of European slavery, and this was partially due to the spreading of information and influence on each other within African diasporic communities. Three years after the Haitian Revolution, both Britain and America abolished African slave trading. By 1860, the last of the European capitalists, in Brazil and Cuba, would legally forfeit slave trading (Thomas, 1997). In addition to defeating the institution of slavery in the Western world, these African diasporic communities reorganized the principles of freedom, citizenry, nationality, and nativism on their own terms and with their own resources. Haiti constructed its constitution to unify African diasporic communities around freedom rather than national-ity. In this way, they expanded the presence of Africa in diaspora through international connections and mutual support.

Second, Haiti's naturalization process for emigrating African Americans identifies a special relationship between diasporic communities. Haitian representatives consistently addressed African Americans as "citizens." Throughout the entire emigration project, African Americans were referred to as the "brethren" of Haitians, wherein the relationship was predicated on both communities having the same mother—being the "children of Africa." African Americans were never referred to as refugees, exiles, or as a displaced community by Haitians. These labels have been applied to African diasporic groups by outsiders or culturally distant insiders. Most importantly for these African diasporic groups, one's place of origin was the determining factor of their unity, not their conditional birthplace.

Third, Haiti identified itself as the "nation for Blacks" in service to the diaspora. As stated in the national constitution, Haiti proclaimed that it would be the haven for African people around the world. Haiti embraced its own independence by sharing it with the larger African community. This is culturally consistent with the African worldview and diasporic conscious-ness in the expression of collective linked fate in orientation to the fate of

Africa as the homeland. This same sentiment would be pronounced years later through influential African world leaders, such as David Walker, Marcus Garvey, and Kwame Nkrumah (Walker, 1830).

Lastly, the overwhelming attraction to Haiti by African Americans should be marked for further study. Little is recorded about this migration, which remains one of the largest voluntary migrations in modern history. The African American emigration to Haiti was ten times larger than that of Liberia, Nova Scotia, or Canada even though, in Eurocentric historical records, the latter are most referenced. The appeal of Haiti requires attention to settle on the fact that African Americans were doing more than escaping slavery. They had long-term plans to build, expand, and develop as a nation-worthy people. The perimeter of slavery in the European mind hinders investigation into the culture and psychology of African potentiality. Haitians and African Americans were engaging in the idea of nation building—nation building as a multiethnic grand *marronage*.

The significance of this review is my connection of diasporic communities to the expansion of Africa conceptually. Africa was and can be explored as a geopolitical and cognitive location that is expanded and located by African people around the world through their *collective consciousness* and cultural expression.

REFERENCES

Ardouin, B. (1853). *Études sur l'histoire d'Haïti: Suivies de la vie du général J.-M. Borgella* (Vol. 7). Dézobry, Magdeleine et Cie.

Bolster, J. W. (1997). *Black Jacks: African American Seaman in the Age of Sail*. Harvard University Press.

Boyer, J-P. (1824a). Emigration to Hayti of the Free People of Colour. In L. D. Dewey (Ed.), *Correspondence Relative to the Emigration to Hayti, of the Free People of Colour, in the United States, Together with the Agent* (pp. 13–14). Mahlon Day.

Boyer, J-P. (1824b). Instructions to the Citizen. In L. D. Dewey (Ed.), *Correspondence Relative to the Emigration to Hayti, of the Free People of Colour, in the United States, Together with the Agent* (pp. 18–20). Mahlon Day.

Burin, E. (2005). *Slavery and the Peculiar Solution: A History of the American Colonization Society*. University Press of Florida.

Carey, M. (1793). *A Short Account of the Malignant Fever, Lately Prevalent in Philadelphia: With a Statement of the Proceedings that Took Place on the Subject in Different Parts of the United States*.

Carruthers, J. H. (1985). *The Irritated Genie: An Essay on the Haitian Revolution*. Kemetic Institute.

Dass, S. (2010). *Black Rebellion: Eyewitness Accounts of Major Slave Revolts*. Two Horizons.

Dessalines, J. (2013). The Second Constitution of Haiti (Hayti), May 20, 1805. In S. Lazar (Ed.), *The Anthropology of Citizenship: A Reader* (pp. 49–51). John Wiley & Sons.

Dewey, L. D. (Ed.). (1824). *Correspondence Relative to the Emigration to Hayti, of the Free People of Colour, in the United States, Together with the Agent*. Mahlon Day.

Du Bois, L. (2012). *Haiti: The Aftershocks of History*. Metropolitan Books.

Du Bois, W. E. B. (1996). *The Philadelphia Negro: A Social Study*. University of Pennsylvania Press. (Original work published 1899).

Ferrer, A. (2012). Haiti, Free Soil, and Antislavery in the Revolutionary Atlantic. *American Historical Review, 117*(1), 40–66.

Fleming, T. (2003). *The Louisiana Purchase*. John Wiley & Sons.

Holton, W. (2007). *Unruly Americans: And the Origins of the Constitution*. Hill and Wang.

Horne, G. (2015). *Confronting Black Jacobins: The US, the Haitian Revolution, and the Origins of the Dominican Republic*. New York University Press.

Hunt, A. N. (1988). *Haiti's Influence on Antebellum America: Slumbering Volcano in the Caribbean*. Louisiana State University Press.

James, C. L. R. (1963). *The Black Jacobins: Toussaint L'Ouverture and the San Domingo Revolution*. Vintage Books.

Landers, J. G. (2010). *Atlantic Creoles in the Age of Revolutions*. Harvard University Press.

Library Company of Philadelphia. (2011). *Colonization and Emigration: Identity and Destiny*. http://www.librarycompany.org/blackfounders/section10.htm

Mackenzie, C. (1830). *Notes on Haiti: Made During Residence in that Republic*. Henry Colburn and Richard Bently.

Marxists Internet Archive. (n.d.). *Constitution of 1801 by Haiti*. https://www.marxists.org/history/haiti/1801/constitution.htm

Meaders, D. (1995). Kidnapping Blacks in Philadelphia: Isaac Hopper's Tales of Oppression. *Journal of Negro History, 80*(2), 47–65.

Moses, W. J. (1996). *Classical Black Nationalism: From the American Revolution to Marcus Garvey*. New York University Press.

Nash, G. B. (1998). *Forging Freedom: The Formation of Philadelphia's Black Community, 1720–1840*. Harvard University Press.

Newman, R. S. (2008). *Freedom's Prophet: Bishop Richard Allen, the AME Church, and the Black Founding Fathers*. New York University Press.

Saunders, P. (1818). *A Memoir Presented to the American Convention for Promoting the Abolition of Slavery, and Improving the Condition of the African Race*. Dennis Heart.

Thomas, H. (1997). *Slave Trade: The Story of the Atlantic Slave Trade: 1440–1870*. Touchstone.

Tillotson, M. (2016, February 18). *Terminal Degree: Institutional Realities and Response* [Lecture]. Temple University Department of Africology & African American Studies Lecture Series, Philadelphia, PA, United States.

Tsehloane, K. C. (1994). *The African Centered Perspective of History and Social Sciences in the Twenty-First Century*. Research Associates School Times Publications.

Ugwueze, U. L-T. (2011). *African Culture, Identity, and Aesthetics: The Igbo Example*. AuthorHouse.

United States (2013). *The Constitution of the United States, with the Acts of Congress, Relating to Slavery, Embracing, the Constitution, the Fugitive Slave Act of 1793, the Missouri Compromise Act of 1820, the Fugitive Slave Law of 1850, and the Nebraska and Kansas Bill*. Hard Press Publishing. (Original work published 1923).

Walker, D. (1830). *Walker's Appeal, in Four Articles: Together With a Preamble, to the Coloured Citizens of the World, but in Particular: and Very Expressly, to Those of the United States of America.*

CONCLUSION
From Griots to Ghettos to Galaxies

Aaron X. Smith

On this journey, we have engaged the power of the spoken word as a liberating force in the struggle against the distorted perspectives put forth by a Eurocentric matrix. The impacts of Afrocentric agency in the digital age were explored. The importance of Afrocentric agency in the process of future production was illustrated. The transformative potential of implementing a multifaceted recognition and deconstruction of phenomena centering African people, culture, and thought continues to be developed and advanced.

Afrocentric Futurism focuses on African and diasporic-African-descended, Indigenous, aboriginal, original foundations for Futuristic thoughts and expressions. An Afrocentric Futuristic, in-depth analysis of the characters, themes, historical context, and future implications of the film *Black Panther* (2018) was offered. The power of asserting Afrocentric, Futuristic, victorious consciousness was interrogated. The Afrocentric Futuristic femininity and creativity stylings of artist Janelle Monáe were powerfully elucidated. The transition of intergenerational, transcontinental, and intergalactic messages was presented. A blueprint, framework, and rhetorical roadmap for centering AfroFuturism within an African cosmological paradigm were skillfully constructed. The practical application of the Afrocentric methodological process of analysis was implemented through a process of excavating the triumphant essence and examples of the Haitian Revolution.

Here, we were able to see the power of *sankofa* through an Afrocentric lens, which utilized the past to empower our present and potentially propel us into an Afrocentric future through innovative insights, aided by our ancestors and previous achievements. Continental, cultural, generational, and spiritually cosmological connections were made throughout this work, and hopefully, the reader has become better acquainted with themselves and the expansive universe through the reading of this text. Each chapter presented an entirely unique yet powerfully interconnected constellation of ideas, constituting a grand galaxy of Afrocentric Futuristic scholarship.

Throughout this text, the reader has been presented with numerous definitions of AfroFuturism while engaging in the many ways Afrocentric thought supports, aligns with, and contributes to the evolution of Afrocentric Futuristic thought and expression. AfroFuturism, like beauty, is often recognized to be defined largely from the perspective of the beholder.

> Some people see it as an aesthetic genre unto itself: SF written by Black people for Black people. Others see it as a way of reading that calls attention to the complex relations between science, technology and race that always undergirded but are not always made evident in SF. Still others understand AfroFuturism as a cultural phenomenon emerging from the relationship between African Americans and Western technology, and they appreciate SF's themes of abduction, displacement, and alienation as fitting symbols for Black experience. Yet others see it as a mode of aesthetic production that merges myth and history to imagine new Black cultures and futures. (Lavender, 2019, p. 1)

What this work has evidenced are definitive distinctions between the popular notions of "AfroFuturism" and the lasting and emerging analytical techniques emphasized in Afrocentric Futurism. The age-old dichotomy represented by Afrocentric communalism in contrast with European rugged individualism plays a part in how many Futurists envision the world to come when analyzing the potential impacts of technological capabilities. In one sense, we have returned to Earth after traveling throughout the Afrocentric Futuristic universe of analysis, speculation, and creative expression. At the same time, we have been properly and powerfully prepared for literary and literal take-off into a future of our making.

Moving forward, we will hopefully see more connections between the mathematical brilliance of aeronautic masterminds Katherine Johnson, Dorothy Vaughan, and Mary Jackson (*Hidden Figures* [2016]) in relation to their formulating African foremother Seshat. Scholars and writers such as Umoja Noble, Ruha Benjamin, Jennifer Williams, and Nancy Farmer will be analyzed within the long history of Ida B. Wells and her red letter and the leadership of Neithotep (ca. 3150–ca. 2613 BCE). This extended historical analysis acts as a predictive slingshot, which could propel thought and have an impact far into the future, for generations to come. The creative genius of Benjamin Banneker and *Black Panther* director Ryan Coogler contrast to the transformative aesthetics promoted by the erecting of the first step pyramid by the architects who labored under the rulership of King Djoser (2780 BCE).

It is of critical importance to remember to maintain and protect the cultural and technological landmarks of our African foremothers and forefathers as we embark on multifaceted Futuristic journeys through space and time. Until then, we will be waiting on the mothership, which could come in the form of a technologically advanced spacecraft (a wheel in a wheel), a return to *ma'at* through a better understanding of our place in the universe, or a shift toward living in greater harmony with Mother Nature. Our transcendental Futuristic deliverance could be brought in the form of proper reverence, protection, and understanding being afforded to the universal mother who carries the all-powerful Eve gene—the Black woman. Whatever form(s) this rebirth assumes, Afrocentric Futurists will be welcoming the simultaneous advancements and reestablishments with open arms and open Afrocentric minds.

REFERENCE

Lavender, I., III. (2019). *AfroFuturism Rising: The Literary Prehistory of a Movement*. Ohio State University Press.

ABOUT THE CONTRIBUTORS

TAHARKA ADÉ is an Africologist and native of Mt. Vernon, Alabama. He is currently an assistant professor in the Department of Africana Studies at San Diego State University. His research interests are wide ranging but include Afrocentricity, Africological historiography, Pan-Africanism, African American history and theory, Du Boisian thought, and AfroFuturism. He is actively engaged in several research projects for publication; most recently he's crafted a treatise, entitled "Africological Historiography: Primary Considerations," published in SAGE Open.

MOLEFI KETE ASANTE is the most published contemporary African American scholar. He is professor and chair in the Department of Africology and African American Studies, Temple University, and the author of *Radical Insurgencies* (2020), *Revolutionary Pedagogy* (2017), and *The History of Africa* (2007).

ALONGE O. CLARKSON is a PhD graduate of Temple University, Department of Africology and African American Studies. As a student committed to service, she was the first woman to teach the course African Americans in Sport, and she earned the Outstanding Service Award. She successfully completed both her BA, as a dual major in political science and Africana studies, and her MA in Africana studies at the University at Albany (SUNY). Her primary research interests include Afrocentricity, African American literature, Africana womanism and feminisms, and African Americans in sport. Additionally, she is an educator in north Philadelphia, providing high school juniors and seniors with the tools necessary for life.

JOHN P. CRAIG is a doctoral candidate in the Department of Africology and African American Studies at Temple University. He is currently completing his dissertation, titled "Wakanda Forever: An Afrocentric Analysis of the film *Black Panther*." His research interests include AfroFuturism, African American History, the Black presence in sequential art, and visual images in the Africana diaspora. He is currently a full-time instructor at Portland Community College in the Ethnic Studies Department.

IFETAYO M. FLANNERY is assistant professor of Africology at Temple University. Her research investigates how the Afrocentric methodological approach has rendered alternative narratives about African American psychology and African diasporic histories. Her edited book, *Introduction to Black Psychology* (2018), offers readers interpretations of the collective consciousness, cultural values, and political decisions of African Americans in relationship to their African ancestry and practices. She has served on the board of the Bay Area chapter of Association of Black Psychologists (ABPsi) and is currently the director of the Diopian Institute for Scholarly Advancement (DISA) International Conference.

KOFI KUBATANNA, grandson of Herman and Helen White, is a PhD student at Temple University in the Department of Africology and African American Studies. Kubatanna is a New Jersey certified K–12 educator; he creates, designs, and develops curriculum for homeschool, independent, and private-school communities. He is Afia's husband and father to Abena, Amma, and Akosua.

LEHASA MOLOI is an Afrocentric decolonial scholar teaching development studies at the University of South Africa. He holds the degree of PhD in development studies. He is passionate about epistemic decolonization debates and the pursuit for rehumanization in the Global South, in particular Africa, against the ravages of the colonial past. His intellectual work is grounded in the paradigm of Afrocentricity and decoloniality as liberatory thinking frameworks to oppose "epistemicides" created by European colonialism. He broadly reflects and writes on Africa, knowledge, development, and decolonization.

m. nDIIKA MUTERE is a scholar, writer, consultant, and lecturer of Africana studies. She has taught at Temple University (her alma mater), Howard University, the University of California at Irvine and Riverside, and at California State University Northridge. Dr. Mutere's "oral-aesthetic perspective" is an Africa-centered toolkit through which she analyzes contributions by Africa's cultural custodians who have transformed ancient aesthetic modalities of African oral tradition into globally consumed genres of pop music while advancing the communal narrative. Dr. Mutere's publications include "Towards an Africa-Centered and Pan-African Theory of Communication: Ubuntu and the Oral Aesthetic Perspective" and "Towards a Transformation Theory of Communication: Ubuntu, Prince, and the Oral-Aesthetic Perspective."

ABOUT THE EDITOR

DR. AARON X. SMITH (AKA DR. JABALI ADE), BA, MA, MA, MED, PHD

It wasn't long ago that Dr. Aaron X. Smith was a student at Temple University's Main Campus in North Philadelphia, merely grateful for the pursuit of higher education. The foundation of his achievement was his God-given athletic talents and a thirst for knowledge gifted to him by his parents. As he progressed though his academic life, he realized that the opportunity for higher education was not readily accessible for most and even more difficult to attain for the underrepresented and underprivileged members of his communities. This realization shaped his personal purpose to dedicate his life to uplifting a new generation of young people, to help them unlock the transformative power of education and to recognize the potential of investing in one's personal growth.

Dr. Smith is an assistant professor of instruction in the Department of Africology and African American Studies at Temple University. As a proud Temple alumnus, he has earned a BA in Asian studies, an MA in liberal arts, an MA in African American studies, an MEd in higher education, and a PhD in African American studies. Currently, Dr. Smith is pursuing an EdD in higher education from his alma mater.

Dr. Smith is the author of "The Murder of Octavius Catto," featured in *The Encyclopedia of Greater Philadelphia* (2015), and "Boundless Baldwin," published in *Contemporary Critical Thought in Africology and Africana Studies* (2015). He has multiple articles in *The SAGE Encyclopedia of African Cultural*

Heritage in North America (2015) and various chapter publications with Springer Nature (2022), Hamilton Books (2022), and Lexington Books (2022).

Dr. Smith is a dynamic and innovative speaker, educator, artist, and facilitator who naturally utilizes his vast wealth of knowledge, uncanny energy, and unique oratorical abilities to translate hip-hop culture into a universal language of leadership, learning, and love. His innovative, artistic presentation style has gained him the name the "Rapping Professor," and a few of his noteworthy clients include HP Inc., Yahoo!, Verizon, and Johnson & Johnson. Throughout his professorship, Dr. Smith has been focused on developing unique and dynamic ways to actively engage the Gen-Z students of today to solidify their love of learning.

INDEX

Printed in the USA
CPSIA information can be obtained
at www.ICGtesting.com
JSHW020445280923
49137JS00004B/22